Cove Bay — A History

Acknowledgements

Many thanks are due to the following, all of which without this book would not be possible:

Bill Martin at the Registers of Scotland Executive Agency, Edinburgh; Laragh Quinney, Peter Milne and Jenny Parkerson at the Map Library of Scotland, Edinburgh; Hugh Buchanan, Secretary of the Local Boundary for Scotland, Edinburgh; Catherine Taylor and staff at Aberdeen Central Library; Judith Cripps, former Head Archivist at Aberdeen City Archives, and current staff Fiona Musk and Martin Hall; the staff at Special Libraries and Archives, Aberdeen University; Mike Craig, curator of the George Washington Wilson Database at Aberdeen University; Catherine Walker of Aberdeen Maritime Museum; Ewan Crawford at Scotrail; The Rev. Peter Lees at St Peter's Episcopalian Church, Fraserburgh; Stephen Cordiner of Cordiner's Sawmills; Fiona Watson at Northern Health Services Archives, Woolmanhill; Joanna Fraser, Head of Photographic at the Press & Journal; John Lyon, caretaker at Loirston Primary School.

Also for their time and knowledge: The late Mr. George Westland; Miss Mabel Guyan; Mr. Fred and Charlotte Cargill; Mrs. Muriel Wood; the late Mr. Alexander Wood; Mr. Ramsay Wood; Mr. Peter Ritchie; Mr. Robert Jamieson; Mr. David Steven; Mrs. Margaret Viera; Mr. Bill and Grace McBain; Mr. Jimmy and Mary Penny; Mr. Dennis and Madge Pickard; Mr. Ian and Evelyn Bowie; and my mother Mrs. Rosemary Gray. Finally, to my wife Sheila, for her patience and understanding throughout the research of this book.

A special gratitude is owed to Mr. Albert Ross for supplying a number of the photographs contained within.

Published by Koo Press, 2008

koopoetry@btinternet.com

ISBN 978-0-9558340-2-8

© Douglas W. Gray

ABERDEEN
CITY COUNCIL

Funded in part by Aberdeen City Council & Cove and Altens Community Council. With acknowledgement of the support of the Aberdeen Energising Board.

Contents

Index of Photographs, Maps and Illustrations

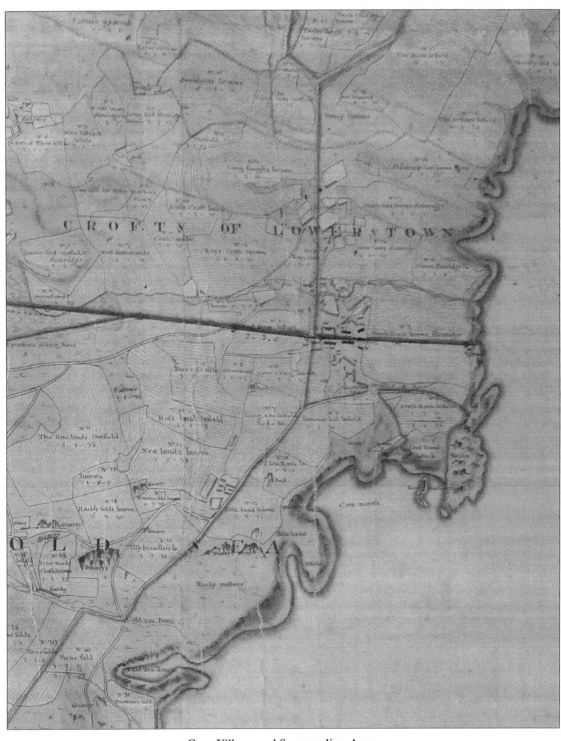

Cove Village and Surrounding Area.
Brown, George, Lands & barony of Nigg, 1777.

Reproduced by kind permission of Aberdeen City Archives.

Introduction

The Cove, Cove Bay, or Cove, where does it all begin? The first inhabitants are mere speculation, but a rich land and plentiful sea hints at a medieval settlement. Cove Bay, however, was never destined to be an independent major development, owing to its isolation and inaccessibility, there being no real access in and out the village, the ferry crossing at the river Dee serving little direct purpose. How times have changed in this former northeast corner of Kincardine!

Following in the footsteps of Janet Murray's booklets 'The Essence of the Cove' and 'Schooling in the Cove, is an attempt to expand on and further the historical roots of this once industrious village; moreover, arising from a 'need to know' is the creation of a sense of place relating to both geographical and physical features, or, to put it bluntly — who, what, why, where and when. Of course, much has been lost, or indeed forgotten, in regards to heritage, identity and lore. Indeed, during the course of this five year quest there have been many frustrations, disappointments and regrets, whereby that up until the mid 19th century little remains by way of estate papers and personal effects, which, no doubt, would have made for both a treasured and colourful depiction of life in the village.

The main focus, therefore, is the period between 1785 and the close of the 19th century, when much was recorded regarding land ownership, religion, education, social welfare and several modes of occupation, but with a detailed description of the austere and relentless life that the fisher-folk led, inclusive of the fishing and everyday events that took place in the terraced rows above the harbour. Indeed, prior to 1863 the village was effectively two separate properties, the tenants paying rent to different landlords! However, more recent events have not been overlooked, such as social welfare and housing development.

For both local tradition and reasons of posterity, on the following pages the village is referred to as 'the Cove', and not the present-day Cove Bay. Of course, this now modern city suburb is simply referred to as Cove, albeit stretching from the old Fishtown of Balmoral by the harbour to within the vicinity of Charleston. Moreover, as in other towns and villages its name has changed, or has been subject to variants over the centuries, such as 'le Coyf', 'Halyman's Coif', 'Coif' or 'Coiff', until the late 18th century when the present-day spelling came to be. By the very late 19th century, however, there is mention of the village as being Cove Bay, which may possibly arise from having a separate national identity from that of Cove in Dunbartonshire, and the hamlet of Cove located to the north of Eyemouth. In addition, and for informational purposes, it has at times been necessary to expand on events elsewhere, such as religion, the fishing, social welfare, etc, in order to give a direct bearing on local interest.

Thus begins an account of reconstruction, industry, communications and a growing population, where events become more intimate, lives more concentrated. So in this walk to yesterday, from perched by the cliffs to a scattering of crofts, lie the salty endeavours that echo a village, with a mansion here and there and a small kirk by the sea...

Douglas W. Gray, September 2008

For those who live here, have lived, and have yet to do so...

Chapter 1: Regional Development

Beginnings

In prehistoric times the North-East of Scotland was inhabited by a long-headed people of short stature, whose dwellings were burrowed out below the soil and the walls built up with stones, on which lay lintels to support the ground above. It is believed they lived upon the land during the warmer spring and summer months, retreating underground in the winter. Traces of these early inhabitants have been found on the south side of the River Dee, of whom most likely ventured into the northern parts of Kincardineshire. Further evidence of early civilisation has been unearthed in and around the Dee estuary, by way of bone hooks and shells, from a people known as the Strandloopers, who roamed the coastal plains at the end of the last great ice age. From these earliest times, through the dark ages, to beyond the first millennium, little has been recorded, proving it somewhat impossible to determine when the area, and more specifically the Cove, was first established. It may well be that by the mid 15th century land-hungry tenants sought to work the fertile soil to the north and west of present-day Loirston Road, with, of course, the additional profession of whitefishing, there being a natural harbour at hand. Nevertheless, it must be considered that up until the mid 19th century most of this area was an uninhabited tract of moss, heath and marsh, profusely strewn with stones.

The Cove was a part of the parish of Nigg, a district within the ancient Celtic province of the Mearns; the former suggesting three Gaelic derivations: 'peninsula', relating to the peninsular-like shape of the parish; 'niuc', a corner or recess; and 'n'eig', the notch, which may refer to the Bay of Nigg itself. Another possibility may be from Cormac de Nugg, a Celtic nobleman who ruled the area in the 12th century. In medieval times the parish of Nigg was known as the Barony of Torrie (Torry), and the area first documented as a result of a gift by King William I (the Lion) to the monks of Arbroath Abbey in 1178, the parish bounds being defined in 1242 by David de Bernham, Bishop of St. Andrews, and containing an area of around fifteen square miles. By the 14th century the Saxon language had swelled from its heartland in the Lothians and superseded Gaelic throughout the lowlands of Scotland; indeed, here in the North-East our dialect is peppered with native and foreign influences. Still in use is 'connach', to spoil, and 'partan', which relates to crab. The Dutch persuasion gives rise to 'dubs', meaning mud, and 'redd', to clean or clear up. Norse has furnished us with 'ness', meaning headland, as in the Hare Ness, and 'kof', which is similar to cove, meaning a hut, or to dwell; moreover, the fishers themselves are believed to have sprung from Scandinavian origin. A further mention of the area, possibly, is given in an ancient poem lamenting the fallen nobles of the Lowland army at the Battle of Harlaw in 1411, where the 'Knicht of Lawriston' was slain in his armour.

The first reference to the Cove is in 1527, by way of the *Arbroath Liber*, narrating the agreement between William Rolland and Gilbert Menzies, Provost of Aberdeen, in regards to renting a number of lands from Arbroath Abbey, in which the Cove is recorded as 'le Coyf'. In 1544 a charter was drawn up by David, Cardinal of the Holy Roman Church, Archbishop of St Andrews, Primate of Scotland, to grant in feu form to Alexander Grahame, lawful son of William, Earl of Montrose, half of the barony of Torrie, its mosses, crofts, mills, boats and white fishings (including the fishing villages of Torry and the Cove). Writing in the mid to late 19th century, Andrew Jervise, a collector of epitaphs and all things antique, informs us that in the 16th century the Cove was described as 'the toun of Coif, callit Halyman's Coif'. He adds that the name had originated from the caves and inlets which abound the vicinity, and from one or more of these caves being 'home' to such self-sacrificing holy men who dwelt there, raising beacon fires to warn mariners of impending danger on this much-feared part of the east coast of Scotland. Indeed, in the Register of the Great Seal, Scotland, 28 August 1581, a document was drawn up at Halyruidhous (Holyrood House) where Duncan Forbes was granted the feu of the 'baronie of Torrie, including Loyrstoun and Coif, called Halymanis-coif'; and again on 12 May 1587, when the feu was in turn granted to Gilbert Menzies, inclusive of Lorystoun and Coiff. Owing to regional dialect, and there being no standard Scots grammar, place names, especially, were recorded as pronounced.

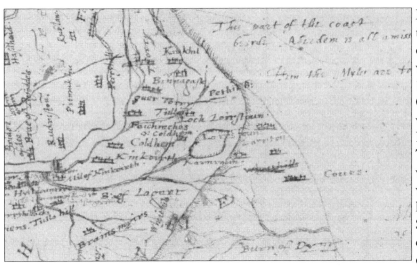

Pont, Timothy, Maps of Scotland c.1590.

Present place names include: Kirkhill, Bannagask (Balnagask), Torry, Kinkourth (Kincorth), Burn of Leggart, Tullo Hill, (Tollohill) Lorrstoun (Loirston) Karnrobin (Cairnrobin) Whitehills, Burn of Dyny (Diney), Hyildountree (Hilldowntree), and of course Coves (the Cove).

Reproduced by kind permission of the National Library of Scotland.

During these medieval times peasant life was one of austerity, and not without ignorance, for in 1607 Isobel Smith of the Cove was charged with witchcraft before the Presbytery of Aberdeen. The evidence showed that when Jonet (Janet) Jack was ill, she was advised by her mother to consult Smith, who would soon diagnose her ailment. A charm was employed to discover whether it was the fevers she suffered from, and a single grey woollen thread wound about her body, at which she would be haillit (healed) thereafter. Jonet Jack died and Smith was accused of her death. One witness said that when the thread was put about her body she was commanded to go once about, in the name of the Father, Son and the Holy Ghost.

Blaeu, Joan, Aberdonia and Banfia, 1654.

The Cove does not appear, the only place names in the parish of Nigg being Lorstoun and Torry.

Reproduced by kind permission of the National Library of Scotland.

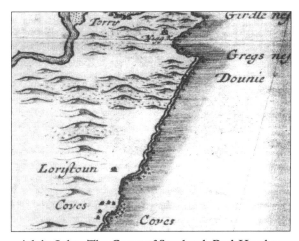

Adair, John, The Coast of Scotland, Red-Head to Aberdeen, 1703.

The Cove appears as Coves, Loristoun (Loirston) is immediately to the north.

Reproduced by kind permission of the National Library of Scotland.

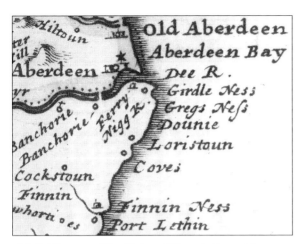

Moll, Herman, The Shire of Kincairdin or Mearns, with the South Part of Aberdeenshire, 1745.

On this smaller scale map the ferry crossing is indicated, with the Cove again depicted as Coves. Port Lethin (Portlethen) and Finnin (Findon) are also given mention.

Reproduced by kind permission of the National Library of Scotland.

Garden, William, A Map of Kincardineshire, 1774.

Cove Harbour is first noted, which suggests a pier is present, with the granite quarries clearly already in operation. A road runs from the Cove to the old Bridge of Dee. Interesting names appear, such as The Stoney Hills and Stotties Dykes.

Reproduced by kind permission of the National Library of Scotland.

Who Owns What?

Securing an area of land appeared to be a cut-throat business and ardently contested, for in 1618 William Forbes of Monymusk was awarded the barony of Torrie, including the Fishtown of the Cove, known as Halymanis-coiff; only for Gilbert Menzies to gain a half share of the said barony on 2 July in 1647, inclusive of the Cove, recorded as Coiff, 'Halymanis' now having disappeared. This see-sawing of property rights contributed to the ongoing Forbes-Menzies feud, which raged for hundreds of years. From 1664 there appears an ongoing battle between Aberdeen Town Council and the Menzies Family, as to who owns what. In 1704 the Town Council of Aberdeen purchased an undivided half of the lands of the barony of Torrie; the other half being the property of Mr. Menzies of Pitfodels. At this time the details of the division of the lands between the two are unclear, but judging by the sheer amount of Court of Session records, was ambiguous to both. It seems the two parties did not divide the land but instead shared profits from it; the system proving both ineffective and frustrating. Following 81 years of regular legal dispute, the situation was finally resolved on 10 February 1785, by way of arbitration, when an agreement was entered into for the purpose of affecting a division of the lands between both parties, the arbiters being master of mortifications Robert Innes, George Moir of Scotstown, and Dr. William Thom of Craibstone. The term 'mortifications' relates to what was originally lands bequeathed to the Church for religious purpose, but was later extended to public benefactions. After what no doubt proved to be a wrangling affair, both the villages of Torry and the Cove were apportioned between the two; John Menzies Esq. retaining the western part of Torry and the southern part of the Cove. In this document the present day spelling of 'Cove' appears:

EXTRACT DECREET ARBITAL BETWEEN MASTER OF MORTIFICATIONS OF TOWN AND ABERDEEN AND JOHN MENZIES OF PITFODELS FOR DIVISION OF LANDS AND BARONY OF TORRY, 1785.

(Excerpts)

"…the fishing town therein called the Cove, consisting of the houses and kailyards possessed by the Fishers together with such further quantity of land not under six acres to each party adjoint to their houses for kailyards and such quantity of moss for their firing as the arbiters or oversman find necessary shall be set apart and divided betwixt the parties in such way as the said arbiters or oversman shall deem to be equal, with power and right to the parties after the Division thereof to use and occupy the harbour of the same in common and to have as many Fishers and fishing boats in their respective shares as they shall think proper…

…that we are to declare the Harbour of the Cove to be common to both parties and equally accessible from both Letts and to reserve a privilege to each party to keep and employ as many boats and Fishers there as may choose".

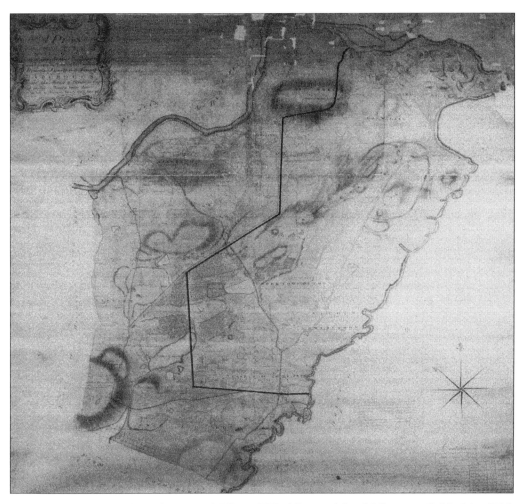

Brown, George, Lands & barony of Nigg, 1777. The parish of Nigg as divided in 1785 between John Menzies Esq. and the Town of Aberdeen. The partition began at the Struak Strype, or Burn, in the north and terminated by dividing the Cove in two. The eastern portion being that of Aberdeen, and the western belonging to John Menzies Esq.

Reproduced by kind permission of Aberdeen City Archives.

However, ownership of the Cove itself was a complex affair, containing crofts and houses that belonged to both John Menzies Esq. and Aberdeen Town Council. Just how deep resentment ran between the two parties may be noted in the finer details of the agreement, where even the most trivial was disputed. For example, the line of division ran through two small houses in the fishtown, whereon, after some deliberation, it was agreed that once the houses fell into disrepair they would simply be allowed to become ruinous. In general, though, houses that belonged to both parties were decided by one paying the other the value of the house; or, if a settlement could not be reached, then an independent assessor would be called and recompense agreed on somewhere in between! Because of the importance of the fishing it was further agreed that access should be made by way of a proper road to the harbour, while the existing road heading from the Cove through Loirston, be kept open. There is no indication whether the fishermen of the Cove would be subjected to any harbour dues when they brought their boats and fish to the port of Aberdeen. The pier repairs were the responsibility of both parties, although in effect was the property of John Menzies Esq., as was the rights to the salmon fishing. Boundaries were marked by way of march stones: A for Aberdeen and P for Pitfodels, while some had impressed upon them A on one side and P on the other.

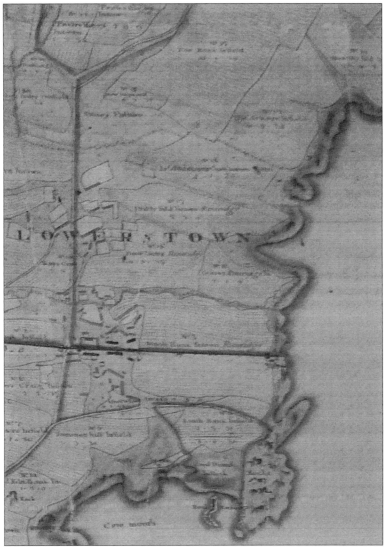

Brown, George, Lands & barony of Nigg, 1777. The Cove.

Reproduced by kind permission of Aberdeen City Archives.

On the page previous is the hand drawn survey map of Nigg in 1777, by George Brown, specifically the Fishtown of Cove and immediate area. These early details render the village barely recognisable from that of today, there being no terraced rows, merely a scattering of crofts and houses, established in no particular order. A little to the north is the Crofts of Lowerstown, and where the road forks became the southern bounds of Loirston House. The Cove Bay Hotel, or the Inn, has not yet been constructed, nor the Endowed School on present-day Colsea Road. The site of the Watch House is known as Card Beard Hillock, while names such as The Arbour (Greenarbour), The Graves, and further to the south, Brownies Fold (Bruin's or 'Broonie's Cave), persist today. The thick shaded lines are boundaries and roads, where on either side of the horizontal delineation lies present-day Spark Terrace, where effectively the ownership of the Cove was divided between John Menzies Esq. and Aberdeen Town Council. The Cove Road is to the left, and the upper end of the vertical line is present-day Loirston Road.

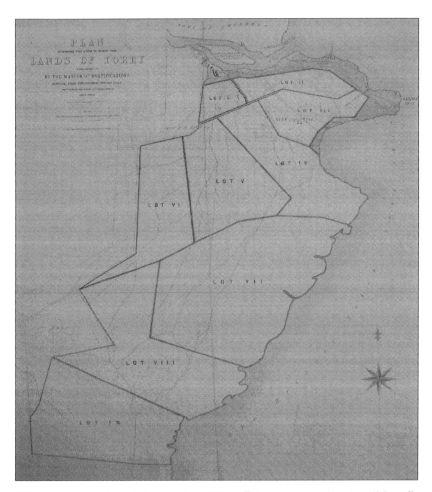

The eastern portion of the parish of Nigg: "Feuing plan of lands of Torry" by Walker & Duncan, C E and land surveyors, Aberdeen, 1896.

The nine lots as divided in 1785, albeit large western portions of lots eight and nine having been purchased by John Menzies Esq, including the eastmost part of Charleston. The village of Torry was of course absorbed into Aberdeen five years previously, and therefore no longer part of the parish of Nigg. Moreover, the western half of the parish, as owned by John Menzies Esq., was also divided into lots and feud.

Reproduced by kind permission of Aberdeen City Archives.

By May 1786 the eastern half of the parish was divided into nine lots by Mr. Ninian Johnston, then master of mortifications in Aberdeen, the boundary beginning at the Struak Strype (Burn) at the heart of the village of Torry, and continuing south in a zig-zag fashion before terminating in a straight line through the Cove, heading due east towards the sea. The lots therein: I North Balnagask; II North Kirkhill; III South Kirkhill; IV South Balnagask; V Middletown; VI Tullos; VII Altens; VIII North Loirstown; IX South Loirstown, in which parts of the Fishtown of Cove lay within. The lots being exposed to public roup and sale by way of feu in the tolbooth in Aberdeen, on Saturday 17 June. Worthy of a mention is the Fishtown of Altens (whose remains may still be seen today), a single row of cottages constructed around 1785, most likely in order to attract a tenantry composed of both farmers and fishermen. However, by 1829 a strip of land on the south bank of the River Dee, including a part of the Balnagask headland, became the sole property of the Treasurer of the Burgh of Aberdeen.

FEUS OF TORRIE NEAR ABERDEEN

(Excerpts)

LOT IX To be called SOUTH LOIRSTOWN, containing some of the southmost parts of Upper and Nether Loirstowns, and what was formerly called the Crofts of Lowerstown, with that part of the Cove and of the Fishtown, now belonging to the master of mortifications by the late division, and the fish boats and pertinents, so far as he has right thereto.

Each lot will have moss assigned to it, and they are as well accommodated with water. And the purchasers will have right to the teinds and multures of their respective lots.

The vicinity of these lands to the harbour and city of Aberdeen; the pleasant and commanding views they afford; the easy access they have to lime, sea ware and other manure, and their other advantages, make feus of them very eligible.

Although both the advertising and the extract decreet between the parties suggests the land made for excellent cultivation, the Crofts of Lowerstown was ill accommodated with water, and much of the soil used by the fishermen was poisoned by over-dunging. Lots VIII and IX did not attract much interest, proving difficult to feu. An upset price could not be met, therefore they were further reduced and once more exposed to public roup. The feu duty for South Loirston (present-day spelling) and the Cove being £60 sterling, 50 bolls of meal and 10 bolls of bear (a forerunner of barley, one boll being enough to sew 0.51 present-day hectares). The feu duties were further reduced at the end of the month — and still there were no takers! It was not until the spring of 1788 before the estate of South Loirston was eventually secured, namely by Mr. William Matthew, a vintner in Aberdeen. He became, in effect, the first owner of the Cove.

The Menzies Family

Having outlined the beginnings and the ownership of the area, it would be an injustice not to further the notable name of Menzies. The Menzies Family could be described as being the first Lairds of the Cove, but they had other, and more important issues, than what amounted to a fishtown in a corner of the parish. They stemmed from a prominent family of Aberdeen burgesses in the 15th century, and from at least the 16th century owned the lands of Pitfodels, situated in present-day Cults, Aberdeen. Around 1534 Thomas Menzies, Provost of Aberdeen, built one of the town's first stone houses, entertaining King James V in 1537; and in 1650 it was occupied by King Charles II on his way south from Moray to his crowning at Scone. They rose in power, ruling over among other lands the barony of Torry by 1520. Gilbert Menzies was created Provost of Aberdeen in 1576. However, in 1618 William Forbes of Monymusk acquired the said barony of Torry, an act which did nothing to appease the resentment between the two families. In 1647 Gilbert Menzies of Pitfodels secured a half share of the lands on the south side of the River Dee, including Torry and the Cove, which proved desirable property, and in time was required for the expansion of Aberdeen harbour, including the development of the town. Although the Menzies family were a prominent landowning family, they did not take part in local politics.

Like most landed gentry their history contained some colourful scenes, none more than the murder of Alexander Menzies on 9 May 1580. Findon had lately been acquired by Menzies of Pitfodels, and it would appear that in these times a species of falcon — probably the peregrine falcon — built their nests in the higher reaches of the cliffs. Alexander Menzies, son of the Provost of Aberdeen, was charged with the preservation of a nest for the service of James VI, who was passionately fond of hawking. That morning an ambush was laid for his life, the Forbes-Menzies feud breaking out afresh when William Forbes of Monymusk and Portlethen, along with some followers, lay concealed behind the Cairn of Loirston, some 200 yards to the east of the loch. Having waited for several hours their victim approached unattended, and placing their culverins (heavy muskets) on rests, they were able to take aim. At the first discharge he fell, pierced through the heart by two bullets. The assassins rushed forward, inflicting no fewer than nine stab wounds on the body, robbing it of sword, hanger, and cloak. Thirty years were to elapse before the perpetrators were brought to trial.

John Menzies Esq.

In more recent times the most well-known head of the family was John Menzies Esq. of Pitfodels, 1756 — 1843. After the division of Nigg in 1785 he was offering crofts of as little as five or six acres, reclaimed from original 'infield', and moor. This was not so much the old order of land use, but a deliberate attempt in regards to settlement, establishing the farming township of Charleston, formerly called Drumforskie, with some 200 inhabitants brought down from the Highlands. At this time the land was run-ridged, or 'run-rig', where the tenants of the different properties of each farm had a right to plough and sow a ridge by turn. A privilege, as one late 18th century writer described, "grossly opposite to common sense... that one is amazed how it could ever have come into the mind of men to claim it." The 'infield' received all the manure of the farm and was perpetually in crop; the 'outfield' consisted of what was called 'rig and baulk', where between the arable ridges lay an interjacent space which the plough never touched. These upper lands to the west of the Cove were rather exposed, being prone to bad harvests, particularly in 1768 and 1782, when the crofters suffered greatly. Nevertheless, water was plentiful by way of the Loch of Loirston, covering 27 acres, thought to have been formed by a block of debris from the third ice age and plenished by means of an artesian well; moreover, at the beginning of the 19th century it was supplying water to the only mill in the vicinity, with a further two in operation during the coming decades.

Like his ancestors John Menzies Esq. was a staunch Roman Catholic, and in 1827 gifted his estate, including the mansion house of Blairs, Kincardineshire, to the Bishop of Aberdeen, on behalf of the foundation of a college for the education of secular priests. Blairs College opened in 1829. In 1805 he exposed the lands of Pitfodels for sale, and with no purchaser forthcoming subsequently feud off several portions. He died in Edinburgh in 1843 aged 87 years, a widower, and the last of his race. A portion of his land at Charleston was bequeathed to the Ursuline Convent of St. Margaret's, Edinburgh, with the eastmost part now occupied by a modern housing development. Not one single representative of this family now remains and their castle, which for so long stood like a sentinel overlooking the countryside, has been completely demolished. Indeed, its site can scarcely be seen, although it is known to have been at a location formerly called Castleheugh, and close to the eastern side of the Norwood Hall Hotel. The area of Pitfodels is commemorated by way of a road and a primary school in Cults, and the name of Menzies in the form of Menzies Road in Torry.

The Coming of the Lairds

To anyone of the Cove, 'The Laird's' was the walled premises containing Loirston House, an impressive structure surrounded by trees and shrubs. Today, of course, it's the private housing complex known as Loirston Manor. The name would have arisen when Mr. Alexander Muir built a modest mansion with commanding views; though smaller in construction prior to Dr. Alexander Kilgour's occupancy, it would have made for an imposing sight against the wee crofts and coastguard cottages strung along Loirston Road.

The first proprietor of South Loirston and parts of the Cove, or Laird, to coin a phrase, resulted from the aforesaid division of the eastern half of the barony of Torry between Aberdeen Town and John Menzies Esq. On 17 April 1788 a Charter of Confirmation was secured in favour of vintner Mr. William Matthew of Aberdeen, who requested a three month delay before taking the feu, as he was to be abroad until the month of July. Whether he ever set foot on his property is uncertain, the estate being acquired by way of disposition and assignation on 27 September 1788 by the Reverend Mr. Francis Johnston, Rector of Vere in Jamaica, afterwards residing in the town of Aberdeen. His sister, Miss Elizabeth Johnston, oversaw affairs. What must be considered is that when obtaining titled land the actual documentation may not take place for up to several years later due to the expense of recording events in the Register of Sasines, a legal binding which covered all such property transactions.

The following February saw Miss Elizabeth Johnston given life rent of the estate, and his nephew James Johnston in fee, albeit not recorded until 10 October 1797. On 13 August 1802 a Charter of Resignation and Confirmation was drawn up by the master of mortifications in Aberdeen in favour of Miss Elizabeth Johnston and Mr. James Johnston, which effectively entitled them to ownership of the estate. Little is known of them, apart from Miss Johnston's residence in the Cove being described as a small mansion, neat and tidy and overlooking the sea. This was in turn Bon Accord Cottage, becoming part of the Cove Farm buildings, and presently a thoroughly modernised dwelling. It would be feasible to suggest that along with Greenarbour (most likely built during the time of the Johnstons) these two houses would make for the oldest standing constructions in the Cove. Elizabeth Johnston held sway until 9 January 1810, when she resigned the estate, selling her residence of Bon Accord Cottage to Mr. James Hector, described as a 'farmer of Fernieflat', who in 1787 leased a part of the lands of Blairs from John Menzies Esq. He was also a salmon merchant, and acquired Miss Johnston's estate by way of disposition, having begun to prosper from being lessee of several salmon stations by the Dee and Don, including those at the Cove and Altens. This would appear to have been his main objective, there being little evidence of any improvements to the village itself (excepting, perhaps, an inn). On 20 April 1813 a Charter of Confirmation of the said estate was recorded in favour of the same James Hector, both Elizabeth and James Johnston having passed away.

On 23 November 1816 the estate fell by way of disposition to baillie Mr. Alexander Duthie Esq.

of Broadford (Kittybrewster), a merchant and ship owner in Aberdeen. He took an interest in the affairs of the village, regularly commuting there from his home, inclusive of presiding over the 'Society of Whitefishers in Cove'. The area to the west of his estate appeared to be of little use, at which he sold a tract of land to John Menzies Esq., who found it most beneficial in regards to the recently established township of Charlestown. A Charter of Confirmation was made in his favour and recorded in the Chartered Register of County Lands on 3 December 1828. Personal misfortune befell him, however, for in February 1832 his estate was being sequestrated by Aberdeen advocate Mr. Alexander Webster, and recorded in the Register of Sasines the following year. It may well be that owing to his plans for expanding and improving his portion of the Cove (including enlargement or construction of the inn), much debt had been accrued in doing so. Moreover, he had married his first cousin, Margaret Duthic, a sister of Mr. Walter Duthie, a notable figure in Aberdeen, and who amassed the wealth which made the family a financial power.

Their residence was No. 34 Maberley Street, producing five children, three of whom died before the age of fifty, Alexander himself passing away on 8 March 1853, aged 76 years. Walter Duthie was a bachelor and produced no heirs, passing away in 1863; at the time of his death there being of the family but Alexander Duthie Jr. and Elizabeth Crombie Duthie still alive, neither of whom ever married. Therefore as representative of the female line the property devolved upon Alexander Duthie Jr. He died in 1877, aged 76 years, leaving the bulk of his estate to his sister, who in 1881 bequeathed the area of land for the setting of the Duthie Park, which opened on 27 September 1883. Interestingly enough, the building work for the walls and lodges was carried out by contractors Messrs. P. Bisset & Son, who made improvements to the piers and breakwater at the Cove that same year. Elizabeth Crombie Duthie passed away in 1885, and is interred with other members of her family in St. Nicholas Churchyard. A commemorative plaque was installed on the wall at her former residence of 34 Maberley Street in February 2005, though the building is no longer of architectural interest, and is to be turned into flatted accommodation by 2009.

The estate was acquired by Mr. Alexander Muir on 29 December 1834 and recorded in the Register of Sasines the following March. Alexander Muir was born at the farm of Netherleask in the parish of Slains in 1793. On 11 August 1831, he married Mary Ann Catherine Kilgour of Woodside, a relation of future owner Dr. Alexander Kilgour; the marriage for Muir being financially favourable. He remained resident in Aberdeen at first, throwing himself into new methods of agricultural improvement on his newly-acquired estate, running his business from No. 36 Union Street. His keen interest of local affairs are recorded in the parish records, where he may be found making donations to various causes and relative issues, taking an active part in appointing a schoolmaster for the Endowed School in the village. His services to the area were recognised in June 1840 when friends and neighbours organised a complimentary dinner for him at the Cove Bay Hotel, then known as the Muir-Arms' Inn. Along with the many toasts was the consensus that he 'understood the welfare of his tenants at heart', while Mr. James Craib, innkeeper, served up a wholly delicious meal. Public achievement, however, was conflicted by private sorrow. His wife Mary bore him two sons, Patrick Kilgour Muir (1832 — 6) and George Falconer Muir (1836 — ?), who inherited the estate on the death of his father. She died in April 1837.

It is most likely that after her death Alexander Muir took up residence at South Loirston, building Loirston House in 1842 at a cost of £800. However, by 1845 a wanderlust was upon him, and he took himself aboard a sailing ship to Ottawa, recording events in a diary. Loirston House was let, his son George being packed off to boarding school. The following spring he was back at his estate, attending meetings at the Nigg Parochial Board. In December 1847 he married Jane B. Ferguson, the daughter of Mr. James Ferguson of Altens, who, like himself, may be described as an improving landlord. This second marriage, too, was short-lived, for she died in January 1849, aged 26 years. Though of a pleasant disposition, Muir would appear to have been a shrewd businessman, for one month after purchasing the estate (like Alexander Duthie before him) he had sold 11½ acres of wasteland in the extreme west of his property, which in turn was the eastmost parcel of mosses pertaining to Findon and Cookston, then known as the 'Groundless Myres'. This acquired land was termed as New Park, and purchased by two local farmers. For reasons unknown, however, he purchased in 1845 Nunnery Croft from John Menzies Esq., situated some 250 yards due west of the northern end of the Loch of Loirston. In 1848 the railway provided him with additional income, the tracks being laid on a portion of his property. By the summer he was chairman of the Nigg Parochial Board, but resigned the following year due to ill health. Alexander Muir died on 13 November 1850, and was buried, as were his two wives and son Patrick, in Nellfield Cemetery, Aberdeen.

For Sale

In his will Alexander Muir had made a number of fellow advocates Trustees of his estate, giving them authority to run his affairs, including the welfare of his son George. He requested that they meet for a yearly audit at Loirston House, or in the event of it being leased, at the then Cove Inn, where they were liberally invited to wine and dine at the expense of his Trust. In 1855 George Falconer Muir began to inherit his father's estate, albeit not entirely, until attaining the age of 21 years. Though now resident in Edinburgh he became active in land transactions, purchasing an area of moss in the vicinity of Charleston. In the March and May of 1857, by way of an Instrument of Sasine, he acquired the eastern part of the Lands of Cove, inclusive of the southern portion of the fishtown. However, the purchase was under the reservation of certain cliffs, rocks, and braes of uncultivated land, which was in effect the rights to the salmon fishing. In the following years Loirston House was let several times, George Falconer Muir having settled in Edinburgh and later becoming a writer.

At this time Dr. Alexander Kilgour, a renowned physician in Aberdeen, had already secured the part of the Lands of Cove which lay to the west of the railway, and was desirous of the remainder, which is further explained in the following pages. Land acquisition was keenly contested, for in 1856, and prior to South Loirston and the Lands of Cove becoming the ownership of one individual, the valued rents were as follows: George Muir £728 South Loirston; Town of Aberdeen £709 South Loirston; John Blaikie (advocate and Trustee for the late John Menzies Esq.) £516 10s. Cove; Dr. Kilgour £294 10s. Cove. Like his father George Falconer Muir would appear to have a keen sense of business nous, for in October 1862 he secured the remaining cliffs, rocks and braes, etc, including the rights to the salmon fishing, from the sequestrated estate of the said John Blaikie.

That same month he was advertising the estate of South Loirston and the whole of the Fishtown of Cove as being just under 340 acres, of which a little over 15 acres was occupied by the village itself. The Cove Moss (the land to the west leading to Charleston) was of considerable extent, being of great value to the fishing population. Loirston House was described as being substantial and in good order, consisting of dining and drawing rooms, parlour, five bedrooms, and two dressing rooms, with kitchen and servants' accommodation, etc, and surrounded by a thriving plantation of hardwood. The garden and grounds were portrayed as being well stocked with fruit trees and enclosed by walls. The quarries, too, were held in high regard, being leased by Gibb & Son. The Lands of Cove were held blench of the Crown; the lands of South Loirston held feu of the Town of Aberdeen. In the event of the whole estate not being sold his intent was to expose the village lands of Cove and adjacent lands as a separate lot:

Part 1. Part of South Loirston: Cove Lands and the Inn; the Salmon Fishings; the Houses, Steadings and Yards; the Fishers' Houses; the Fish Manure.

Part 2. The Lands of Cove: Village Lands of Cove; Garden Land; Pasture Land, Sea Braes, Salmon Bothy and Icehouse; Preventative Water Guard House (Coastguard); Quarries; Fishers' Houses; Fish Manure; Roads.

Until the above proceedings ownership of the Cove had always been divided, bearing in mind that the southern portion of the village was not originally part of the estate of South Loirston, and rather the Lands of Cove. Moreover, in Part 1 the Fishers' Houses consisted of those that lay between present-day Colsea Road and the northern half of present-day Spark Terrace; Part 2 being from the southern half of the said Spark Terrace to present-day Stoneyhill Terrace.

On 17 July 1863, by way of an Instrument of Sasine, Dr. Alexander Kilgour acquired the whole of the above, in effect creating a single proprietor for South Loirston and the Lands of Cove.

Dr. Alexander Kilgour

A name upon a page can hold little significance until further exploration, and such is that of Alexander Kilgour. Dr. Alexander Kilgour was born on 28 October 1803, and rose from poverty to become a well-liked and greatly respected Aberdeen G.P. He started in practice at the age of 23 in 1826, soon after receiving the diploma of the Royal College of Surgeons, London, living above his drugstore in the Gallowgate. Records indicate he was rather an imposing man, having a deep interest in educational institutions. In his early years he was a great Reformer, being described as bluff and 'a Whig and something more'. He had advanced political opinions

and was looked upon with little favour by people of established positions, including authorities in the City and University. He spoke his mind very freely and boldly, regardless of the consequences to himself, enjoying a social drink with friends and being rather partial to 'partan taes' (crab claws). He possessed a force of character which in turn gained the confidence of his patients, and may be described as a mixed bag of authority, being of clear judgement, caustic, yet with a quiet humour. Examples of his wit and thought could be seen in publications of the day, such as the *Aberdeen Magazine,* the *Censor,* the *Herald* and the *Aberdeen Chronicle.* It appears he was as candid in practice as he was in ordinary life, and surprised the more medicine-loving of his patients by his contempt for drugs in which they had put their trust — issuing fewer prescriptions than his contemporaries of the day, and being met with more success towards their collective health!

Dr. Alexander Kilgour.

On the establishment of King's College Medical School he was appointed lecturer on the Practice of Medicine, an office he held for a number of years, and was a physician of the Royal Infirmary in 1838, where his qualities as a clinical lecturer were universally recognised. In 1840 he set up to enquire into the sanitary conditions of the poor, with a view that cholera — quite rightly — was closely related to the existence of open sewers. He was also Chairman of a committee of citizens whose aim was to promote the union of the Universities and continue the independence of the Colleges, becoming bitterly disappointed at the suppression of Marischal College as a School of Arts, and the means of a cheap and easy University education for the youth of Aberdeen.

His first wife was Miss Marjory Dyce, daughter of Mr. Alexander Dyce Esq., of Tillygreig in Aberdeenshire. Sadly, she died in childbirth of her firstborn, which was also stillborn. His personal life was steeped in his profession, and at the age of 44 he married Mary Elizabeth Duncan on 6 January 1848, the daughter of Thomas Duncan, an Aberdeen advocate. She bore him one son, Alexander, born 25 May 1852. His business address became No. 158 Union Street, and, in his sixties, was a force in regards to the founding of a new school in the Cove, a man devoted to literature, his pen always ready to champion what cause he had in his heart. Dr. Kilgour resigned his office of physician in 1864, but was appointed consulting physician until 1871, when ill-health forced him to retire altogether. He became very poorly and in great pain during the last year of his life, and wished release from it all, being more or less confined to his bed. He had enjoyed good health until the summer of 1870, when seized with a serious and a painful illness from which he never recovered, and died on 19 February 1874, survived by his wife and son. His wife Mary Elizabeth Duncan, died on 22 January 1894, aged 93 years. He was reputed to have built up the best consulting practice in the north of Scotland, with an annual income of £3,000 per annum — an amazing figure at the time.

Estate Acquisition

As mentioned, in December 1854 Dr. Kilgour purchased 229 acres of the Lands of Cove lying to the west of the railway line from Mr. John Blaikie, advocate and Trustee for the estate of the late John Menzies Esq, Mr. Blaikie having purchased the whole of the Lands of Cove in 1848 for £11,350. It is worth noting that in the preceding year a sum of £3,500 was granted by the Land Improvement Act to the Trustees of the late John Menzies Esq. for improving drainage and enclosure, including those tenant farmers who held what was known as an Improving Lease. The results of the labour from the aforementioned Act may be witnessed by the many drystane dykes still standing today.

The property now belonging to Dr. Kilgour comprised three farms of sound condition: the Cove Farm of 89 contiguous acres; the Farm of Calsies, or Calsay Croft, of which two plots of land measuring six acres were leased to tenant farmer Mrs. Janet Sinclair; and that of South Blackhills. There was also the western portion of the quarries. The land, however, still required extensive trenching, drainage and dyking. What appears rather odd, though, is that the Loirston Moss was actually situated on the Lands of Cove, and consisted of a rectangular piece of ground a little over 13 acres in area, located to the west of the railway line, and stretching between the middle of the Braedens (the precipitous cliffs opposite the harbour) to the Colsea Yawn. Dr. Kilgour immediately set to work, and being a visionary physician with an infant son, Seaview House was built by summer the following year, set in half an acre, with Dr. John Ferguson (previously residing at No. 11 the Cove) installed to oversee the medical needs of the people of the village and surrounding area. The said Dr. Ferguson commuted over an extensive area, and could be witnessed being pulled along by horse and sledge during severe winters.

There appears to be a serious wrangle between John Blaikie and Dr. Kilgour regarding the purchase of the Lands of Cove, for the moss that lay to the west of Wellington Road had to be mutually divided between the two parties by way of a Decree Arbitral in May 1855. Once settled, John Blaikie was allocated an area of just over four acres, beginning at the Checkbar and continuing for a length of 220 yards along the road; Dr. Kilgour being granted just over 5 acres, with a length of around 300 yards; the areas being demarcated by way of march stones. Resentment between the two was furthered in December 1855 when a Mr. Matthews of Nigg sent a list of the valued rents of the parish, where Dr. Kilgour's portion was stated as being £69 12s., and Mr. Blaikie for his part the same sum. Moreover, Dr. Kilgour owned at least 75% of the property in question! A reason, perhaps, for such legal rancour, is that the adjoining lands of Charlestown and Drumquhale were not being offered for sale, and were in fact bequeathed to the aforementioned Ursuline Convent of St. Margaret's, Edinburgh.

Dr. Kilgour, however, wished to acquire the remainder of the Lands of Cove, inclusive of the fishtown, and became frustrated at Mr. Blaikie, who had at first indicated his intention to sell, but for reasons unknown withdrew the offer. In the December of 1856 Dr. Kilgour was pressing for an answer. He was never to receive one, the eastern portion of the Lands of Cove, inclusive of the fishtown, being acquired the following year by George Falconer Muir. Nevertheless, he was soon to have his way, purchasing from the said George Falconer Muir in July 1863 the estate of South Loirston and the remaining Lands of Cove, inclusive of the rights to the salmon fishing.

Having secured both properties, he was to show his character and intentions by hiring land surveyor Mr. James Beattie, describing to him in a letter that he was 'rather ashamed at the look of some parts of my property', and immediately launched into a great many improvements during the time of his ownership. Though Loirston House was part of the South Loirston estate Dr. Kilgour remained resident near his practice in Aberdeen.

Loirston House

Part of a postcard sequence of the village during the mid 1960's.

Although Alexander Muir was responsible for the construction of Loirston House, it was somewhat smaller than the later photographs indicate. In November 1863 Dr. Kilgour had plans drawn up to greatly extend both the house and enclosure walls, whose perimeter stretched to less than half of what is seen today; there being no trees to the north of the bounds adjacent to Langdykes Road. The area that lay to the north of the house was in fact open ground, and was known as the 'house field', measuring 3.3 acres, the total area of the bounds of Loirston House being around 6.5 acres. Plans for the lodge at the northwest corner were drawn up in 1864. Dr. Kilgour, however, did not get possession of Loirston House until June of that year, the tenancy being occupied by Mr. George Yule, an elderly merchant whose business lay in Aberdeen.

In September the plans for extension and modernisation had been drafted and fully realised, the ground floor comprising: drawing room, bedroom, spare room, porch, dining room, corridor, kitchen, butler's pantry, bath and w.c., wine cellar, closet, larder, pantry, milk house, scullery, wash house, laundry. The upper floor: bedroom, closet, bedroom, dressing room, landing, store room, laundry, bedroom, bedroom, bedroom, dressing room, servant's rooms, drying loft. Huge bay windows were to be added to the exterior of the additional wings.

Two years later estimates were still being tendered for the required extensions, amounting to just under £1200. In October 1866 things were finally underway, though some difficulty arose in regards to obtaining stone for the frontage, there being a dispute, or some misunderstanding, pertaining to the working of the stones from the Cove Quarries. Of course, the original building itself was composed of local granite, though the additional masonry was from granite elsewhere. In November 1866 the redesigned hall entrance pushed the estimate for the work up to £1287. During the extensive

Loirston House in autumn. The central and original portion of the building was constructed by Alexander Muir; the wings and extension being added by Dr. Alexander Kilgour in 1866. Inset view of the premises today.

interior reconstruction it is believed that Italian artisans were hired to create ornate stucco ceilings and frescos, with entry being gained to the premises by the summer of the following year. Additional buildings included stables, a coach house and a piggery; the house garden now inclusive of a croquet lawn for the amusement of young Alexander. In essence, though, Dr. Kilgour would have spent no more than the remaining three years of his life at Loirston House, living in quiet seclusion.

An aerial view of Loirston House, circa 1950's. On the right there is located a piggery and outhouses. Market garden operations may be seen to the left of the house itself.

The full glory of the bounds of Loirston House may be seen on a sketch map of 1888, and depicted as fully walled. The layout then, within the present-day perimeter, being as follows: the house itself was set southwest from the centre of the bounds, with the rectangular house garden to the immediate northwest, stretching to the outer wall, inclusive of a conservatory. There was a smaller garden situated at the extreme southeast, with the remainder of the land on the east, and as far as the north boundary wall, consisting of 3 acres of arable land, separated by two narrow belts of trees. A road ran through the bounds, leading from the lodge on the northwest corner, curving through the grounds to the main entrance on Loirston Road. To the southeast was a huge tree-enclosed lawn, and to the northwest a further large area of arable land. The entire perimeter of the grounds was thickly lined with trees and shrubs. A house as such, however, required a great deal of attention, and by the mid 1890's was beginning to register many repairs, especially to the roof and drains. In 1904 the house was vacated and lay empty for nineteen years, and in 1922 a great deal of the furniture sold off by public roup within the bounds themselves. Further details appear in the following pages.

Overseeing Affairs

At the death of his father, Alexander Kilgour Jr. was aged 21, and began to manage the estate. Among the day to day business affairs was the upkeep of the Cove. In 1878 he financed the constructions at the harbour, which was of great benefit to the fishermen, and also improved the sanitary conditions of the village in general. Remaining a bachelor, he was an educated man, recording two accounts of his travels abroad, mostly by way of train, the first being 'A Three Month Tour of the Continent', published in 1877, followed by 'A Spanish Diary', published in 1882. There were of course other property interests in and around Aberdeen, including the landed estate of Dunnydeer near Insch. Sadly, Alexander Kilgour was committed to an asylum at Woolmanhill in 1904. He died there on 30 March 1921, aged 68 years, and is buried, as are his mother and father, in St. Peter's Cemetery, Aberdeen.

Such statistics, however, merely scratch the surface, and the troubles of estate management are manifold, beginning with the inadequacies regarding the sanitation of the village, which, by the close of 1878, gave Mrs. Kilgour cause enough to pen, 'we find our health will not stand such continued worry', and that both she and her son wished to sell the whole of the estate. Such letters, incidentally, were headed *Loirston House*. Of course, what must also be taken into consideration is the expense and the construction of the harbour that year, highlighted by a letter written on behalf of Mr. Kilgour: '… for some years past the fishing population has become very troublesome and he feels (Alexander Kilgour) all the more as he personally looks after the fishing village. During the last five years he has devoted himself to the improvement of the sanitary condition of the village. He has improved the roads, he has built several new dwelling houses for the fishermen. Unfortunately for him, the fishermen do not appreciate these improvements, but have become, if possible, more obstinate and difficult than before.' It appears that by 1880 more than £1,000 had been spent on upgrading the middens and privies, and that a man called Ferguson was being paid 15s. per week to empty the manure, albeit insufficiently.

The main reason for the antagonistic attitude of the fishermen was because of the recent harbour constructions, whereby the collective rent of the houses in the village was increased by around £100 per annum. This was detailed in a letter proposing that each man who went to the deep sea fishing or the herring fishing, whether householder or not, would have to pay £1 10s. per annum in regards to interest of the money laid upon the piers and breakwater, as the government would not allow for the charging of harbour dues. For the convenience of the fishers the additional rent would be collected on the second Monday of September at the termination of the inshore herring fishing. Other factors evolved, in that each man was requested he take a tack of nineteen years on his house, and that the houses of older men who have given up the fishing be put into the name of their eldest unmarried son. This in fact caused uproar, with mention of a threat of the fishers leaving the village as a whole.

It appears that resentment ran deep, for at the close of 1879 a rather bitter memorandum was sent to Alexander Kilgour (most likely written by his advocate), directed at the fisher-folk of the Cove: 'Don't build any more houses, never give any repairs unless where you are made certain that they are absolutely required… they will tell lies in your very face… let them understand that they will have to pay additional rent on every repair… if they say they are poor and cannot afford to pay for repairs tell them that they must go away as their houses can be easily let to others… persons leaving their houses in a dilapidated condition will be handed over to the public authorities for prosecution.' Ironically it was soon after that the method of trawling drew a number of tenants to Torry, the line fishing being in decline, at which the houses were no longer being occupied.

Alexander Kilgour and his mother were still agreeable to sell the estate, and 'cut their losses', so to speak. Family advocate Mr. Patrick Cooper replied that it would be inadvisable to do so as this would incur a considerable loss of income, there being 'legal technicalities' written into the will of the late Dr. Kilgour in regards to the power of sale in which the Trustees of the University of Aberdeen were in some way the beneficiaries, even though the Kilgours were each left a half share of the estate. Nevertheless, they wished to proceed with the sale and relocate to a steading near Banchory, but again were discouraged by the steep cost of the premises, and that the price of beef had fallen quite sharply. It was advised they sell a part or parts at first, without impacting on the remainder of the estate, the foremost being the village itself, along with Balmoral Place and the salmon fishing rights, which would 'free him from all further bother with fishermen and the harbour'. Particulars for the sale of the estate were drawn up accordingly, its location having a special value of being within the 'Milch Circle' of Aberdeen. Even then Patrick Cooper again advised they at first sell only the fishtown, the fishings, the quarries, the inn, and a small quantity of land between the railway and the sea. With no purchaser forthcoming, the Kilgours were to advertise the whole of the estate of South Loirston and the Lands of Cove in both the local and national press, under the heading: 'Valuable Seaside Residential Estate for sale', by public roup on 13 July 1882, with an upset price of £52,000, the property being measured at a total of 613 acres.

However, problems appeared to erupt intermittently in regards to the fishing population, and in August 1881 there was an abundance of rent arrears in the village, which may be interpreted as either poor fishing, animosity towards the proprietor Mr. Kilgour, or simply down to the fact that many would soon be relocating to Torry, therefore unwilling to pay the last instalment of their rents. If partly through resentment it appears that the fishermen had lost heart, or indeed their faith in the Cove, and Mr. Kilgour, having been away on the continent, would have returned to a very different picture of the village. Indeed, in June 1886 the rents collected at Whitsunday were described as 'but a middling collection', along with a great deal of complaint. He was advised by his advocate to seriously consider the condition of the village, as there were many empty houses, amounting to around one fifth in total, and so much discontent amongst the remaining tenants that something would have to be done. It was also stated that as the fishermen got nothing to themselves for the manure, they were simply cleaning the fish at sea and throwing the guts overboard, rather than bring the offal home. It was suggested that in place of this long-standing rent in kind, a monetary offer might be made for the manure, as was the custom at Portlethen, where the farmers brought in cart loads of moss and mixed it with the fish offal at the village, which created a valuable compost, and in turn was purchased at a fixed price.

There was trouble concerning the land tenants, too, and in February 1880 farmer Mr. William Walker of Westerton, Whitehills, was still seeking recompense from Alexander Kilgour for damage incurred by workmen in his fields two years previously when laying pipes for conveying water to Loirston House, for abatement of rent at losing a 'slice of land', taken off for the burn carrying water to Cove village above the school, and for cutting 400 yards of small drains in the field in which the water was conveyed for the fountain at Loirston House. The above being merely an extension of the disagreements regarding the plans drawn up for Westerton Farm House in the March of 1866.

Though other incidents arose, a rather amusing aside occurred in 1886 concerning damage inflicted by workmen to grass in a field leased by then innkeeper Mr. Richard Hallglen. At this time the lease of the inn included sowing crops upon the land attached, of which may be barley, turnips, etc. Alexander Kilgour wished to supply piped water to the houses in Balmoral Place by the harbour, and was advised by two elderly fishermen, John Robertson and John Webster, who were resident there, of a disused well which had never been known to go dry. Located at the edge of the field, by an old footpath leading north from Balmoral Road, it appears that the workmen trampled the grass in order to clear this well of boulders and debris, at which Richard Hallglen took umbrage. The incident continued when a civil engineer (who had conducted operations regarding the piers at the harbour) met at the inn with the aforesaid fishermen and innkeeper Hallglen, and jovially remarked to Hallglen that "Kilgour was going to take the water across to Balmoral", at which Hallglen retorted, "This would be like taking away the water that he mixed his whisky with." The two fishermen added that the well had indeed been used for mixing whisky and, "More gold was therefore taken out of it than they had any idea of." Letters ping-ponged back and forth, each with a difference of opinion — from Mrs. Hallglen calling at Loirston House stating that the field had contained barley, to one of Mr. Kilgour's workmen being adamant it contained no more than grass, and the oldest grass in the field at that! It proved no laughing matter, however, and was pursued to the bitter end by the prickly Hallglen, who took the matter to court and settled for compensation by way of £2 2s. Nonetheless, the following February a 430 yard pipeline was laid across the aforementioned field, beginning at the Langburn by the Cove Hotel. A clash of personalities ensued and, needless to say, by 1889 mine host Hallglen had departed.

Yet further stubbornness with the fishers continued, and in 1890 several non-payment of rents occurred, at which a summons was raised against certain tenants. The fishers by this time found that trawling was much more beneficial, and relocated to larger ports, especially that of Torry, which, in effect, was the beginning of the end for a number of the houses in the village. Frustration and bitterness came in response from Mr. Kilgour, who in the following year declared: 'regarding the fishers who are not satisfied, the sooner they are informed they go to Torry the better, and they will be little loss… all the improvements in the village over the years, have been a dead loss. No more complaints are to be listened to during the rent collection'.

In Mr. Kilgour's absence maintaining the property was essential, and carried on regardless, albeit under the authority of a factor. An extensive array of repair bills are testament to this, a number bearing ornate designs and flowery fonts. There was also the serious business of rent collection in the village and revenue for the estate, inclusive of letting selected fields for grazing. Besides the more matter of fact aspects of maintenance such as carpentry, masonry, slating, etc, in March 1875 the drain and burn by the Cove Hotel was cleaned out for the price of £1 11s. — the cost equating to 3d. per yard, the length of the burn being 124 yards. Of course, Mr. Kilgour had local manual assistance in running the affairs of the village, and in the mid 1880's a Mr. Charles Bain was employed as superintendent of the village, whose work involved draining, repairing and re-pointing the houses, besides keeping everything tidy in general. It was through no fault of his own, though, and rather a lack of enterprise, that he was made redundant in the February of 1893.

As for the life of Alexander Kilgour, he was privately tutored at Loirston House, and as a young man would no doubt have been seen around the village in his horse and carriage, as even after the coming of the railway overland excursions were still as such, including the hiring of cabs for special occasions. Indeed, in 1885 a bill was presented for the use of an omnibus and cabs to Mr. Kilgour from Mr. A. Campbell of No. 6 Diamond Street, who described himself as a 'horse hirer for all occasions'. There was an extensive wine cellar at Loirston House, including fine brandies, ports and whiskies. Good food also prevailed, with trout and salmon being supplied by Mr. Routledge, then lessee of the Cove fishings. Photographs were taken of Mrs. Kilgour and Alexander at Loirston House by the famous George Washington Wilson, though sadly none have been traced. It would appear to be one of an opulent lifestyle, though stinted by Mr. Kilgour's suffering from rheumatism, which, at the early age of 27 years, gave rise to many letters being written in a spidery hand. Still, he took an active part in the affairs of the area, and when the 'Nigg Mutual Improvement Association' was formed in 1884, he became a patron, along with Mr. David Sinclair of North Loirston and Altens, the Rev. Robert Fairweather, and William Michie Esq., M.D. (who some years ago condemned the sanitation in the village). They met in Kirkhill Public School every Wednesday at 7.30pm, the evenings consisting of both Speakers and Essayists, with an allocated time for each. It is not known how long the association ran for. Among his many local public appearances was in July 1889 when he was invited to support the 'Nigg Picnic and Games' being held at Newlands Croft by the Loch of Loirston.

Commissioned bust of Dr. Kilgour.

Reproduced by kind permission of
Aberdeen Medico-Chirurgical Society.

Things, it appears, had began to take their toll, and in August 1892 he wrote in a business letter remarking that he had been very unwell, and that a doctor treating him could do no more. Apparently he felt that he 'was done with the world and its affairs', and continued by stating that he'd had a good life, with no reason to complain, and was very well nursed and taken care of. However, he suggested, if he was to take other people's advice, then he ought to keep to his bed and not come down the stairs at all! By 1892 his mother's health was ailing, and the tribulations of estate management greatly contributed to a mood of gathering insularity, a serious rift developing between himself and his remaining closest relations, excepting an aged aunt with whom he had regular correspondence. It is not unknown if this rift was ever healed. That same year he commissioned a sculptor to create a marble bust of his father, which was unveiled at the Infirmary on 9 October 1893. By all accounts, though, he adored his mother, and never fully recovered from her death the following year, and for the time being withdrew from public affairs, though the estate was to be intermittently advertised throughout the decade.

In 1903 it was again on the market, albeit Mr. Kilgour had withdrawn it later that year, giving rise to the furtherance of erratic behaviour. On 16 July 1904 he went as a voluntary patient to Elmhill House in the Royal Lunatic Asylum, Aberdeen, and was later described as 'labouring under morbid mental depression of an active type, accompanied by uncontrollable impulses'. There did not appear to be any likelihood of him being able to reside again in Loirston House, or indeed manage his affairs. That year an inventory and valuation of the household furniture was drawn up, including silver plate, books, etc. In 1905 Loirston House was in need of extensive repairs and unlikely that a tenant be found, the Trustees unwilling to spend the considerable sum needed to rectify the situation in order to make it habitable; the house, therefore, remained empty until the sale of the estate in 1922. In his will Alexander Kilgour bequeathed all the pictures in Loirston House to Aberdeen Art Gallery, and the books to Aberdeen Public Library, though for reasons unknown the pictures were never received. Most of the furniture was to be sold as seen fit by the Trustees, with certain items being given to Mrs. Elizabeth Dempster, his housekeeper, along with the capital sum of £500. Various hospitals received cash amounts, as did several nursing associations. Of course, the bulk of the estate went to the University of Aberdeen.

End of the Line

From 1905 the estate lay in the hands of the Curator Bonis on behalf of Alexander Kilgour until his death in the March of 1921, Loirston House lying empty until 1923, albeit a gardener remaining resident in the lodge at the northwest corner, keeping the grounds in a manageable condition. After his death it was placed in the care of the Trustees of the University of Aberdeen, and offered for sale the following year; The Aberdeen Fish Manure & Oil Company Ltd. purchasing both the house and estate in December 1922, installing works manager Mr. John (Jock) Catto in Loirston House the following April. However, he remained in residence for a few years only, relocating to his former address at Burnbutts Croft on Loirston Road, and in 1927 Mr. William Ellis, a market gardener, became tenant of the premises. After the event of the company going into voluntary liquidation (details given in chapter six), in May 1939 Mr. Ellis bought Loirston House and the grounds within, including the field to the immediate east of the walled periphery. On his death the business remained in the family, managed by younger son John, who employed several local men on a part time basis. His wife Dorothy having passed away in 1967, he continued to trade until ill health forced him to retire, dying a few years later at Woodend Hospital, Aberdeen, in December 1972. Technically, he may be considered as the last of the Lairds, Loirston House being demolished earlier that year, which, on reflection, amounted to no less than an act of architectural vandalism.

After the demise of the now Aberdeen Fish Meal Company in 1937, both South Loirston and the Lands of Cove were effectively broken up. The housing stock in the village became the possession of private landlord Mr. Charles G. Kennaway, a solicitor based in Auchterarder; the outlying crofts to Mr. Henry J. Kennaway, and sold by way of disposition. Burnbutts Croft and areas of land were acquired by Mr. John Catto, with tenant Mrs. Ruby Spark becoming proprietor of the Cove Bay Hotel. Further acquisitions are detailed in the following chapters, though the estate as a whole was lost forever. Nevertheless, the Kilgour name lives on, by way of a monument in the form of the breakwater and piers, and in the Kilgour Scholarships at Aberdeen University, a legacy of the Doctor's passionate belief in education.

Greenarbour

Some 10 yards to the east of the former bounds of Loirston House lies Greenarbour, purchased by Dr. Kilgour as part of the estate; his sister Miss Jane Kilgour residing there until her death. It is believed to have been constructed around 1800, initially a but-and-ben type cottage, though like the terraced rows of houses in the village, it is unknown if the property had at first a thatched (thackit) roof. Moreover, in 1777 the land on which it stands was known as the Arbour Infield. Little is revealed of its early history, though it appears to have been worked as a farming enterprise, and in 1856 James Valentine of South Loirston rented the farm of Greenarbour, excluding the house itself. On Dr. Kilgour's acquisition much improvements were carried out, and in October 1864 the enclosure walls of the garden were constructed. After the death of the said Jane Kilgour in March 1872, the following month it was let to Mrs. White, a Mother

Superior, who had requested that Dr. Kilgour feu her a portion of land for a proposed orphanage, which was to be built behind Burnbutts Croft. The exact location was to be to the immediate east of present-day Catto Park, with the existing burn diverted. It appears that Mrs. White ran a school for orphans from Greenarbour, albeit for no more than a period of three years, the proposed orphanage never having materialised; the main reason, perhaps, being the death of Dr. Kilgour in 1874. The school's brass bell, however, still survives today, the engraving having faded, albeit the bell itself in good working order.

After the departure of Mrs. White, the house required further repairs and improvements, and was advertised for lease in the *Aberdeen Herald* in February 1875, the accommodation comprising of two sitting rooms, three bedrooms, with kitchen and servants' accommodation. In this same year the removal of a huge rock in the adjacent field was undertaken for the princely sum of £20. A number of tenants followed, one of the first being John Colville, a retired coastguard who had been stationed at the Cove. In December 1886 drainage improvements were carried out, including a 325 yard sewer pipe leading to an outfall a little to the south of the Black Cove inlet.

In 1901 salmon fisherman Mr. James Marr became tenant (though in the summer months only of 1905 it was rented by Mr. W.S. Cook of the engineering company Barry, Henry and Cook, who was granted permission to keep his motorcycle and sidecar in the coach house at Loirston House for 10s. per month, on the understanding that no petrol was to be stored within), followed by his youngest daughter Mary in 1914. Mary Marr was well-known in the Cove, and in her later years recognised as a very neat and petite old woman. She became owner of the property in 1939, letting rooms to many lodgers over the years. Remaining a spinster, she died in 1964, with ownership falling to the Simpson family, and latterly Mr. Colin Simpson, who in turn sold the property in 1998 to current owners Mr. Ian and June Stark.

Mr. Simpson revealed that having been in the employment of a notable family in England, Mary Marr had become acquainted with the nanny of the children of Nicholas II, Tsar of Russia, and owing to her having to leave Moscow during the 1917 revolution, offered her a room at Greenarbour. He adds that Miss Nellie Sinclair, daughter of Mr. William Sinclair of North Loirston, informed him that during the time of the railway construction her father and some of his men entered the cave at the Black Cove inlet, believing it to reach beneath Greenarbour, and that iron bars were driven into the rock at the entrance of the cave. This may have been for the purpose of hanging seabird boxes in order to collect their eggs, as opposed to climbing up difficult and dangerous ledges. However, on most occasions the cave is completely blocked by driftwood and debris.

North Loirston House

At the very least there remains in the area a structure of historical significance, in the form of North Loirston House, built in 1870 for Mr. David Sinclair, then factor and tenant of North Loirston and Altens, by Mr. Alexander Crombie, proprietor of the said estates. Early records of the Sinclair family begin with Mr. Donald Sinclair, born 1775, who married Janet Milne. He died 8 May 1835 aged 60 years, leaving widow Janet Sinclair, described as a farmer and resident in the Cove. She lived in present-day Colsea Road, along with sons William and David. It would appear they had little to do with the fishing, and had leased a croft in neighbouring Charleston, including 12 acres of a triangular piece of ground located on the northern side of the Cove Road, adjacent to the site of the old Cove School, and the field between the old quarry road and the sea, currently owned by market gardener Mr. Roy Jamieson. By 1851 Janet Sinclair was the tenant at North Loirston, employing eight servants of various description, which would indicate an upturn in prosperity. Though North Loirston House is recorded in the 1861 census, this was in fact a smaller construction, and part of the farm buildings. She died 30 October 1866, her younger son David inheriting the family business. As well as running the farm and estate he had an avid interest in the local community, especially that of education, becoming Chairman of the Parochial Board and Parish Council, a County Councillor and Chairman of the School Board. He stood as a conservative Candidate in the Parliamentary Election of 1880.

In 1881 David Sinclair acquired the lands of North Loirston from the aforementioned Mr. Alexander Crombie, along with the estate of Altens; the Sinclairs, in effect, becoming gentlemen farmers, owning in addition Redmoss Farm to the west of Wellington Road. The estate had also a small granite quarry (though not extensively worked) located a short distance to the northeast of the farm buildings.

The funeral of Dr. William Sinclair of North Loirston. The huge number of mourners were a veritable who's-who in Aberdeen, Kincardineshire and surrounding areas.

Reproduced by kind permission of Aberdeen Journals Ltd.

David Sinclair died in 1911, the estate falling to son William, each of them aspiring to letters after their names, William boasting M.B. C.M. J.P. His other son, Edward, whose occupation was a tea planter in Ceylon (Sri Lanka), died in 1920. William died 1 October 1933 and was buried according to his wishes, two of his farm horses conveying him in a cart draped in black to his final resting place. In turn his son David Sinclair B.Sc. (AGRI). J.P. inherited the estate, selling North Loirston and Redmoss Farm to Aberdeen City Council in December 1966, though remaining resident at North Loirston House until the early 1970's. It was inevitable that North Loirston would be taken out of Kincardine, as Aberdeen was looking to extend its city limits, and had been an 'interested party' the previous year. Of course, today North Loirston House is the modernised Altens Community Centre, providing a meeting place for sundry events, ranging from a crèche to a club for old age pensioners.

On 24 August 1985 David Sinclair died aged 80 years, his wife having predeceased him. They had no children. The last of the Sinclair family was Miss Helen McKenzie Sinclair, who lived at Redmoss Farm before relocating to 'The Cottage' on Loirston Road in 1947. She was 'weel kent' in the Cove and went by Nellie Sinclair, being fond of cats and a good friend of Miss Janet Murray, author of 'Schooling in the Cove'. Nellie lived to the ripe old age of 93 years, and died on 6 August 1994. Like the Menzies family before them the Sinclairs left no descendents, there being but Sinclair Crescent, Terrace and Place in the Cove, and Sinclair Road and Place in Torry, to commemorate their importance to the area. Indeed, as in Loirston House, tragedy to 'those of means' is certainly no stranger, the Sinclair family headstones bearing testament to this. Nevertheless, a fondness for the past lives on, whereby the older residents of the Cove still refer to North Loirston House and its bounds as being 'Davy Sinclair's'.

Chapter 2: Order Within

An Early Sketch of Fisher-folk

In medieval times the authorities in Aberdeen had trouble ensuing that fish caught locally in Fittie, Torry and the Cove, were brought to market, the fishing fleet of the town itself containing few boats. White fish was a particularly important source of food, especially for the poorer people, who needed to afford it in small quantities for themselves. Measures were repeatedly taken to ensure that the fish was not sold at the shore or to landsmen (merchants who came to the town to buy fish in bulk, in turn selling it inland and in other towns and villages for a marked price increase), or in large quantities to retailers in the town itself, but that it came to the market and was available for everyone. In general the fisher-folk were regarded by urban dwellers and those who lived outside of the fishing communities as somewhat alien, of an inferior standing. This, of course, was very much unfounded, as history proves in regards to their social identity. In the mid 18th century a typical North-East fishing village had between 100 and 300 inhabitants, the fisherman retaining small plots of land on which he grew vegetables to supplement his diet. Though fishing villages may be less than a mile apart, they remained distinct, both in physical boundaries and community uniqueness. Perhaps a tale may attest to this, even as recent as the 1930's, when the late Mr. Willie Westland of the Cove stood a pint of ale to a fisherman from Downies, at which the latter remarked, on draining the last of the glass, "the finest point I ever tastit", in a rather mixed accent, if not with a little sarcasm!

Much is indebted to the Reverend Dr. David Cruden for recording events within the parish of Nigg in the first Scottish Statistical Account 1791 — 1799. In an air described as being healthy, though somewhat chilly nearer the sea, the fisher-folk of the Cove were understanding, industrious (they had to be to survive), and appeared resigned, if not content, with their lot, as it was all they knew. Unlike other fishing communities such as Torry and Portlethen, the Cove wasn't noted for giving by-names. They were decent, *sober*, charitable and honest, and would not take so much as a mussel that did not belong to them, or keep back a penny from a share of the fishing. Indeed, if one man was ill another would take his lines out to sea, from which he received all the fish on them; if a woman was sick, then another would bait her lines for her. In 1785, however, there was some devilment — or wanton vandalism — in the form of young boys from the crofts inland, or 'Herds of Loirstouns', who, on having gone to the Cove and drawn the fishermen's nets for crabs and fish, deliberately cut the ropes in the process. Of course the fisher-folk were open to argument with each other, but soon settled their differences, albeit not with the crofters. Above all they held great sympathy and spirit, as was noted some years before when a sudden storm forced the boats to return from the fishing, one being capsized on nearing the harbour, the men clinging to the hull for their lives. Other fishermen who had but some minutes ago returned looked pitifully at the spectacle, one brave soul crying, "We live together, let us die together;" at which a boat was launched and three of four men were prevented from drowning.

Indeed, it was a perilous life, where the sea took its toll, leaving families near destitution, with many donations being given by the church towards the bereaved. In the February of 1768 five men from the Cove were lost at the fishing, leaving five widows and a number of orphans who could 'neither work nor want'. In 1787 three fisherman were lost in the near proximity of the harbour, leaving widows, children, and other dependant relatives. In 1790 six men perished, leaving five widows and twenty-five children; collections in the nearest parishes, and principally in Aberdeen, raised the sum of £131 (Scots money). The new century brought little difference, for in the May of 1803 a Cove fisherman was lost on a voyage home from Aberdeen. These, however, are merely but statistics, with more details emerging by the fourth decade. On Friday

17 May 1839, a fishing boat from the Cove was homeward bound from Aberdeen when run foul by the smack *Guthries of Dundee*, being instantly swamped by the main boom. There were six of a crew aboard, three of whom quickly perished; the other three fishermen clinging to the keel for their lives, being picked up in due course by another Cove boat. The incident was placed under legal investigation, it having been stated that no boat was lowered by the smack to save these unfortunate men. And on Thursday 31 March 1842 a fishing boat from the Cove struck a sunken reef to the north of Burnbanks (believed to be the Hasman Rocks), after having taken refuge in Aberdeen harbour during a southeast gale. Five were lost as the boat capsized, with one man rescued by another boat fishing from nearby Altens Haven.

Such was the life of the whitefisher and his family, which in effect was no more than slavery to the sea, where, in poor years of fishing, and after the necessary expenses of bait and lines, might yield no more than 10s. annually. During some months of a winter the subsistence of the entire family depended much on the work of the women. More dangerous than any long hours of toil, though, was the commencement of the French and American Wars in 1778, when men were press-ganged into service. It's little wonder that the fishermen would disappear and the fishing interrupted from their fear of being seized; and small compensation when an 'agreement' was reached, from which only one man be taken from each boat. To elude being pressed into service, the fishermen could buy their way out, whereat ten crews in the Cove paid £106 14s. (Scots money), a considerable amount, and one that left a heavy debt on these families for years.

At the turn of the century, however, the ongoing wars with the French gave rise to many Cove fishermen becoming patriots, who 'enrolled themselves to serve with their boats for any purposes judged expedient'. Furthermore, they were not entirely helpless, and in 1772 the fishermen of Torry proposed they give 2s. 6d. (12½p.) annually towards their inevitable retirement from the sea. Known as the Friendly Society, this may be described as being an early form of an old age pension. A familiar institution commenced in the Cove a few years later, when in 1802 the 'Society for Whitefishers in Cove' was founded.

The Society of Whitefishers in Cove

In 1793 King George III entitled an act for the 'Encouragement and Relief of Friendly Societies', and on 29 May 1802, the Society of Whitefishers in Cove, or the Cove Society, became established. This fund was by voluntary contributions, its objective being to provide relief towards the poor among them, and those unfortunate enough to leave widows and children. The president was the Rev. Dr. David Cruden, minister of St. Fittick's Church, with each man having to sign his name; those who were illiterate were requested they place a mark or initials next to their names as written by Dr. Cruden himself. However, no man over the age of fifty years was permitted to join. Fisherman Robert Robertson was the Box Master, or Treasurer. Most likely the meetings took place in the rudimentary village school, with an initial £120 donation from the Treasurer of Aberdeen being gifted. George Caie put forward £1.1s. (a guinea). There was £3 cash from Dr. Cruden, plus £1 5s. 2d. from the Treasurer. Interestingly enough, there was a donation of 2s. 6d. from Mr. Peter McEwan, schoolmaster. The half-yearly collected dues amounted to £4 10s., giving a total of £129 13s. 8d., and the initial distributions awarded to Anne Brand, widow, for 10s., and Ann Morrice, for 10s. The transactions were signed by Dr. Cruden. Accounts were diligently kept, an unnamed clerk being given the initial payment of 5s. for his efforts. The following entry in January 1803 has James Webster as clerk — receiving only 3s 6d!

On 24 February 1807 a general meeting was called to discuss the disaster that beset the fishing villages on the Moray Firth on Christmas Day past, when 37 fishermen lost their lives in a sudden storm, leaving 31 widows, 89 children and 56 aged parents or dependants. The purpose of the meeting was approved regarding the 'terrible situation', as well as remembering what had happened to the fishermen of the Cove some 17 years previously. The sum of £2 12s. 6d. was to be donated, with treasurer Robert Robertson giving 7s. and 6d. of his own, making for the round figure of £3. There was in addition a collection at the church the coming Sunday towards this purpose. Many familiar names of the Cove appear in both the collection and the distribution, such as Morrice, Caie, Webster, Guyan, Robertson, etc.

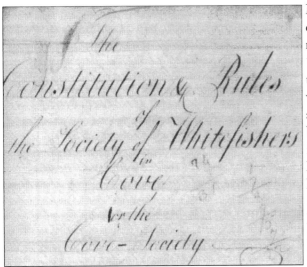

The document heading as drawn up in 1802.

Much of the recorded details relate to yearly dues and monetary distributions, with scant mention of everyday life in the village. In 1817, however, Alexander Duthie Esq. began to preside over meetings when Dr. Cruden was unable to attend owing to illness and old age. It appears he took a keen interest of both the presidency and the welfare of the fishermen. In May 1822, the current clerk, Mr. Patterson, wished to share the burden of his duties, being inconvenienced at times, (most likely the weather) and proposed that Mr. Ferguson, the teacher at the Cove School, might be admitted as joint clerk. In 1826 Dr. David Cruden died, the Rev. Alexander Thom succeeding him.

Some five years later it was decided by Alexander Duthie, and agreed by present members of the society, that there were insufficient funds to support their expenditure. On 30 January 1827 it was proposed that the Society be dissolved and the remaining funds divided accordingly. A meeting was called on 5 March, and by the written consent of each member, was forwarded to Mr. Duthie, who paid out the remaining funds in the first of four instalments, relating to what was owed, including long-serving members, short serving-members, widows, children and aged relative dependants. He also gave a 'handsome present' at each of these instalments. On 2 June 1827 each man who had been a member for less than seven years was given only the amount that he put in. Those who had not been members for seven years shared what remained in the funds. In a touching moment the members of the Society blessed Mr. Duthie and his family for all the assistance he had provided in this venture. The Society of Whitefishers in Cove was no more.

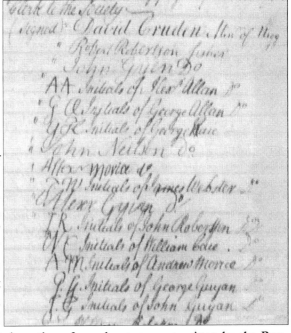

A portion of member names as written by the Rev. Dr. David Cruden, with most Cove fishermen placing their initials to the left. Prevalent names being Allan, Caie, Guyan, Morrice and Webster.

A Terraced Fishtown

At the end of the 18th century the Cove was but a clutch of crofts and rudimentary houses with thatched roofs, there being no proper roads leading through the village. Very few houses from before this period survive in the fishing communities of the North-East. Indeed, the present-day village east of the railway is a product of the improvements in the early 19th century when the custom in simple Scottish housing became the two-roomed but-and-ben, the fireplaces being at the gable-ends. As witnessed, the original part of the village, or 'fishtown', consists of terraced rows of houses built gable-end to the sea, exceptions being present-day Bunstane Terrace, which runs parallel to the railway, and Balmoral Terrace by the harbour. From the 1820's it would be reasonable to suggest that the 'new' Cove had begun to be built towards, rather than away, from the sea, the main street being present-day Colsea Road, which, in the late 19th and early 20th century, was known as the 'sand road' owing to its poor condition. The construction of the school and the inn would have proved this road to be the hub of the village.

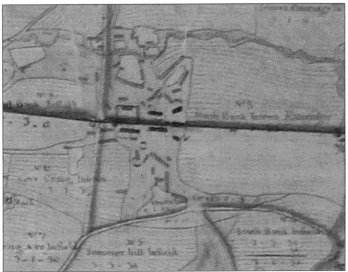

The Cove in 1777. No roads exist through the village itself and the uniform terraced rows as seen today are almost 50 years in the future. There is, though, a road that leads to the harbour.

Reproduced by kind permission of Aberdeen City Archives.

As yet no date has been found to indicate when the first of the uniform terraced rows were constructed on the north side of the village, though it is thought to be around 1822 when Alexander Duthie Esq. began to make improvements to his portion of the fishtown. The same may be said of Alexander Muir from the mid 1830's, with additional houses being built. Again, it must be considered that the greater part of the village belonged to John Menzies Esq., beginning on the south side of present-day Spark Terrace, and the probable construction of these particular rows dates to around 1824, when the crofting township of Charleston was being established. Later, though, in an outline for the proposed sale of the village in 1854, then proprietor John Blaikie (a former Trustee of Mr. Menzies' estate) stipulates the rent of eight *new* houses being set at a uniform £2 7s. 6d. each, which is most likely the construction of present-day Bunstane Terrace the previous year; therefore by 1855 — excluding Seaview Terrace, which lay some 25 years in the future, plus the demolition and construction of several but-and-bens — the village would more or less have looked as it is today.

Outside the nucleus of the village a row of six thatched houses was constructed by the harbour c.1856, and named Balmoral Street, in effect becoming the first proper address relating to the Cove. Two more were added in 1870, and in 1874 it was renamed Balmoral Place. By 1933, however, a few had fallen into a ruinous condition, Nos. 7 & 8 being used as a net store. In 1962 only two were occupied, namely by Mr. George Milne and Mr. Robert and Isabella Adam, and by the mid 1960's Nos. 1 — 6 were no more than masonry shells, being demolished in 1975 and turned into modern houses, to be renamed Balmoral Terrace. Since 1988 Mr. Fred and Charlotte Cargill have been resident at Nos. 7 & 8, redeveloping these into a single dwelling, with only the walls remaining as part of the original construction.

In 1863 there were 75 houses in the village, augmented by a further 13 at the expense of Dr. Kilgour in the next few years (none of which exist today), situated for the most part between present-day Craighill and Stoneyhill Terraces, and present-day Colsea Square. In 1873 he built an additional five, these being present-day Nos. 2 and 4 Springhill Terrace (the adjoining house to No. 2 being demolished in 1968) and Nos. 11a and 15 Stoneyhill Terrace. On their construction these houses were initially Nos. 78, 79, 80, 87 and 88 *Loirston Road*. In that same year John Fyfe held the lease for the Cove Quarries, acquiring half an acre of ground for the purpose of accommodating quarrymen and their families. By the autumn of 1879 a row of six adjoining houses had been completed, financed at a cost of £420 by Mr. Alexander Kilgour, the name of Seaview Terrace first appearing in the valuation rolls of 1885/6 and deriving from Seaview House, located some 80 yards to the west. Moreover, these houses were never recognised as fisher-houses.

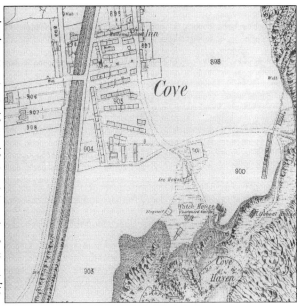

The Cove, 1864. The village is more or less as it is today, excepting present-day Seaview Terrace, Nos. 2 and 4 Springhill Terrace, and Nos. 11a and 15 Stoneyhill Terrace. The original Balmoral Street (Terrace) is also present, as are the Ice House, the Flagstaff and the Boat Shop by Balmoral Road.

Seaview Terrace was indeed the last of the houses built in the village, until those constructed by Kincardine County Council in 1968. Furthermore, in this same year the terraced rows were given an identity, rather than the houses being no more than a numerical address relating to the village, i.e. No. 45 the Cove. Below are explanations for their individual names:

Colsea Road: from Coldsea Haven, which appears on the 1822 Topographical and Military Map of the Counties of Aberdeen, Banff and Kincardine. The origin of Coldsea itself may derive from the temperature of the sea in the Colsea Yawn, which, due its precipitous height, gathers little by way of sunlight. This was the main street in the village, simply knows as 'the Street'.

Spark Terrace: from proprietor of the Cove Bay Hotel, Mrs. Ruby Spark, who purchased the premises from the Aberdeen Fish Meal Company in 1939.

Hasman Terrace: from the Hasman Rocks, a tidal reef to the north of Altens Haven; locally pronounced as the 'Hessmins'.

Springhill Terrace: from the many springs that issue forth east of the railway.

Craighill Terrace: from Craighill Wood and Quarries, which were located to the southwest of the present-day Remoss housing estate.

Stoneyhill Terrace: from Stoneyhill Wood and Quarries, which were located to the northwest of the present-day Redmoss housing estate. Another source (although unlikely) may have been the condition of the road, which, until the late 1960's, comprised of a rough surface of granite stones sunk into the ground.

Bunstane Terrace: from the Bun Stane, a table-like outcrop of rock located half a mile north of the Cove.

Balmoral Terrace: from the re-designed and extended Balmoral Castle in 1856 on Royal Deeside; there being, incidently, a Loirston Hotel in Ballater.

What is interesting to note that all are coined as Terrace, apart from Colsea Road, which, with its stepped-to-slope construction, is indeed more 'terraced' than Balmoral and Bunstane. Such names, of course, were never fully accepted by aged and life-long residents of the Cove.

However, a more dense and varying layout was being mooted in 1869 when Dr. Kilgour hired a land surveyor to draw up a plan with his proposed improvements and additions to the village. Each house was to have constructed a timber peat store of dimensions 12 ft. by 10ft. by 6ft. high, complete with padlocked door, as supplies by then were somewhat limited. A number of additional houses were to be built, eight of which were to be located between present-day No. 11a Stoneyhill terrace and Stonecraft Fireplaces, plus three more at the south end of Craighill Terrace, complete with individual peat stores. There was also a proposed new road (an extension of present-day Springhill Terrace), inclusive of a covered drain, leading west from present-day Colsea Road to around 60 yards south of the Railway Bridge, continuing through Bunstane Terrace and effectively cutting the row in half. Two additional houses were to be built on the northern end of Bunstane Terrace, with a further three to the south of the proposed new road. For some unknown reason the blueprint refers to present-day Colsea Road being 'Union Street'. Of course, this was but a fleeting notion, for later that year Dr. Kilgour had notified the tenants of the village stating that the fishing population was sufficiently large enough. Moreover, if he did decide to build, then it would only be on certain conditions, and that any proposed houses would have slated roofs, and not be thatched.

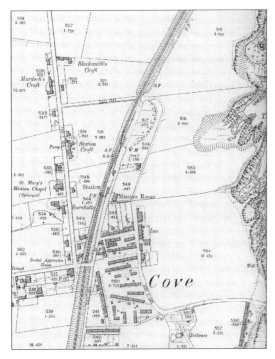

The Cove, 1901. The first of the houses are beginning to fall into ruin, with the centre portion of Hasman Terrace and the northern end of Springhill Terrace having disappeared.

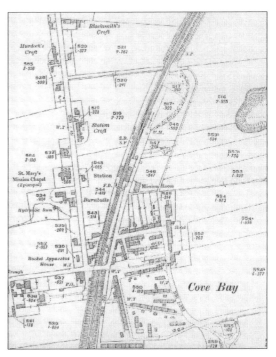

The Cove, 1923. Further depletion of the village may be witnessed. Little development has occurred as yet on Loirston Road.

From the mid 1880's the drift to trawl fishing and a general migration to Torry was impacting on the village, there being no new tenants taking up residence in the vacated houses; present-day Spark Terrace and Springhill Terrace the first to fall into serious disrepair. The decay of the village continued, and in 1922 there were 73 houses, 11 of which were in disrepair, followed by a total of 59 houses in 1963, 4 of which were unoccupied. However, in 1968 the downward spiral began to reverse when Kincardine County Council cleared the sites of existing ruins and built single-storey, one bedroom houses in the village: 4 on Stoneyhill Terrace, 3 on Springhill Terrace and 2 on Spark Terrace, with 5 small garages constructed on the west of the latter.

By the mid 1960's modernisation of the village was thoroughly underway, and besides the ongoing renovations, 1971 saw the construction of Nos. 37 to 47 Colsea Road, with Nos. 25 to 35 taking place the following year. Later additions being the private dwellings on the south side of Stoneyhill Terrace in 1977 (part of the Cove Farm lands, and ground initially purchased in 1969 by Kincardine Council for additional council housing), Colsea Terrace in 1992 and Colsea Square in 2001. More recently, and in the vicinity of the hotel, are two semi-detached houses (Nos. 11a and 11b Colsea Road) and a single spacious dwelling house (Colsea House), having been completed in 2007.

Thus the older part of the Cove as we see it today, albeit special mention must be given to former county architect and planning officer of Kincardine, Mr. Alistair J. Sturrock, who in the mid 1950's prepared a plan for the gradual redevelopment of the village. Aimed at recreating the traditional atmosphere, he stated that it must be preserved, and that some of the houses be classed as listed buildings. Indeed, 18 B-listed houses exist today, plus the 6 C-listed houses of present-day Craighill Terrace, which, incidentally, prior to 1855, remains the only complete row left in the village. His suggested measures have been for the most part successful, and with the old village of Torry falling victim to the bulldozers in 1974 (the same year the Cove was being removed from Kincardine), as suburbs of Aberdeen only the Cove and Fittie remain testament to a way of life that is undoubtedly gone forever.

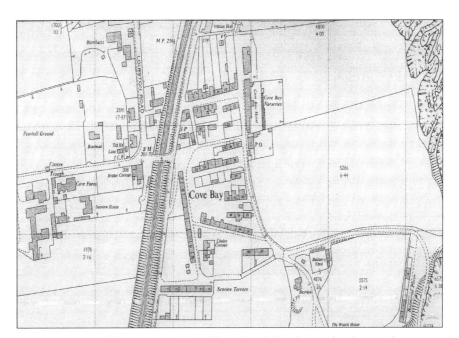

The Cove, 1962. The heart of the village has fallen into ruination, as has most of Balmoral Terrace.

Reproduced by kind permission of the National Library of Scotland.

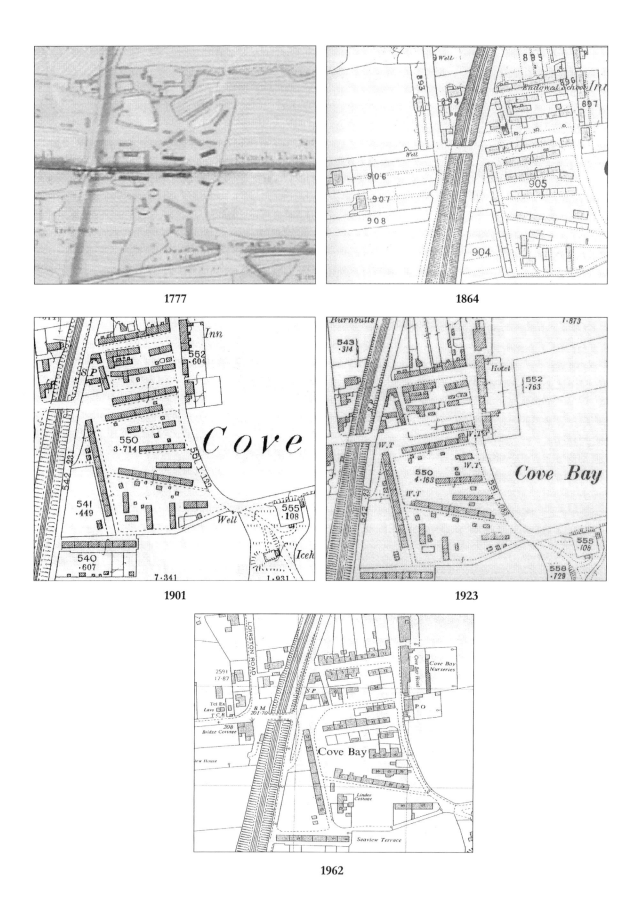

1777

1864

1901

1923

1962

Five map plans of the development and deterioration of the Cove.

Place Names

In established settlements there is a need to identify with significant locations, such as the christening of geographical features, or perhaps in honour of some notable deceased. Place names in the Cove and its vicinity abound, some being self explanatory, others proving impossible to trace; but on the coast, beginning at the southern edge of the old parish boundary, and heading north towards Burnbanks, are the following:

The Bunstane Rock.

The Horse Shoe is about ¾ of a mile south of the Cove, and so called after two small inlets either side of an outcrop of rock, forming a U shape; the railway bridge some yards from the cliffs being known as the 'Horseshoe Brig'. *Bruin's Cave*, or locally, *Broonie's Cave*, may derive from a piece of cultivated land above its entrance, once known as Brownie's Fold; what the cave has in relation to anything ursine, is a mystery. *The Braedens* is the Cove Shore or Mouth, effectively being a deep den at the end of the brae above the harbour, although the sandstone cliffs themselves are more recognised with this name. *The Berryhillock* is a high knot of rocks midway along the pier where, during the time of the coastguard, a flagstaff warned the boats of impending danger. One definition of 'berry' is a mound, or indeed a hillock, and may also refer to connotations regarding lifting, or to hoist. In the late 18th century the name also appears as a salmon fishing station to the north of the River Don. It is most unlikely that blueberries, or some other hardy form of shrub, flourished here. *The Crawpeel* arises from 'crab pool', a shingle beach some yards to the north of the harbour. It has previously been recorded as the 'whelk bay'. There are also several good fishing locations known as holes, such as the *Dog's Hole* and *Meg's Hole*, which are merely dips in the seabed, the former being dramatic in depth a few yards from the shoreline. *The Poor Man*, or *Peir Man*, is a geological stack, and did indeed resemble the lonely figure of a man. The 'Man' lost his head, so to speak, around 1950, during salvage operations on the steamship *Trebartha*, scuttled directly beneath the Cove Bay Hotel during World War II. Explosives were used to free the more valuable parts such as bronze and brass, and following one severe detonation, the shockwave disengaged the tip of the stack. However, one puzzling feature is the *Mutton Rock*, a tidal reef due east of Balmoral Road; an obscure source may derive from the Anglo-Saxon 'mott', a meeting place, where in medieval times boats may have gathered here, as the strong tides can produce good fishing. Though now referred to as the *Mountain,* owing to its triangular peak, this is indeed a fitting description.

On land, too, names abound, and today's *Loirston* has several variations: in 1654 it is cited as *Lorstoun*, while 1703 reads *Loristoun*, and in 1774 becomes *Lowerstons*. One map of 1822 indicates *Lourston,* while another, quite separate, reads *Lowers Towns*. It has also been suggested that *Loirston* is derived from *lobhars,* a Gaelic word for leper, and was an area where these poor unfortunates could live together and be provided with food and fuel, therefore removing the need to encroach upon the neighbouring communities. On St. Fittick's Church at the Bay of Nigg there are narrow slots in the masonry of the southeast wall known as 'lepers' squints'.

As the Cove expanded addresses were required, and to the west of Loirston Road lies *Sinclair Terrace, Place* and *Crescent*, in memory of the Sinclair family of North Loirston, while *Catto Crescent, Walk and Park* commemorate father and son, Charles and Jock Catto, local landowners and works managers at the Aberdeen Fish Meal Company. Jock Catto, incidentally, became a member of Nigg Parish Council in 1931, and a District Councillor for the area three years later, representing Nigg on Kincardine County Council from 1935 until his death on 14 February 1947. The street and road names of Altens derive from coastal locations between Aberdeen and Montrose, such as *Soutar Heads, Usan Ness,* and *Bervie Brow;* while later housing developments were given a more local feel, as in *Earsheugh, Langdykes, Lochinch* and *Charleston;* others being more thematic, such as *Cormorant* and *Creel.*

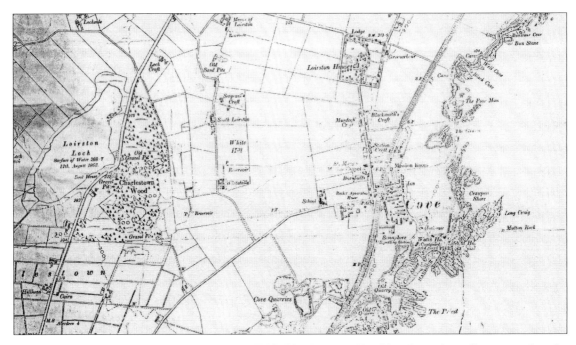

Between the Cove and the Loch of Loirston, 1904. Charlestown Wood has long since disappeared, and the fields and open pasture given way to modern housing development.

From simple fishing village to modern city suburb, yet within the construction, statistics and nouns lies the every day affairs of these earlier times; or, inasmuch, the daily sweat of flesh and blood. The following pages portray the environment of this hardy fishing breed, including that of peril, at which our present-day existence would deem both the domestic and occupational conditions as wholly unacceptable.

Location and Population

In a number of cases the fishing village is actually some distance back from the shore, as in the Cove, which is in contrast to settlements being as near to the beach as possible in order to minimise the work of carrying the weight of fish and equipment between the boats and houses. As to why the actual village was not located in the field adjacent to Balmoral Road, is a mystery, there being both fertile soil and a location more at hand. A reason, perhaps, may be that the elevation was not sufficient to counter the spray from roaring easterly winds. Then again, there is a strong presumption that in cases where the settlement is back from the shore, fishing was originally only part of the activity of a 'ferm toun', the settlement site being more centrally placed among the cultivated land. This would be unlikely in the Cove, owing to the stony proliferation and the many springs that run down the rather steep inline. Albeit the village was to be laid out in uniform rows, fishermen retained small holdings to subsidise the fishing.

Fishing and farming have proven to be the main supports of the economy of the North-East, the people of the two occupations living in intermixed groups, with the fishing villages strung along the edge of the agricultural belt. At social levels they held strictly apart — fishermen married only their own kind, since every boy born into a fishing family expected to become one, perhaps even to live in the same village, and to marry a woman of the same group. Nobody would be received into the community who had not been brought up in it. This was the result of necessity. The fishermen were totally dependent on the sea for their livelihood, and had to marry and intermarry with those who had been born to this mode of life, who could work shoulder to shoulder with them, keeping what was earned in the family; or, more importantly, the money 'in the boat'. The men remained in the village, though it was common for the wives to come from outside, sometimes from considerable distances, such as from Gourdon to the Cove. Due to space constraints a family of six was considered quite large, though children were looked on as a source of gain, allowing a fisherman to take a larger share in a boat, therefore a larger share of the fish; while a daughter was at hand for household tasks and baiting the line. It was common place for first cousins to marry, and as a result the majority of the inhabitants became blood relations. Of the 75 houses in the village in 1864, 63 were occupied by 9 families, namely: Allan, Brand, Caie, Craig, Guyan, Morrice, Robertson, Webster, Wood.

Between 1790 and 1850 the population in most fishing villages doubled and even trebled. Such increases hint at an occupational migration, at least between villages, and, on the whole, would suggest that their isolation as self-supporting communities was nearing an end; perhaps with in-migration from rural areas. In 1755 the parish of Nigg had a population of 1289, while some 40 years later it had diminished to 1090 owing to the ongoing naval wars and a general relocation to other districts, though slowly increasing in the following years. The census records for the parish being as follows: 1801 — pop. 1143; 1811 — pop. 1213; 1821 — pop. 1281; 1831 — pop. 1684. This latter statistic indicates a significant rise of 403 of a population, almost by a third, and may be attributed to a boom in housing construction, inclusive of the Cove. Moreover, by 1840 the Cove was the most populated settlement in the parish. Such expansion, though, abruptly ceased, and by the 1851 census there is little sign of people living in any one of these villages who had been born outside the fishing community.

Further insight into population numbers may be gleaned from a letter written in April 1881 by the minister at Nigg on behalf of Captain Sir William Wiseman, in regards to the Royal Naval Reserve for HMS Clyde, and in particular the statistics for male children in the village. Besides there being 30 Cove fishermen noted on its books, there were also 42 fishermen's sons aged between five years and fourteen; 21 under the age of five years; 21 between fourteen and nineteen years of age, making for a total of 84 boys in the village. Nineteen being the age at which a fisherman (after five years service at sea) may become eligible for the second class of the Royal Naval Reserve. And in a deed describing the particulars regarding the sale of Cove and South Loirston in June 1882, the following statistics are given: 52 houses occupied by fishing tenants; 28 by labourers and other various tenants; 12 houses then being empty, which, as previously mentioned, was the beginning of the exodus to larger ports.

There being no population recorded for the Cove prior to 1840, statistics for the village (excluding Loirston Road and Balmoral Terrace) are as follows: in 1841 there are 79 houses — pop. 354; in 1851 there are again 79 houses — pop. 415; in 1861 there are 75 houses — pop. 412; in 1871 there are 86 houses — pop. 417; in 1881 there are 86 houses — pop. 365 (a significant reduction). After 1879 there was little by way of construction in the village, and this, coupled with the decline of the fishing, saw many houses being vacated, giving rise to the following decreases: in 1891 there are but 67 houses being occupied — pop. 304; in 1901 there are but 58 houses being occupied — pop. 266. Moreover, it must be considered that when new houses were being erected during the mid to late 19th century, the older and dilapidated buildings were being pulled down.

At this time, however, transformation was in the air, both socially and economically, though the Cove as a community adhered to its individuality, its physical and characteristic nature, as Father William Humphrey, who from 1864 'lived and laboured' as a parson for three years among the fisher-folk of the village, ably describes:

> In my time I 'stood in the midst of the years'. The old systems were passing away during my residence at the Cove, and were giving place to new systems in the spheres both of education and of religion. Railways had been for some time bringing Scotland into closer communication with England, and English ideas and methods in both spheres were creeping towards the north… This was what I found on my frequent visits to Aberdeen from my solitude at the Cove. I returned to them to the Cove as to a haven of rest, with its bracing salt sea breezes, its simple ways, and the stick-in-the-mud conservatism of the fisher-folk. Little did the fishers care about the changes that were taking place outside their community in the educational and religious world. They were not aware even of the existence of those changes. Few of them could either read or write, but they could catch fish, cure fish, carry fish to the market, and in a bargain for the sale of fish could beat those who had more school learning than they had. They were wise in their generation. They were educated for their state of life… The fisher-folk, both men and women, were by no means averse to a dram, or glass of whisky, but they were not drunkards. They were too frugal and thrifty to waste their money by continual drinking. They knew that their boats and nets were at the mercy of the sea and might any day be lost, and that boats and nets must in any case wear out and have to be renewed before many years were over. I have known a fisher-family stinting themselves even of their ordinary food in a time of scarcity, although they had over a hundred pounds in the house stored up against a still more evil day.

As opposed to the compact fishing community there was limited development to the west of the village, Loirston Road being no more than a rough cart track, part grass, part mud, and having no pavements, with two burns flowing freely over its surface. By 1830 there was but eight coastguard cottages and a few crofts interspersed the length of it, each having their own midden and a stack of peats at hand. Following the construction of St. Mary's Church and the Rocket Apparatus House in 1867, a note of interest being that, excluding the houses built by Kincardine Council in 1939, only two are attached.

Living Conditions

Around 1750 the traditional abode of the fisherman and his family was cruck framed (curved wooden timbers) and had a thatched roof, with a peat fire burning in the middle of the floor. Owing to the low social status that the fisher-folk often had, it may well have been that the construction of the walls would have incorporated the use of convenient materials such as turf and peat, as well as undressed stone. Information suggests that the house, or 'black hoose' was primitive and unsanitary, aggravated by the fact that much of the necessary work of baiting, gutting and cleaning the fish, was carried out in the vicinity of the living area.

A late 18th century description of Fittie speaks of 'comfortless low thatched houses, sparsely furnished and beset around with dunghills, fishing gear and drying fish'; and in a paper by the Rev. William Paul, a vivid, if not despairing, picture is given of the village of Stranathro (Muchalls) regarding the need for improvement of the living and sanitary conditions, in which the houses are described as 'wretched hovels built of compacted clay and thatched with straw'.

The walls were damp and cracked and the floor consisted of clay; the rafters being exposed and black with soot. They offered poor shelter in stormy weather, for the turf was visible beneath the thatch itself and the rain fell upon the floor in filthy black drops. Outside the house fared no better, there being minimum drainage and the 'roads' ankle-deep with mud; not to mention the dunghills placed by the doors, containing fermenting heaps of fish offal and other household aversions. The only source of water was drawn from a well around a quarter of a mile distant. Meanwhile, rents in general did not exceed £1 per annum, but were paid irregularly, and with much difficulty.

Balmoral Place, c.1910. Only the two houses on the far end of the row survive today, and were in fact later additions to the original row built in 1856, being constructed some twenty years later. Smoking lums are still in place for the curing of haddocks.

By the early decades of the 19th century, landlords often took the initiative in housing improvements, especially in new planned villages. When the terraced rows of the Cove first appeared the dwellings were but-and-ben, the but being larger than the ben and containing one or two box-beds; shelves laden with crockery in rows (the pride and joy of the housewife); a long table which served as a sideboard; a clock, most often slung on the whitewashed wall; a few chairs and a kist (chest) for the Sunday clothes. If the roof was tiled it often let in water when raining, with pails and basins positioned around the house to catch the drips. The ben, not being required for work, was a smaller room than the but, and contained one or two wooden beds and several kists. It was not uncommon for the spars connecting the rafters to support nets, sails, or dried fish. With the fireplace removed to the gable-ends, an early covering for the earthen floor could be canvas, in the form of an old boat sail, perhaps even timbers from a wreck washed up in the vicinity.

The fire burned on the hearth of the roomy fireplace, with cooking done by way of a 'swee', an iron rod on which pots could be hung and swung over the fire. There was also the 'rantle-tree', on which was the 'crook', a pivoting iron bar with suspended hooks or chains for hanging the cooking utensils. In this room the family lived, ate and slept, besides doing a good deal of their day to day business. Evenings were passed by doing various chores, singing songs or telling stories; any children attending school might busy themselves with schoolwork. It was common practice to invite a neighbour or two to join in the social proceedings. Here fish livers were boiled and the oil extracted stored in the 'uillie pig', or 'eely dolly', to be used as fuel in cruisie lamps. Here, too, the wife shelled mussels and baited the line, which in turn was redd by the man; again, housework and cooking taking second place — the essential work came first. Another source of light was by 'fir-cunnels' (candles), which were thin splinters of bog-fir around three feet in length, fixed in a form of candlestick, called the 'peer-man' or 'peer-page'. The 'peer-man' was of various shapes, more commonly a small round block of stone, perforated with a hole in the centre. Redding up for the wife entailed whitening the hearth and chimney, sweeping up the earthen floor and strewing it with fresh sand, the floor having become fouled with trampling and other work related to the fishing. This was a custom which survived in the Cove until the 20th century; another being the 'straw bed', where the mattress was filled with chaff purchased from the Cove Farm, and refilled twice a year. The bed at first would be around two feet in thickness, though decreasing to no more than a few inches in the following months. The mattress, on emptying, had to be disposed of 'ower the brae heids', i.e. over the cliffs, owing to the rather messy flurry that ensued.

Colsea Road c.1900, looking on to the Cove Bay Hotel. The plaque in the centre, high above the door, reads 'messis ab alto' — food from the sea.

Things were not always quite so primitive, for new houses built to replace the older houses were rather more comfortable, the walls being plastered, if not lathed, with the floor of the ben consisting of wood and that of the but from concrete. The roof, too, was snugly slated and weatherproof. Even so, in the first half of the 20th century some houses were occupied by two separate and unrelated families, a room being apportioned to each. Such domestic tolerance, if not acceptance, are reflected in the words of Miss Mabel Guyan, "You just had to crawl in somewhere, that was the way of it then!" Though the houses themselves were more habitable due to various improvements, in the mid to late 19th century they were warm but draughty, the fire at times requiring the door be opened to 'draw the lum'. In 1849, however, it must have felt like the end of the world for those in the Cove, due to the intensive blasting programme needed to construct the railway, at which the granite bedrock would have quaked, and in turn gave the terraced rows a 'richt shak'.

On the whole homes became exceptionally spruce, by way of a 'spring clean' two or three times a year, including a thorough wash down of the interior. Usually a cat was kept to prevent the mice nibbling at the fishing gear stored in the loft, inclusive of the oars. Owing to the bedrock there was a sweet and abundant water supply from several pumps and wells. At the close of the 19th century lighting was by way of paraffin and wax candles, replacing the rush pith and fish oil of the sputtering cruisie lamp with its malodorous flame. Heating was commonly by driftwood and coal, the moss and heath in the vicinity of the village being more or less exhausted. Evidence of peat cutting may be seen by the Checkbar, adjacent to the old Wellington Road. The people were of a robust nature, as described a century earlier by Dr. Cruden, with a typical meal consisting of copious quantities of small fish and potatoes, besides some butcher meat and other foodstuffs containing a high degree of starch. In addition there was 'hairy tatties', the flesh of the cod teased out and mixed with mashed potatoes. Provisions could also be had from either of the two shops in the village, or by weekly groceries brought home on the train. Because of the nature of their occupation the men became creatures of habit and were highly superstitious. Women, being the purse holders, would on occasion bring their husbands a pint of whisky or rum, spirits at the time being around half a crown (12½ pence a bottle), albeit the hotel made for a brisk trade at weekends. Drunkenness existed, though seldom by females. Another factor to disposition was the prevailing winds from the SSE, which were relatively free of land germs and dust. Although exposed to both haar (sea fog) and sunshine, the Cove is perhaps afforded a little shelter by way of promontories to the north and south, in the form of Soutar Heads and Findon Point, respectively.

Cove fishwife, 1900's.

Details of proprietor and tenant were quite straightforward. In 1874 the rents for the houses in the Cove were paid twice a year, namely in June and December, with the average rent per household being around £1 10s., rising to a little over £2 13s. by 1883. At this time rents and leases in general usually began on either Whitsunday (the seventh Sunday after Easter, and around 15 May) or Martinmas (11 November), two of the quarter days in Scotland, with Candlemas (2 February) and Lammas (1 August) being the others. Interestingly, in 1880 John Lewis paid £4 15s. for house and boathouse, and Robert Thomson, of present-day Posties shop, £9 for the shop and £14 for the house attached. It appears that the rents were collected at a central point in the village, most likely the hotel, by an agent representing Alexander Kilgour. Upon occasion in 1893 the rent agent had stated that all the land tenants appeared and paid their rents in full. The tenants of the fishtown, however, were of an 'average collection'. The lease did not automatically descend to the heirs of the tenant, except with the landlord's permission, and if no son was within the household on the death of his father, then the husband of a married daughter may be allowed to continue with the tenancy.

With regard to roofs, the old school on main street remained thatched, even after repairs and refitting in 1867, in an attempt to accommodate prospective tenants. And in October 1874 there is a repair bill for thatching houses Nos. 33, 34, 35, 37 (Hasman Terrace) and No. 47 (Craighill Terrace), which suggests that many of the houses in the village did not as yet have slated roofs. The straw for the thatch came from the surrounding fields, with cart loads of clay provided by the Cove Farm. Burnbutts Croft was thatched at this time, though the lodge at Loirston House was fully slated. It would be fair to presume that as from the mid 1860's any house of a sound thatch would remain so, by way of small repairs; or, if the overall state of the roof was in poor condition, then it would receive a full covering of slates. By the end of the 1870's thatch was still being mended, and in 1878 a complete repair list was carried out on the whole of the village, with very few houses escaping attention. The work survey was summed up by stating that in general the houses were poorly maintained, especially the roofs, which were covered in a 'most careless and untradesman-like manner', there being too little cover for such exposure as experienced by the houses in the Cove. A note of interest being that the front door lock on each of the houses was to be renewed. By the mid 1890's, though, it would appear that slates had been applied to all but one or two.

In the mid 19th century the sanitation in fishing villages on the east coast of Scotland left a lot to be desired, giving rise to the typhoid epidemic experienced at the Cove at the close of 1840. Further evidence is revealed, such as in one acidic document describing the village of Torry in 1854, and directed at the inhabitants themselves: 'filth in your village is trodden upon at every step, inhaled with every breath, and is, in a word, impregnated with the very means of the existence of many of you'. And again in a report from the Aberdeen Branch of Ladies' National Sanitary Association in 1862 — Dr. Kilgour spoke at a number of their meetings — at which typhoid and other diseases were discussed, including the filthy conditions of the day among the poor in general. There was, though, a flash of humour, in the form of one poor fellow being admitted to hospital with a cut on his arm. It appears that a layer of collected filth had been washed away in order to reveal the extent of the wound, at which he howled in protest at being deprived of heat, as the dirt was like a greatcoat to him!

In the Cove the drainage was rather poor, consisting of semi-circular channels constructed from pebbles and other small stones; albeit the Cove had gravity on its side in the form of a steep gradient eastwards. In earlier decades 'middens' were filled with the household refuse, and water waste simply flung out the door. Indeed, seldom is heard of the everyday sanitation habits of a typical fishing village, including the more unsocial aspects of the toilet, whereat the men would 'drop anchor' at the nearest secluded location from their homes. The women, too, would follow suit, and for the most part wait until after dark; or, at the height of summer, make use of a pail and deposit the faeces elsewhere. There is little doubt as to malevolent odours and the problem of rats, the refuse being infrequently carted away by farmers and used as manure. An interesting quirk being a stipulation from the Board of Health in 1877, where the tenants and their families were expressly prohibited from keeping fowls, though oddly enough, ducks were permissible!

Cove fisher couple John Morrice, known as 'Coffee', and his wife Betty Inglis, c. 1890.

Nevertheless, not every household had a midden, and in 1876 there were thirteen located throughout the village, giving an average of one per five households, and by now being regularly emptied; as were the ash-pits, of which the cement base of one may be found on present-day Craighill Terrace. Middens as such were capable of holding several cart loads, and were constructed of stone and lime, on one side there being a coping of dressed stones. Some four years later the ash-pits and middens were redesigned to a specification already in use in Fittie and other fishing villages north, which allowed for water to run into an adjacent channel, their floors being 'cassied' with local granite.

Worthy of a mention is that Balmoral Place had its own separate 'dungstance', or midden, and was contracted as the Fishtown of Balmoral. In 1864 the method of selling the fish dung in the Cove was by way of lots, the average price per lot being £1 4s, though uncertain how much weight was contained in a lot. Early lessees of the fish manure were farmers in the vicinity, and in 1867 William Walker of Westerton, Whitehills, had the contract for £63 per year, and in 1871 William Coutts of Newlands Farm, sited to the northeast of the Loch of Loirston. At this time the fish guts were partly rent in kind, and to the great consternation of the seagulls, none were to be thrown in the harbour, rather the fishermen brought them up the brae to deposit them in the middens; but not those of herrings, which proved too oily for manure purposes. Under no circumstances were the fishermen to sell any of their fish prior to gutting.

In 1878 Alexander Kilgour began to improve the collection of manure and the sanitation in general. However, on inspection of the village in August 1880 Mr. William Michie, a member of the regional Medical Board, was appalled at the conditions: 'it was far from polite to have ash-pits planted at the doors. It impairs and stints the health of their children and renders them constantly in danger of having an epidemic, or an endemic, as at present, hovering over the place. I strongly condemn the sanitation in Cove village and it must be improved. Typhoid fever has been endemic in the fishing population for over six months, and supposed that the putrid odours emanating from the decomposition of the filth in their pits and the stagnant water in the gutters'. These conditions were also witnessed by other members of the said Medical Board, who had compared the huts of the natives in India as having better conditions of sanitation than that of the Cove, which, they stated, exceeded the former 'twenty fold in wretchedness and in filth'. Mr. Michie rounded off by protesting, rather pointedly, to Alexander Kilgour: 'I hope, sir, you will have these poor wretches of fishers under your tenancy in the Cove village placed in a more healthy atmosphere than they are at present living in'. This was indeed a differing depiction from that of 1871, in which conditions were cited as 'favourable', and a measure that environmental standards were in fact being considerably raised.

By the close of the year there were four new privies, a large communal midden, and a tool house for the village handyman, situated side by side on present-day Stonecraft Fireplaces, which, during the summer months, must have proved somewhat daunting! In November 1881 a contract was drawn up for emptying the ash-pits and ridding the middens of manure, inclusive of mussel shells, and that only liquid waste be thrown into the gutters and channels. Relevant points of the contract included: the middens be neatly trimmed up and covered in moss or mould and lime, and emptied once every two days; they be deposited at the communal midden (later known as both 'the dungers' and 'the diters'), until further collection and disposal; to periodically lime and wash the privies at least twice a year, and during the summer months disinfect the new ash-pits with Mr. Dougal's carbolic preparation, no less!; the grounds of the houses be kept clear of nettles and grass, and the main street of the fishtown ridded of any debris; to regularly clean and clear out the branders (drains), especially that of the one in front of the hotel. Such work was carried out by the 'scavenger'. The above was agreed to be contracted by John Valentine, tenant farmer at South Loirston since 1855, who also held the leases for Sergeant's Croft at Whitelhills (so named after one Sergeant Campbell), along with Blacksmith's Croft (12½ acres) and Murdoch's Croft (12¾ acres) on Loirston Road; in 1890 he took over the tenancy of the Cove Farm. He also retained the right to purchase the village manure at a cost of £20 sterling, payable in two yearly instalments.

The Cove, nevertheless, has always been blessed with a commendable supply of water, though in 1864 a sample was analysed and found to contain a small portion of suspended insoluble matter, which quickly subsided when the water was at rest. Indeed, the organic portion found within resembled that which is found in most mountain streams, being of a woody or mossy origin. A similar report occurred in 1885, stating that the general water supply at Cove village was good, though between thirty and forty of the population on the north side of the village had no drinkable water within a reasonable distance. In 1870 Dr. Kilgour proposed the laying of pipes to various wells located in the village, as unlike the country folk the villagers were described as being wasteful in their habits. By 1871, however, the water at Balmoral was described as 'unwholesome' by the residents, the well having to be regularly cleared of filth and debris. In 1881 the particular well that served Balmoral was to be covered over so as to keep it clean. Additional plans were made to excavate the small well at the harbour as an alternative source of water, which would effectively deepen the pool. The well is still in existence today, situated adjacent to the Boat House, though rather than having being excavated, a few stones were utilised in order to retain a small amount of drinking water. A new sewer was piped in the summer of 1891, the pipe being eight inches in diameter and three feet below the surface of the ground. The sewer began at two separate points in the village, one being at the north side of the hotel, the other at the south end of present-day Bunstane Terrace, with the pipes converging by Stonecraft Fireplaces, before continuing down Balmoral Road and leading to an outfall some yards into the sea a few yards north of the Crawpeel. Indeed, pumps and wells supplied the older part of the village until the introduction of running water in 1962.

Working Life

During the 18th and 19th centuries the fishing community was of a single occupation, in that they had much the same income and the same social standing. A typical day for the Cove whitefishers would be a long one. In summer, from midnight to the early hours in the morning, the men would regularly go to sea, laying their lines at dawn (the optimum time for fishing) and returning home with the catch. The fishwife was active by 3 or 4 o' clock, fetching home fuel or fitting in domestic duties; if at school, then boys and girls up to 14 years of age would assist by doing various chores, including fetching up mussels for bait. Before the boat came ashore it was the duty of the fishwife to run out the ropes on the capstan in order to winch the boat up the beach, at times an operation both difficult and dangerous if breaking waves prevailed. The boat was pulled down the beach on wooden rollers and launched stern first into the sea, the bow being turned in the direction of the sun. The fishwife would carry the fisherman aboard the boat, keeping his feet dry, a practice known as 'humphing'.

This, of course, was down to superstition, in which almost every aspect of the fisher-folks' lives was interrupted, including weddings, births, funerals and other domestic issues. When at sea words such as minister, kirk, swine, salmon, etc, were simply not to be spoken, and would have alternatives such as bell-house, himself, curly tails or the red fish, respectively. Indeed, if a boat was wrecked with loss of life it was allowed to lie and rot, for no fishermen would care to own it, or indeed use it as firewood, though the boat may be repaired and sold on to someone from another village. Much the same applied, albeit more of principle, if a boat was to be repossessed and sold under legal warrant, as befell a Cove fisherman in 1885, who was unable to meet with his rent — quite simply no other fisherman would dare submit a bid. Linked with superstition is the sighting of 'monsters'. When fishing from the rocks the head of a seal might bob out the water, at which one Cove fisherman described as, "A man from the deep, plain as day"; or, as in June 1922, while three miles offshore, "A head and two humps appeared not half a mile distant", was how two Skateraw (Newtonhill) fishermen, Peter and James Masson, described what they saw. 'Nessie fever' didn't become a worldwide phenomenon until 1933.

As mentioned, some years the fishing would fail, and the church be required to distribute money for the benefit of the fishermen and their families, particularly in the January of 1829 when the fishing population were in dire need of assistance due to the continuing bad weather, at which the spring allowance for the poor had to be distributed among them. Returning home, though, could prove to be quite an event if the boat was laden with fish, at which much excitement ensued; or, on the other hand, unable to land due to a heavy groundswell and be driven onto the rocks. On 19 August 1848 a tragedy was witnessed at the Cove. The herring fleet was fishing to the south of Stonehaven, the day previous being warm with a moderate wind when the boats were caught in what was described as a hurricane. The gale gathered in strength throughout the evening, the sky black and not a star to be seen, an inch of mercury having fallen on the barometer. Some boats made for Stonehaven harbour, while others ran north in mountainous seas, the wind being SSE. A Portlethen boat aimed to put into the Cove, but at the mouth of the harbour heavy seas threw her onto the rocks. Most of the crew initially managed to scramble to safety, though one man thrown overboard and drowned. The skipper was flung upon the nets and fish, which, on capsizing, fell upon him and prevented his escape. He was found drowned a few hours afterwards, still in this situation. The two who perished were brothers. The consequence of the gale then was without parallel in the annals of the east coast of Scotland, in which from Wick to Gourdon, 93 men lost their lives. A sum of around £20,000 was requested from the government to replace boats, nets and fishing gear, with further aid for the widows, children and other dependents. No loss of life was recorded from the Cove itself.

On winter mornings the men would return soaked and frozen to the bone, and, if under sail, the fabric stiff with frost. A dram would be provided by the women, though not as a celebration of landing with a catch, but rather to 'warm the cockles of the heart' and get the circulation going again. Having had a meal, the men had to 'tip' the line and clear it of old baits and seaweed, leaving it for an interval to dry, then 'redd' it and undo all the tangled parts in order that it run easily back into the scull when baited. Two lines were always in use on alternate days. When a storm prevailed the unwelcome leisure was exploited in all sorts of ways: they cut hazels to make hoops for creels, made good repairs on their boat, wove baskets from willows and brought home 'spreeth' (driftwood) for the fire. At the Cove the tide dictated the order of the day, and if the harbour was dry during early morning darkness, then the boat had to be 'tided down' beforehand in order to keep her afloat, giving rise to a trek over wet and treacherous rocks by lamplight bearing a scull — or several sculls — of lines, where one slip could result in a day's work being destroyed.

Baiting the hooks was a cold and laborious task, and even a small line took three to four hours to complete. This was the work of the women, and with deft turns of fingers and wrist the mussels were prised from their shells by means of a 'shieling knife'. She'd be hunched on a stool or some rudimentary chair, flanked by a bucket and basin, immersed within the all-pervading smell. Once the line had been redd and the hooks turned into the snoods, a long wooden pole was set horizontally at a convenient height and fixed by inserting one end into a shallow hole in the outside wall of the house, with the other being rested upon a trestle. Known as a 'spilltree' the line was looped across it and pulled towards the baiting woman as required, in effect spilling into her hands. Lines were also hung across the 'spilltree' to dry. The mussel had to be intact, and was twisted round the hook in a particular way, the heart being skewered on the barb. The hooks were carefully arranged into tiered rows, sometimes bull grass being used as a means to keep the mussel from adhering to the surface of the scull. This, of course, was a most important part of the procedure, requiring great patience and awareness, for one misplaced hook could result in the whole line going over the side of the boat at once, in what later became known as a 'funnel gush'.

In the Cove there were no natural mussel beds to speak of, there being insufficient quantities of fresh water, attempts having failed to grow them in the past, and rather the fishermen went to Montrose, sometimes two or three times in the summer months. The mussels were then cast upon rocks and pools within reach of the tide — known as 'scaups' — the objective being they took hold and would remain so until required. If rough seas prevented this, or indeed they withered and died, quite simply the fishermen had to replace them. What must also be considered is that if the fishing failed in January, as it occasionally did in the 1780's and 90's, then the fishermen could be greatly out of pocket, and not even make the value of the mussels themselves! An alternative bait (though not as efficient) was the limpet, usually gathered by the children from the rocks, another being offal from the butcher. In small creeks like the Cove, both perseverance and resilience were the order of the day, especially when the locality was far from self-sustaining, and long sojourns had to be undertaken in order to supply the means of a livelihood, i.e. the bait itself.

The Fishwife

Once the fishermen returned to the harbour and the catch was divided out, the focus fell on the Cove fishwife and her creel. These women carried loads of anything from eight to twelve stones of fish up the steep incline to their homes, the men behind lugging heavy sculls laden with lines. After smoking and curing they went by 'right of way' to Aberdeen, and did not encroach upon Loirston Road, the 'land street', at all. To supplement their income they'd gather badderlocks (a seaweed composed of long brown-green swards), dulse and pepper dulse, which was relished by the townsfolk. Woollen stockings were also knitted in numbers, both for the family and to be sold on to agents based in Aberdeen.

For the most part the route they tramped ran parallel with the east side of the railway, crossing Tullos Hill (Loirston Country Park) and the Vale of Tullos (East Tullos Industrial Estate), arriving at the ferry crossing at Torry and on to Aberdeen. The opening of the Wellington Suspension Bridge in 1831 replaced the old ferry crossing between Torry and Ferryhill, though they did not exercise this route. On journeys there and back they'd occupy themselves by knitting, and always have a song in their heart, tighten or loosen their load by means of a wooden toggle, which, on twisting, was in effect a Spanish windlass. The constant bearing of such heavy loads, however, induced a physical effect on these women, albeit partly hereditary, giving rise to enlargement of the pelvic area and exaggeration of the hips.

Cove fishwife Isie Caie, c.1950.

In the late 1840's there is mention of them having to make both an unscheduled and unwelcome detour during the construction of the railway. When the railway became operational at the Cove in 1850 they were at first reluctant to utilise this method of transport; for one, it only ran as far as Ferryhill, which still left some distance to be tramped, another being that the fishwife could not carry any heavier a load, as it still had to be taken by foot and be sold at places such as the Green. A further issue may have been the cost, which at the time was 4d. return, or for an eight mile excursion, a ½p. per mile for the round trip! As opposed to the material comforts of today, one may only imagine the austere life these women led, or indeed the inner strength of character they needed to possess to survive. An authentic description regarding the fisher-folk of the Cove is given by Father Humphrey around 1866, recorded in his wonderful book 'Recollections of Scottish Episcopalism', some thirty years later:

On the sea the fishermen were themselves and quitted themselves like the manly, sturdy, and self-reliant men they were. On the instant that their boats touched the ground the men were abject in their subjection to their womenkind. The fisher-women and the fisher-girls waded through the surf, and took possession of the fishing boats and of all that the boats contained. The men went straightaway to home, to refresh their wearied bodies and to make up their arrears of well-earned sleep. On land the fisherwomen reigned supreme over every fisherman, whether husband, or son, or brother, or father. The fish found in the boats they regarded as their own unquestioned and unquestionable property, and with their administration they would brook no interference. The fishermen might form a House of Lords on sea, but the fisherwomen constituted on land a House of Commons, and in their hands were held the purse-strings. Those strong, sturdy women carried the fish upon their backs in creels, or large baskets of wicker-work, to Aberdeen — a distance of four miles — for sale. All the fisherwives were dressed alike in short petticoats of blue stuff, with wrappers or bodices of the same or other material, and with mutches, or caps of well-starched linen, not unfrequently edged with lace. This was their uniform, and it had been the uniform of their ancestresses for generations. In it they looked picturesque. Without it they would have looked sordid and loathsome. The physical strength of those fisherwomen was extraordinary. I have known a fisherwoman, three or four days after her confinement, carry on her back, a distance of four miles into Aberdeen, a creel of fish which her husband could scarcely lift. The chastity of the fisherwoman was almost perfect. The fishermen were for the most part chaste, but they were not immaculate. When they failed, it was not in their intercourse with the fisherwomen at any rate of their own village. This would have been 'working folly in Israel'. Their occasional misdemeanours were generally with the inland women, who were not of their race. Even then, if a fisherman had got a country woman into trouble, he was held bound by the fisher code of honour to marry her, and so make her what they called an 'honest woman'. The honest woman had, nevertheless, for the future an evil time. Never, to the day of her death, was her past forgotten by the fisherwomen, nor did they permit her to forget it.

There is, of course, the human element in regards to such women, who at times were looked on as little more than animals, of whom certain walks of society held a great mistrust and disdain. Again, social standing plays its part, and in the fact that these women were lovers and wives and mothers. There is no better summary in general than that of 'Harvest of the Sea', by James Bertram, first published in 1865, where she is described as 'of necessity extremely masculine in character':

Then the nature of their calling makes them bold in manners, and in speech rough and ready. Having to encounter daily all sorts of people, and drive hard bargains, their wits, though not refined, are sharpened to a keen edge, and they are more than a match for any 'chaff' directed towards them either by purchaser or passer-by. So long, however, as they are civilly and properly treated, they are civil and fair-spoken in return, and can, when occasion serves, both flatter and please in a manner by no means offensive. Altogether, the Scottish fishwife is an honest, outspoken, good-hearted creature, rough as the occupation she follows, but generally good-natured and what the Scotch call 'canty'. She does not even want feeling, though, it may be, her avocation gives her little opportunity to show it. But who is so often called upon to endure the strongest emotions of fear, suspense, and sorrow, as the fisherman's wife? Every time the wind blows, and the sea rises, when the boats of her husband or kinsfolk are 'out', she knows no peace till they are in safety; and not seldom has she been doomed to stand on the shore and look at the white foaming sea in which the little boat, containing all she held dear, was battling with the billows, with the problem of its destruction or salvation all unsolved.

As a rule, and as far as was possible, the women had to be presentable in appearance, including personal demeanour, which very much impacted on the sale of their wares. Nonetheless, this hard, unchanging ritual of the fishwife may be summed up in one sentence: "Mony a week oor een niver steekit on a pillow!"

Speldings and Smokies

Once the catch had been divided out a portion would be preserved for winter use and, after gutting, splitting and salting, was spread out upon rocks or shingle to dry. Sometimes a number would be connected by means of a wire. If the rain came on the fish had to be turned over, their skins facing upwards in order to prevent the salt being washed away. This was the work of the women and children, laying them out in dry weather and frequently collecting them when wet, a process of which may be done several times a month in order to complete the curing of the fish.

By 1830 the curing of haddock by smoking was common practice on many parts of the coast. In the Cove the haddocks were gutted, split open and rubbed with salt. Smouldering peats were laid upon an earthen floor in the corner of the house, then sprinkled with wet sawdust in order to prevent them catching fire, producing a thin bluish-grey smoke which pervaded the room. They were hung upon a 'hake', a triangle of wood studded with nails, and from each nail hung a haddock. If the fish were to be eaten immediately, or locally sold, they would be smoked for a brief period only. For more distant markets in the south they'd be smoked much longer, in turn being thoroughly cured. At their most delicious they were lightly salted and smoked to a golden yellow. However, smoking was not without its drawbacks, and when the occupants attempted at times to gain entry to the house, they were 'smorred oot'. Towards the middle of the century wooden kitchen 'lums' arose, followed by smoke-houses, low, black-tarred sheds with tall wide chimneys built adjacent to the house; thus dozens of fish could be skewered and placed into

Speldings at Cove.

a wide open hearth and cured over slow-burning peats. When deemed as being smoked the fish would be for sale and classed as 'Finnan haddies', tied with rushes in bundles of three. Perhaps the Findon taste had something to do with the peat grown locally, for the Cove, and other North-East fishing villages, were smoking fish in much the same way. In addition, whitings were cured by this method also, and known as 'speldings'; though of a sweet taste they proved to be much less popular than that of the haddock.

Fisherman's house with peat stack.

It is thought that the root cause for the disappearance of the Finnan haddie was the serious depletion of the peat stocks, as was the case in 1869 at the Cove when the amount of peats taken from Loirston Moss had to be reduced, with each of the fishermen's houses receiving no more than 5 loads, as stipulated by Dr. Kilgour; the allocation being further reduced in 1877. In 1879 proprietor Alexander Kilgour is recorded as having to chastise the Moss Grieve, the man who oversaw the cutting and supply from the Lands of Cove on the west of the estate. It appears that black peats were presented to a number of households, being quite unsuitable for the purpose of curing fish, and that favouritism was prevalent towards certain individuals of the fishing population — the fishers wanted grey peats, or what they termed 'fittocks', as black peats were best adapted for fuel only. Moreover, the tenants as a whole were most displeased, and in 1885 were bitterly complaining about their overall quality, a sure indication that supply was nearing an end.

Nevertheless, the village of Findon became the national identity when it came to smoked haddocks, and remains so even today. Some insight to the Findon process is that having been gutted and cleaned the fish were laid out in a tub and sprinkled with salt, there they remained for some time before being allowed to dry in the open air, then hung on spits over a large hearth covered with pieces of smouldering peat. A rough or heavy curtain was drawn around an ample wooden smoking chimney (though at first in a corner of the room), the wife or woman kneeling to the fore and sprinkling sawdust upon the peat. For two hours a dense smoke was created, rising slowly, and by means of the depositing of pyroligneous acid, cured the haddocks, imparting them with a yellow colour and of course, a flavour unmatched. Thousands of haddocks were prepared by inferior methods, and from areas far removed from Findon, in turn being sent by curers to markets in the south, which did much damage to the reputation of the genuine article. Those days may be forgotten, but still there lingers an old adage regarding the smoking of haddocks, which all but conjures up a succulent smell:

"The hindmost words the haddock spak were roast my belly before my back."

Social Beasties

In the 1850's, as in most fishing communities on the east coast of Scotland, fishermen in the Cove sported more clothes than those of other professions, perhaps up to three ordinary cotton shirts below their distinctive surcoat, which was of a coarse blue serge and opened out at the front. Above this was a double breasted waistcoat with sleeves. When pulling at the oars the topmost garments were discarded, but immediately donned when at sail. Completing their attire was heavy blue cloth trousers, with a form of knee breeches being worn during leisure hours in the summer months. Before putting to sea tapes were tied round the knees, and thick woollen stockings drawn over them. The leather sea-boots were made to measure and reached to the top of the thigh; the leather, kept well-oiled, moulded itself to a man's leg and was impervious to water. Ashore the boots were often replaced by slippers. A black or brightly coloured silk handkerchief tied twice round the neck was as popular with fishermen as it was with gypsies. A hand-knitted jersey and a blue bonnet with a tassel, shaped like a tam-o-shanter, completed the working rig. In certain localities, the blue bonnet gave way to a peaked 'cheese-cutter' cap. Cloth suits or Navy blue serge with bell-bottomed trousers and a double-breasted jacket being the attire of young fishermen on Saturday nights and Sundays.

When a wedding took place it was accompanied by much rough pleasantry and rituals which varied from village to village. The jollities of a typical mid 19th century wedding could last a week, starting with the 'bidding', where almost everyone in the Cove was invited by word of mouth. As in today gifts would be presented for the wedding, and a viewing arrangement known as 'seeing the bonny things'; a tub or pail belonging to the bride would be filled up with whisky, the men partaking of numerous drams. The night before the wedding the fishermen had their own version of a stag night, where the bridegroom was pinned down and a feet washing ceremony performed. It was not unknown for some of the fishermen to get carried away and scrub the soles of the bridegroom raw by the liberal use of a besom (stiff sweeping brush). Prior to 1829 most wedding ceremonies in the Cove would have been conducted at the house of the father of the bride, St. Fittick's Church being three miles distant. However, if a wedding took place at Nigg Parish Church, then it was back to the abode of the married couple and the abundant wedding feast, the bride having slipped a coin into her stocking or her shoe in order to bring good fortune when her foot first touched upon the floor. In the course of the festivities the happy couple would be ushered into the next room for the 'bedding' ceremony, a sixpence or shilling being placed beneath each pillow of the box-bed beforehand. The door was shut and the newlyweds left in comparative privacy as the guests continued with the serious business of toasting and general celebration. Some understanding of the wedding proceedings is offered in the form of a poem, 'The Cove Marriage', written in his native tongue by George Caie, while at sea in 1853. The narrative consists of the unfolding of the day's events, from the feasting and toasting to the somewhat raucous celebrations, albeit perhaps with a few drams of hyperbole, as the penultimate verse suggests:

> An hotter still the battle grew,
> The women fighting with the men,
> An through the house the skink pot flew,
> Faith crippled some 'twas in the ben.
> An "Murder!" they were crying out,
> Pelting tither wi earthen ware.
> Faith, Muddelie, he anither plan took,
> From them he tore the hide an hair
> > Wi a Clip that night.

Once more an historical gratitude is owed to Father William Humphrey, who in this honest observation brings a village custom back to life, though above any words is the sheer humility of the man himself:

> It was a custom among the Cove fisher-folk in my time that if a fisher-lad and a fisher-lass were going to be married, they should, in company with their more immediate relations, go in state and formally give notice of their purpose to the Laird. I remember that on one occasion an engaged couple went with their following to tell the Laird (Dr. Alexander Kilgour). When he playfully rebuked them for bringing stale news, which I had given him a month before, their answer was, "Eh, ay, but then ye ken he's ane o' oorsells." This was, I thought, the greatest compliment I had ever received in my life, and it would not have been a greater compliment to me if I had been admitted into one of the most exclusive clubs of London. So exclusive were the fishers in their own society and in their pride of race, that the fisher-children would not even play with the country children.

In accordance with weddings funerals in the first half of the 19th century could be rather drunken affairs. Immediately after death the corpse was laid upon a table, with two lighted candles in the room and a plate of salt upon the deceased; no matter the inconvenience the body would be lying due east and west. Some relatives and neighbours sat up in the room where the corpse lay for the whole of each night until the day of internment, and during this, the occasion of the lyke-wake (the period between death and the funeral), a portion of the bible was read and psalms were sung. Due to there being alcohol refreshments, at times the decorum of the watchers could be described as improper, though it was considered disrespectful to the memory of a deceased friend if a quantity of strong drink was not consumed at his funeral — and quite a bit at that! In consequence a number of the guests became intoxicated. The women, however, were given to loudly expressing their grief, with much bodily gesticulation. Before the funeral procession, which in the Cove would have meant a six mile round trip to St. Fittick's Church at the Bay of Nigg, those present in the house were invited to have a last look at the corpse before the coffin lid was screwed down. Thus done, those closest to the deceased would bear the coffin a short distance in the procession towards the kirkyard, before being relieved of their burden by others. At the graveside it was somewhat melancholy to witness the contrast between the sorrow of the close family as opposed to the sheer apathy and boisterous nature manifested by some of the guests. Moreover, around 1830 one particular minister decided to limit the funeral refreshments to a single glass of whisky, at which one of his well-known parishioners quipped, albeit rather miserably, "A funeral wasna worth gan till noo-a-days!"

Chapter 3: The Fishing

A Creek becomes a Harbour

From the Bay of Nigg southwards the coastline is one of a precipitous nature, there being no real break in the cliffs until Stonehaven, albeit out of necessity the small creeks within were a haven for a means of survival. They were difficult to access and offered little protection from the elements, yet no less than nine fishing settlements were established on this dangerous stretch of rock-bound coast, namely, Altens, Burnbanks, the Cove, Findon, Portlethen, Downies, Newtonhill (Skateraw), Muchalls (Stranathro), and Cowie, making for the most densely populated coastal region in the North-East, if not in Scotland. If, however, there was no natural harbour fit for boats, then the Cove may have become more of an agricultural centre than one of fishing, with perhaps Altens or Burnbanks increasing in size, as apart from the 'Bonny Shore' at Gregness, between the Cove and Aberdeen, there is no geological scope for another village arising along the coast.

Since medieval times there has been fishing at the Cove, from what amounted to no more than a parting of the rocks and an infill of shingle. Moreover, there are two natural harbours, back to back and less than 100 yards apart, therefore a more suitable name for the village may have been the Coves, as depicted on earlier maps of the area. Indeed, it would have been less toil to winch the boats up the Crawpeel, the beach having a more gentle slope than that of the harbour. However, owing to the low lying rocks to the east being exposed to northerly winds, and a boulder-strewn beach with a minimal channel, this proved most unsuitable.

Until around the mid 18th century line fishing was pursued on inshore fishing grounds in relatively small boats. In 1709 Robert Brands and Alexander Masson obtained a tack-agreement to fish from the Cove with one boat and crew as fit, for a period of seven years at 20 Scots Merks yearly, from the master of mortifications in Aberdeen (a Merk being the equivalent of 13s. 4d. (66½p), in turn decreasing to around 13d. (6p) English sterling as the 18th century progressed). In 1711 the same procedure applied to Alexander Gyan (Guyan), followed in 1747 when a number of skippers and crews of the Cove were granted permission to fish by the master of mortifications for £20 Scots yearly, including 10 Merks of teind silver to the minister of Nigg, and houses at 5 Merks yearly. In 1762 there were five boats in the Cove, four of which belonged to the Town of Aberdeen and one to John Menzies Esq, the rents being £73. 6s. 8d. and £13. 6s. 8d. Scots money, respectively. In 1795 the total rent from the whitefishers in the Cove to John Menzies Esq. amounted to £50 exactly. By 1785 a pier existed, composed from blocks of stone, albeit much smaller than that of the present; legend has it that the natural formation made for a better harbour, reducing the drag of shingle in adverse weather. This may be so, but as it stood, offered scant shelter. At this time the smaller boats sailed out between the Berryhillock and Port More, a tidal reef extending immediately south, the flood tide running south-west by south, and the ebb north-east half north, at the rate of three to four knots.

Following the herring boom and a requirement for bigger boats in the pursuit of whitefish, by the mid 19th century the fishing in the Cove was at its peak, though improvement was needed to enhance the harbour, not least against the winter storms that roared in over the low lying rocks, causing a great deal of damage to the boats upon the shingle. In December 1874 a plan was drafted showing the proposed harbour constructions, there being three capstans equidistant along the crest of the beach. The pier was to have initially been of a curved construction with a rounded termination, and the slipway for the salmon coble to the *east* of the small pier, and therefore within the main harbour itself.

On 30 December 1874 the initial blueprint was drawn up for the Cove harbour. After almost four years of negotiation and alteration, in 1878 proprietor Alexander Kilgour financed the construction at a cost of just over £3,000, two thirds of which was required for the piers. The work included filling up the gaps in the low lying rocks; a breakwater and pier along the line of rocks forming the east side of the harbour; making level its approach to Balmoral Road; the deepening of the harbour; and a small boat pier on the west side of the harbour. The small boat pier on construction measured 100 feet long and nine feet broad, part of the existing rocks having to be blasted away. The gravel and loose stones in the harbour were dug out and used in the various constructions. On the formation of the main pier there was a sea wall some 23 yards long by 4 feet high, with 200 feet of oak beams measuring 8 inches by 6 inches, hot dipped in vegetable tar, and bolted to the edge of the pier itself. It is not known whether the existing pier was retained, though the contract states that 'any materials unfit or improper for construction should be removed'. What must be considered is that cement and other materials had to be transported from the station by way of horse and cart, and that all of the above completed by 1 July that year. Delays arose, however, while improving the section of Balmoral Road leading from the village, for which a pitch-lined drain was required, plus another located at Balmoral Place; the additional cost amounting to £225, though in operation by the end of November. The constructions were upon land by way of a feu from the Crown for the initial sum of £5, plus a yearly payment of one shilling (5p.) — a token gesture which was never to be exacted.

'On The Cove Shore', 1867, by James Cassie. To the left is a construction formed of stone blocks serving as a rudimentary pier, while beyond the Berryhillock are the sails of herring drifters. The foot of the Berryhillock itself juts well into the harbour basin. In the foreground are some heavy wooden creels, and a pool which may have been used for cleaning the fishing gear.

It is with some significance that from the outset of operations Alexander Kilgour did not intend to apply for a Provisional Order to levy dues for the harbour against the fishermen, and that besides the aforementioned manure problem, a quite separate dispute arose in regards to a rent increase for the proposed constructions and improvements to the harbour. In the November of 1877 a deed entitled 'Of Conditions by the Fishers of Cove Village of the Proposed Harbour Improvements', was issued, of which all fishermen were requested to sign: 'We the fishermen of Cove have agreed to have our harbour repaired by Mr. Kilgour Esq. according to the plan shown to us on the following conditions: 1st. That we are to pay £100 yearly. 2nd. That we be allowed to sell our white fish to a curer as they are caught. 3rd. That we have the right to use the whole of the harbour including the part where our herring boats are drawn up. 4th. That we are not to be responsible for any damage that may be done to the harbour by storm'. A few were obviously dragging their heels, for on Christmas Day Mr. Kilgour advised his advocate that any fishermen who did not wish to pay the rent increase were requested to leave by Whitsunday next.

It appears that a number of them had openly expressed their intentions not to do so, and during the constructions, and all of that year, resentment between the two had grown as such that in February 1879 Mr. Kilgour had stated he was having 'no more to do with them', whereby negotiations regarding the increased rent had completely broken down. In August, however, he requested that each fishermen should present a paper signed with his name, agreeing to pay one pound yearly in lieu of the manure held at present as rent in kind. The following month the arrangement was revised, at which the fishermen were to pay only 10s. each via the skipper of the boat in the form of a yearly payment; there being twelve large boats at the harbour, and with each skipper paying £3, amounted to £36 per annum. It was also proposed that each of the old men in the four smaller boats pay 5s., making for a total of £42. This was agreed, albeit the fishermen requesting that the pier be extended to the outer rocks of the harbour by seventy feet, stretching to Port More, and that the beach be broadened to accommodate the 12 larger vessels with ease. The former, of course, was never to be implemented.

Cove harbour in the mid 1880's. Large vessels with masts sit by the pier. The two salmon cobles to the right of the smaller boat pier were not allowed access to the main part of the harbour, which was in fact reserved for the whitefishers only. Inset as seen today.

In regards to the harbour itself, the main purpose of Mr. Kilgour was that he foresaw the prospect of the Cove becoming a herring curing station, Aberdeen having rose to prominence as a major herring port some five years earlier. He had also stated that there would be no more work done to the Cove harbour until it became a regular herring curing station, and therefore a worthwhile investment that yielded an assured return. It would appear that he altered his strategy, though, for a contract was drawn up in the March of 1879 for further improvements, including a concrete walkway leading from the footpath on the beach to the smaller pier, of which a few yards of rock had to be blasted away in order to accommodate its access. Other tasks included the removal of loose stones from the harbour and a filling up of the northern end of the beach where the boats lay, as it was somewhat sunken and covered in mould. For the latter clean pebbles from the surrounding area were utilised in raising it to a more accessible level. Towards the end of April, though, Mr. Kilgour himself had to prompt the workmen to quicken the procedure of removing large boulders from beneath the line of low water, the spring tides being the only time of the year in which this operation could be carried out.

A herring fishing station firmly in his mind, by August Mr. Kilgour had hired the services of Mr. Norman Ferguson at the weekly wage of 15s. per week, with a view to take complete charge of the harbour operations. Among his duties were to prevent the fishermen causing damage to the newly constructed piers, and from throwing rubbish onto the beach; that they keep their berths in good order; in no respect should they interfere with the salmon fishers, or indeed the men of the Coastguard. Once fully operational then Mr. Ferguson was to oversee the incoming and outgoing of the boats, including where they were to go to unload their respective catches. Besides effectively becoming the harbour master he was also given the task of looking after the village in general, including seeing that the tenants kept their houses in good order; albeit he was given no power to do so west of the Railway Bridge, the hotel, or upon the premises of the salmon fishers, as mentioned. Though allocated a house in the village his employment was brief, for by November that year Mr. Kilgour had given up any further thoughts on making the Cove the 'seat of a herring station', and had relieved him of his duties. Moreover, Mr. Ferguson had previously ventured that the Cove would best flourish if given over to the curing of haddocks. Indeed, had the Cove become a herring port, then the impact on the area would have been enormous, with most likely the suburbs of Aberdeen City stretching significantly further south.

Even though the Cove was not to be a curing station it became apparent that the height of the breakwater was insufficient to prevent the crashing waves, and in 1883, in the aftermath of a storm, it was raised to its present height of 24 feet above high water. A small gap in the rocks near the Berryhillock was also filled, and a portion of ground on the landward side of the breakwater floored with concrete for the purpose of the salmon fishermen drying their nets. The beach, too, had been severely damaged some days before, and was repaired and made level by Mr. John Fyfe, then lessee of the Cove Quarries.

Perhaps the words of Mr. Ferguson had a struck a chord some seven years previously, for in the August of 1886 a lengthy discussion had taken place between Alexander Kilgour, his advocate, and a Mr. Johnstone, outlining the establishment of a haddock curing station at the Cove. If the fishermen would be prepared to sell to Mr. Johnstone — as was done in many other places — their fish fresh by the hundredweight, then he would be prepared to establish a station and buy at market prices, in turn curing any haddock and whiting immediately. He would, of course, be willing to give a reasonable rent to Mr. Kilgour for a harbour stance. The fish offal would continue as before, the guts being deposited in the village middens and collected for use as agricultural manure. However, the following month he stated that he could not commit himself to a station at the Cove, as there were far too many trawlers to unload at Aberdeen. He suggested Mr. Kilgour advertise a curing station in the local press, which he did, though it brought little response. Another curer was contacted, but again was reluctant to set up at the Cove, as there was a constant supply of fish at Aberdeen. More emphatic, though, was the reply from Mr. G. Angus, a curer based in Aberdeen, ominously stating that 'centralisation is the order of the day', and with fish at Point Law from all quarters, and in all weathers, he could not entertain such a proposal. Perhaps because of there being a fifth of the village empty Mr. Kilgour wished to establish a curing station in order to tempt fishermen back to the Cove, as business in general was suffering.

Yet another dispute arose in regards to the harbour, albeit not from the fishing community. In August 1887 Mr. David Sinclair of North Loirston lay claim to having 'certain rights', offering to sell these to Alexander Kilgour for the sum of £200. Mr. Kilgour explained that Balmoral Road was not a public road and maintained by himself at his own expense, and that recently a traction engine for towing the larger fishing boats up the beach was granted permission to traverse its length, though only on his direct authority. Indeed, as confirmed in a document outlining rights of access on the division of the parish in 1785, no mention is given as per the collective upkeep of the road leading to the harbour, or indeed the harbour itself. However, the feuars on the eastern half of the parish most certainly had access, albeit John Menzies Esq. and William Matthew (inclusive of their successors) were liable to pay half each towards the general upkeep. Mr. Sinclair, it seems, had no more to do but drop his pursuit.

The harbour, though, still had its problems, and in December 1888 fisherman George Morrice complained to Mr. Kilgour of a rock which obstructed the boats at low tide, and that it would prove a great benefit if blasted clear. This, plus a ridge of rock at the point of the main pier, was therefore to be removed. The work was contracted to John Fyfe, and ten quarrymen hired, operations commencing during the following March ebb tides; the fishermen being requested to help carry the debris up the beach for disposal. The foundation at the point of the smaller boat pier also required some attention. In the aftermath of a severe storm further repairs were undertaken, and in the summer of 1892 a spur breakwater, leading eastwards from the pier to the neighbouring rocks, was added, with another adjoining the Berryhillock; the iron reinforcing supplied by John Fyfe from his blacksmith shop at the Cove Quarries. Again, this became an extensive operation, requiring 12 tons of dry cement and 40 yards of jute. Though the bulk of the construction had been completed by the end of August, in September work continued by excavating the beach between the piers at times low water. Additional men were drafted to complete the operation, with further work to be carried over to the west side of the lesser pier in the coming month.

Cove harbour in the 1920's. To the right of the main pier may be seen the two spur breakwaters in their entirety. The northern end of the smaller pier has already began to disappear.

After all the harassment, intentions and expense, came the irony, for at the time of the harbour constructions the coming demise for small creeks like the Cove had been forecast in a short press report on the haddock fishing between Aberdeen and Stonehaven. Some haddock boats were being decked over and equipped with beds and a store, the objective being to fish overnight for herring to serve as bait for the great line boats, the writer being of the opinion that cod and ling fishing was much more advantageous if a commodious harbour with an on-hand market was available for the disposal of such large fish. Thus the beginning of the end for settlements with tidal harbours, the Fishtown of Altens having been abandoned in the 1830's owing to its poor harbour and a lack of moss for curing haddocks.

Left. The ruins of the fishing settlement above Altens Haven. Right. Fishermen's houses at Burnbanks Village, of which there were around twenty. Bad harbour facilities and a lack of peat for smoking purposes became the root cause of their abandonment as fishing villages.

Little by Way of Shelter

Winter sea at the harbour.

As man encroaches on the sea, so shall she encroach on he — in all of her majestic fury! There have been countless storms at the Cove over the centuries, one of the earliest descriptions being on 1 January 1784 when great pieces of rocks were rent off and thrown into the harbour, the sea rushing in forty yards further than the oldest man in the village could ever remember, with a great deal of lightning, along with the wind. However, no storm has been as fierce, or reported in depth, as the one on 17 February 1900. During the course of the afternoon the sea began to rise, greatly assisted by an easterly gale. The harbour was soon a seething mass, huge rollers crashing over the breakwater and the piers. All that evening, and through the night, the fishermen struggled to haul their boats beyond the reach of danger. The salmon fishers, along with lessee Mr. John Hector, struggled to save the two salmon cobles berthed behind the smaller pier. Indeed, the lives of the fishermen were in constant danger. At about two o' clock in the morning it was fully high tide and the storm at its height when a barrel was hurled over the breakwater, shattering upon the beach. Seconds later a gigantic wave swept over, threatening to engulf all that lay before it; two brothers, David and John Robertson, were dashed against their boat, receiving serious internal injuries. The storm did not abate, and besides the crash of waves came a rumble of falling masonry — the sea wall at the entrance of the harbour had been hurled down, with fifty yards of the pier being torn away. This would have made for a hellish spectacle, for the waves rolled in unchecked, the water rushing up the bothy brae to a height of around forty feet. Both salmon cobles suffered severely, few boats escaping the fury as stem-posts, bows and gunwales were smashed during the onslaught. It was estimated that 100 tons of pebbles were swept from the beach. In fact, the very rocks themselves were torn and broken, chips and other fragments being hurled a considerable distance.

In daylight the damage was better ascertained, the main pier being in a shattered condition, the shore littered with the wreckage of boats, three of which were entirely destroyed, and seven others seriously impaired. The extent of the damage was calculated to be around £500, quite a sum, considering the cost of the breakwater and pier twenty-two years previously. The oldest fishermen of the Cove at the time, John Robertson, George Webster and George Morrice, men in

One of the last photographs taken of the Cove harbour in its entirety, c.1920, before the onset of storm damage. The sweeping curvature of the main pier is most discernable, and the smaller pier is all but intact.

their seventies', declared that "Many a storm had they witnessed, but could not recall one that had been so disastrous to property on land". During the above events Cove fisherman Mr. Robert Wood was born, and locally known as 'Stormy Morning'. In the following days Mr. Kilgour visited the harbour and examined the damage. He arranged at once to begin clearing up the debris. In fact the fishermen themselves did a considerable amount of the work, with Mr. Kilgour paying £120 towards damages and wages. The restoration work was undertaken by Sellar and Company, contractors in Aberdeen, the pier being restored and made considerably stronger. There was also repairs to the breakwater east of the main pier, which, in southeasterly gales, effectively took the full brunt of the waves. Compensation was sought for the fishermen of the Cove, and Mr. John Freeland, fishing organiser, contacted Mr. J. W. Crombie, M.P. for Kincardineshire, with a view to obtaining money from the Greenwich Hospital Fund to help repair and replace the boats. Nothing could be done, however, as the fund was confined entirely to the relief of sailors in the Royal Navy.

Further storms ensued, notably in 1902, and c.1940 when the end of the main pier was again torn away. Over the 20th century the lesser breakwaters have been dashed down, inclusive of the one due east of the main breakwater itself, with the pier being extensively repaired on several occasions, most recently in 1959, when the sea wall was seriously damaged. Indeed, had it not been for extensive

Cove harbour looking north, c.1940. There is serious storm damage to both piers — the curving frontage of the main pier has been broken off completely. Its southern section is of a hollow construction.

concrete blocking, then the main pier may not be present today. In one such storm the curved termination was broken off and never restored to its former glory, portions of which may be seen at low tide, in the form of large concrete slabs. It is essential that the pier be maintained, and in 1990 Mr. Hugh Moir, then lessee of the salmon fishing, employed local man Mr. Walter Fraser to lay a skin of concrete on the central section in order to prevent further fissures and cracks. However, the pier is in deterioration, an iron boat ladder being removed, another replaced as they slowly rust away. On both its harbour and seaward sides there is constant erosion by the friction of the waves. Sadly, the smaller boat pier is in a ruinous condition, being completely submerged at high tide, its 'hearting' having long been spilled upon the beach.

Since the initial construction and repairs no further additions have came into being, other than a means of hoisting the salmon fishing equipment onto the pier. After the First World War a small wooden sheer legs was installed for this purpose, in turn replaced in the early 1950's by a more substantial hand-cranked, swivel-based iron crane. As well as hoisting the fishing gear, it had the capacity to raise the coble upon the pier when stormy weather prevailed. However, being constantly exposed to salty winds, it was deemed to be in a dangerous condition and removed in 1993. At present the harbour is privately owned, though at the forefront regarding the heritage of the Cove, therefore its preservation of the utmost importance.

Aerial view of the harbour, 1981.

The Fleet

As was common in the North-East, the Cove on establishment had no more than a handful of boats. The fishermen possessed the barest of equipment, yet it was known for them to propel a 25ft open boat, with a crew of six or seven, many miles distant, remaining continuously at sea for two or three days. Smaller boats were more commonplace in tidal harbours, as they had to be continually manhandled into and out of the sea, more so in adverse weather. From the mid to late 18th century most would have measured between 15ft. and 25ft., owned and crewed by whitefishers, so named after the colour of the flesh of the fish they pursued. In the mid 1790's there were twenty-four men in four boats, with fourteen boys and older men in yawls (a half-decked fishing boat 15ft. to 20ft. in length). Torry had thirty-six men in six boats, both as fishers and acting pilots, along with nine boys and older men in yawls. At this time a boat of around 25ft cost £25, and had a working life expectancy of around ten years or so.

Below is an excerpt from the 1777 survey of the lands and barony of Nigg, by George Brown:

> There is easy access to the Harbour of the Cove for bringing in lime, tho' indeed they have more fine fishing dung than they can use. The Toun of Cove comprehended originally six fishing boats, and just now there is nearly that number, tho' the town of Aberdeen has more than Pitfoddels; the fishers have no land but what they take from the Tenants for sowing hemp; they have houses, and some of them yards, for which they pay to the Proprietors along with the boat rents.

Several types of fishing were pursued, with statistics given regarding the number of boats at the harbour. During the early 1820's the Cove would have possessed only one class of boat, these being owned and fully manned by local fishermen. By 1838 there were nine boats, each crewed by six or seven men, with numbers increasing in the following decades. In 1882 the fishing had peaked, there being thirteen first-class boats (over 30 feet), twelve second-class boats (18 to 30 feet) and five third-class boats (under 18 feet), with ninety-eight resident fisher men and boys, making for an industrious location. Even with its piers, the Cove remained a tidal harbour, which therefore dictated the size of the boat. Though a manageable size of vessel had to be considered, in the late 18th and early 19th centuries, the boats were significantly heavy enough to require more than their crews to pull them up and down the beach. It became necessary to install a hand-operated cable winch, or capstan (two of which remain at the harbour), and by inserting spars into the slotted axle a few men (or women) could with ease wind the boat up the beach. It would be favourable to await the tide, as the low water line could present quite a distance. The boats themselves were on wooden rollers.

'Scaffies' on their way to the fishing grounds.

However, the harbour proved unsuitable, especially during the herring boom in the second half of the 19th century, and the fishing industry demanded bigger boats for greater distances. In 1857 there were 70 fishermen from the Cove and surrounding district in the Kincardineshire branch of the Shipwrecked Fishermen and Mariners Royal Benevolent Society, out of a total of 136 members. What may have compounded this was the severe storm which hit Scotland in August 1848, sinking 124 fishing boats in the process, undermining the belief in the open boat by

Scottish fishermen in general. This gave rise to decked vessels such as the 'Scaffie' (Moray Firth) and the 'Fifie' (Firth of Forth) in the following decade, and later the 'Zulu' (so named after the ongoing Zulu Wars) in 1878. Boats such as these, and many tons burden, may have been owned and crewed by the Cove fishermen, but were operated from the deep water docks at Torry or Aberdeen. Most of these vessels were 45ft. to 50ft., albeit with recorded lengths of up to 80ft. or more. There being a reasonable road to the harbour, by the end of September a few such vessels belonging to the Cove were hauled up the beach by means of a steam engine, then berthed until the following season.

Around 1880 a four oared haddock boat was worked by five share fishermen, and a six oared boat by seven men. Haddock boats cost around £40 to complete. Larger boats were fitted with mast and sail, costing in the region of £220, and carried a crew of seven sharemen, working longer lines further out to sea than the smaller vessels. A boat was considered to be doing well if averaging three shots per week. In the past the fishwife had taken possession of the boat

Fishermen stood by a yawl at Cove, c.1920.

on its arrival, landing and disposing of the catch; by this time, though, and especially in Torry, Fittie and Aberdeen, it had become common for curers to engage the boats at a fixed rate, inclusive of a bounty (a lump sum at the end of the season), in the same manner as those at the herring. For boats from the Cove it would have proved no different, the fishermen selling their catch to a number of curers and merchants at Aberdeen harbour.

A fishing yawl berthed behind the breakwater.

In 1882 an Aberdeen syndicate bought an old Tyneside-built tug called *Toiler* at Dublin for £1,550, converting her into a steam trawler. On 23 March that year she made her first paying trip across the bay, the catch being three boxes of haddocks, with a value of 37s. In the first month *Toiler* took over £200, and almost instantly steam trawling began in earnest. Due to their swelling numbers, and the damage inflicted upon the inshore fishing grounds, meetings were being held the length of the east coast of Britain; from Lowestoft to Golspie line fishermen railed at this threat to their livelihood. In regards to the North-East The Commission of Enquiry was set up at the Courthouse in Aberdeen on 30 August 1883, to 'inquire and report upon complaints that have been made by line and drift net fishermen of injuries sustained by them in their calling owing to the use of the trawl net and beam trawl', there being witness accounts from line fishermen at the Cove:

George Caie Sr. said that he had been a fishermen for 39 years, and caught less fish each year, stating that he 'never got so few haddies', and that they had ever decreased since trawling was introduced, especially that of steam trawling. His wages, too, were on the wane, earning little more than eight or nine shillings per week, as opposed to a few years earlier when it was considerably more. He continued that the whitefishing as a whole had been falling off rapidly since steam trawling commenced, and that the line fishers tolerated the sailing trawlers due to what little impact they had upon their fishing grounds. He was also aware that the steam trawlers had destroyed a number of nets and lines belonging to the fishermen of the Cove, but instead of compensation for the damage incurred, the trawlermen merely laughed in their face. Trawlers also destroyed vast number of crabs, taking immature and 'mother-partans', which no local fishermen would ever do. His solution was total abolition, as it was impossible that line fishermen and trawlers could ever work together. His son George Caie Jr. agreed with what his father had said, adding that as well as taking partans, the trawlers took away their partan creels, and that trawling by night did more damage owing to the partans being more active. George Robertson admitted that he'd rather the trawlers were prohibited from fishing at night, as opposed to by day, but would prefer to see the steam trawlers abolished altogether. George Morrice thought that lights on the trawlers would be of no service, as they would still be unable to identify the name of the boat, and that the only remedy was to ban this type of fishing. James Craig was rather more blunt: "I would prohibit trawling altogether, although a sea of sailing vessels was better than a few steam trawlers." Regarding the dwindling amounts of fish being taken, Torry line fisherman Andrew King spoke for the community as a whole, stating that while they used to get up to thirty score of haddocks on one line, they now caught between two and eight score, and that he personally had had his lines twice broken and once taken clean away.

Later that year Mr. G. Balfour, M.P. for Kincardineshire, proposed that the line fishermen on the east coast of Scotland were a singularly isolated body without influential friends to put in force any acts of Parliament, therefore he wished that legal officers be authorised to take up their complaints against the loss of their fishing gear. He also requested a coastal body of public officers, who, on given power, could enforce the law against any trawlers which not only took away the fishing gear but also tore up the bait beds. The appeal was further strengthened by Alexander Kilgour, who as the representative of several hundred fishermen, penned a letter to the Right Honourable W. G. Gladstone M.P. First Lord of the Treasury, outlining their plight.

It appears that initially the sailing trawlers did little harm to the fishing grounds, but the consensus among the line fishers of Scotland was to be rid of steam trawlers once and for all, 'less they all come to poverty', their main grievance being that the trawlers were a constant presence on the age-old fishing grounds, where they tore up the feeding beds of the haddock, cod and flatfish, and from the dwindling fish stocks there was little left for them to catch. Effectively the trawler was ruining in a few seasons what ecologically took thousands of years. Indeed, the introduction of steam trawling was the death knell for the line boats in small havens. Moreover, the scope of the fishing was growing as a whole, for in 1860 boats were mostly undecked and could be easily hauled ashore, though by 1890 ambitious fishermen had a larger, and sometimes fully decked vessel, which had to be taken to the nearest harbour for security in bad weather. This impacted on villages without adequate harbour facilities, effectively losing their fishermen to the nearest recognised port, and in the Cove, as mentioned, may be evidenced by the number of houses becoming unoccupied and falling into disrepair. Though the Cove and other similar fishing villages struggled on for a surprising length of time, the inevitable had been realised.

REGISTERED SAILING BOATS AT COVE, 1914

Reg	Name	Owner	Ton
A19	Cruden Bay	William Webster	1
A42	Maggie Ann Mary	James, John & Robert Craig	2
A99	That's Her	James Craig	2
A171	William Webster	John Wood	1
A276	Leader	George Robertson	3
A330	Annie Caie	R. Caie	1
A543	May Flower	R. Allan	1
A558	Nellie	George Guyan	1
A689	Gratitude	John Morrice	3

REGISTERED SAILING BOATS AT COVE, 1920

Reg	Name	Owner	Ton
A19	Cruden Bay	William Webster	1
A42	Maggie Ann Mary	James, John & Robert Craig	2
A99	That's Her	James Craig	2
A171	William Webster	John Wood	1
A276	Leader	George Robertson	3
A330	Annie Caie	R. Caie	1
A429	Be In Time	G. & D. Robertson	2
A543	May Flower	A. K. Stott	1
A558	Nellie	George Guyan	1
A689	Gratitude	John Morrice	3
A732	Family's Trust	William Stephen and others	2
A886	Boys' Delight	William Stephen	3

After the end of the First World War inshore fishing began a serious decline, thus the number of boats operating out of small tidal harbours. By 1954 there were but two registered boats in the Cove. The first motorised boat in the Cove was the *Family's Trust,* by means of an inboard diesel engine. From the 1940's outboard engines became the norm, the most popular being the single cylinder, three to six horsepower Seagull, a simple but reliable means for inshore fishing. Towards the end of the 1960's the yawls had all but disappeared, with only *Mabel,* owned by Mr. Albert Ross, and *Nellie,* owned by Mr. Fred Cargill and Mr. David Steven, remaining, both being sold a few years later. Moreover, testament to the age of the yawl lay in the form of *Golden Arrow,* heeled over on the shingle and rotting away, a victim of the elements and time. The wooden rollers on which the boats were launched had also disappeared, having been replaced by two-wheeled beach trailers with a greased wooden slipway. The capstan, too, became redundant, compact diesel-powered winches being the order of the day. By now the open boat of fifteen to eighteen feet was predominant, being lighter than the yawl and easier to handle, and much more manoeuvrable afloat. Such boats became known as 'partan backs', owing to the shape of the stern, which indeed resembled a crab. In the 1970's the traditional wooden boat was being gradually replaced by fibreglass, whereat a mould was taken from an existing hull and fitted out. Boats like these required little maintenance and were virtually watertight, and not subjected to rot and springing timbers. As evidenced at the harbour today the boats are of a fibreglass construction, excepting *Crawpeel,* owned by Mr. William Adam, a traditional clinker of larch and pine, built by Mr. James Adam at the Cove in 2003. Presently the boats are propelled by twin-cylinder outboard engines in the eight to forty horsepower range.

Line Fishing

Fishing has been pursued at the Cove from at least the 16th century, albeit with scant recorded documentation, though from the late 18th century onwards details are given describing four distinctive pursuits: whitefish, salmon, shellfish and herring. At first, and for at least two centuries, whitefishing was the more prevalent, and from sheer necessity the fisherman was forced to work whenever the weather permitted; sudden storms were a particular risk, with periodic loss of life at sea. Indeed, by this time his occupation dictated there was no set hours, the work long and the hours irregular, and engaged by means of line fishing, of which there were three variations.

First was the *small line,* or *sma' line* (as in all other forms of line fishing initially made from hemp), sufficient for a man to manage both at sea and on shore, containing 720 hooks on snoods of horse hair, one yard distant from each other, with a value of 15s. (75p.). Boats from sixteen to twenty feet were the order of the day, usually with a crew of four men and propelled by oars, each trip lasting no more than a day. Sometimes the lines were tied together and could number 3,000 hooks. Fishing for smaller species such as haddock, whiting and codling in inshore waters became the occupation for the greater part of the year, particularly in autumn and winter. When the boat reached the fishing ground the line would be 'shot'. First a buoy with a rope attached to a stone or small anchor was dropped, followed by a lead-weighted 'tow rope'. The line uncoiled itself from the scull, being pulled over a metal runner, the speed dictated by the tidal drift and paid out along the sea-bed. A further tow rope, anchor and buoy at the opposite end completed the process. Hauling the line was a simple task, the fish being removed from the hooks and the line coiled into a wicker basket, and in the Cove known as a 'murrlin'. However, should a sudden squall develop, the line might have to be cut and left in situ. On reaching harbour the catch was arranged according to size and species, then cleaned and smoked as per custom. In January the haddock had roe, and came to the coast by the shoal; in March various flatfish, including plaice, were plentiful on the sandy bottom. By early summer the fishing of haddock and whiting were good, and from November the cod was at a premium, caught on coarse and rocky ground.

There was also the *dog line.* In August the voracious dog fish would consume all before it and swim to within the fishing grounds, having the capability of totally destroying both the fish and the line. It was taken in considerable quantities, where twenty good dog fish livers could yield one Scotch pint of oil, with a value of around 1s. (5p.). A heavier gauge of line and larger hooks was the order of the day, there being 480 hooks at one to four yards distant. Usually this type of line fishing required a boat 25 feet long by 9 feet wide, having two small masts and a crew of six men.

The third being the *great line,* or *greatlin,* and from March or April, weather permitting, the fishing commenced. The fisherman had intimate knowledge of the fishing grounds, and in 25ft. boats with crews of six men (and sometimes a boy) sailed thirty miles or more to find the larger species. Besides being propelled by oars, boats such as these had means of a sail. As the year progressed the ling was first more plentiful, followed by the turbot, then the skate during May and June. Large cod, known as 'keilling', were caught through the spring and summer. This line was considerably stronger than the small line, containing 3,600 hooks, being 1½ fathoms distant from each other on snoods one fathom in length. Unlike the small line the hooks were corked and coiled into baskets and baited with half a mackerel or herring. The lines were prepared on the outward voyage, with the shooting one of a rhythmical process of uncorking the hooks and handing to the baiter, who in turn slung the line into the water. On arrival at the fishing ground lines could be shot and hauled several times over, though the distance made it impractical to return to shore, therefore the boats would be in situ for two or three days at a time. In 1792 parish minister Dr. Cruden suggested that a few larger decked vessels should be employed at the more distant fishing banks, whereby smaller boats could unload their cargoes and have recourse to in adverse weather.

Cove fishwife Elizabeth Morrice baiting a line, c.1930's.

There was also the politics of the whitefishing to consider, and if a boy was employed he would pursue only special duties, drawing a minor share of the proceeds. Becoming a man meant taking a full share in the boat, which preserved a life-long livelihood. The usual rules applied, such as in a crew of six, where the division of the catch was one equal share to a man, the seventh being that of the boat. Nonetheless, inflation sails by around 1830, as recorded when a successful catch by a boat from the Cove fetched a price at Aberdeen market double that of 30 years ago! At this time cod was beginning to be sold uncured from the boat to various merchants for pickling (which required much salt and barrels), a more costly process than the traditional splitting, salting, and drying in the sun, and a method never undertaken by the fishermen themselves. The cod were mainly prepared in this way for the London market during the month of February, with curing at its height in the spring months. Where traditionally haddocks had been smoked in-house, by the 1830's some of the catch was also being sold directly to curers. Thus in the mid 1840's the normal price for a box (eight stones) of haddock was 4s., rising to 8s. in the 1880's.

It is with some significance that after the first half of the nineteenth century the golden age of inshore whitefishing was all but over, and by 1865, in 'Harvest of the Sea', local fishermen along the east coast of Scotland were collectively unanimous in that thirty years ago the inshore haddock stocks were plentiful, with little distance being required to catch a sufficient quantity. Indeed, yet bigger boats were required, having to go further out to sea in order to catch what was once abundant locally, with the ratio of baited hook to captured fish, or 'hook power', ever diminishing. So, too, the cod, and at the same time mention given of the state of the inshore grounds between Kincardine and Burntisland, from once being in their thousands, to 'not a cod now to be got'. In essence, the demise of the fish stocks was primarily due to an ever-increasing demand, which had expanded from personal use, to local market, to one of a national supply.

By the third quarter of the 19th century larger vessels were being used and, in late spring, the Cove fishermen in boats with a crew of nine men each, worked on the fishing grounds known as the Long Forties. This was an area of the North Sea with a fairly consistent depth of around 40 fathoms, thus, on a nautical chart, a long area with many '40' notations. It lies between the northeast coast of Scotland and the southwest coast of Norway, centred about 57°N 0°30'E; the Shipping Forecast area 'Forties' being so called after it. Long sojourns like these would give rise to exposure in the most cramped conditions, with only cold sustenance for the crew, such as oatcakes, loaf, smoked haddocks, or dried herring — wrapped in cloth and soaked through during inclement weather. Other times there was but hard ship's biscuits, which were softened when dipped into tea. For the most part, though, the men were home at weekends. As noted, if crewed by fishermen of the Cove, then boats as such would operate from deep water harbours at Torry or Aberdeen, being laid up for nine months of the year, with the crews resorting to smaller craft on fishing grounds nearer the coast. Large boats, however, were more frequently being used to coincide with the start of the herring season in July. Of course, if the dogfish prevailed then the usual consequences applied.

Great line fishing lessened towards the mid 19th century, there being more profit in haddock fishing, but in the 1870's, was revived somewhat, owing to a demand for cod. The root cause may have been the railway, now providing direct transportation to markets in the south. Indeed, haddock fishing in small harbours such as the Cove occupied more fishermen than that of cod, even in the spring months when the cod fishing was at its

Fishwives at Cove, with 'speldings' in the background.

height. At this time the common cycle for the fishing year in the Cove, and throughout the North-East, was as follows: spring for the cod; summer for the herring; autumn and winter for the haddock. Of course, in the following decade the trawl net loomed, drawing the crews of the line boats to an occupation which had less physical work for superior wages. Line fishing had founded the Cove, and as it declined so too did the number of boats as the fishing began to focus on larger ports. Nevertheless, it stubbornly persisted, though increasingly pursued from seldom further than Findon Ness or the Hasman Rocks, inevitably dwindling to that of a part-time basis. Having ceased in the mid 1980's its methods were essentially unchanged, albeit with improved equipment such as plastic, polypropylene and nylon.

Herring Fishing

From the Firth of Forth in the 1790's, the herring began to migrate north to Caithness. Indeed, the name of herring is derived from 'heer' or 'herr', and relates to an army. An unpredictable fish, the herring lives on plankton, moving along the coast by a form of mass instinct. It was believed that they appeared around the Orkney and Shetland Islands in the spring, moving slowly southwards, until around midsummer when they were off Peterhead and Fraserburgh; by the autumn they had reached East Anglia. In 1807 work began on the expansion of Wick, including many curing yards, with the government encouraging the use of the Scottish herring buss, a large vessel of 50 tons burden and more, which in effect was the mother ship for smaller craft to unload their catches. This flourishing industry swept down the coast into the long established centres of whitefishing; in fact the men of villages like the Cove, whitefishers by tradition, turned collectively to the new prospect of profit in herring.

By 1830 most fishermen along the east coast of Scotland were active in the herring fishing, but apart from a small number who followed the herring farther south, it occupied no more than two to three months in the year. At this time a typical herring boat measured 30 to 35 feet and was clinker built, some weighing ten to fourteen tons burden. In 1838 there were nine boats from the Cove working the north coast herring grounds, fitted up with masts, sails, cordage, and nets, and at considerable expense — it's unlikely such boats would be regularly launched from a tidal harbour, there at the time being no more than a rudimentary pier at the Cove. They each were crewed by five or six men, engaged to provide a certain number of crans, perhaps around 200. The preceding year, however, proved most unprofitable.

Of course, the Cove wasn't noted for landing herring, but throughout the 19th century this was to prove a predominant source of income. Indeed, the herring bonanza may draw a parallel to that of the oil boom in 1970's Aberdeen. The fishing began in the middle of July and would last until the beginning of September, the profit being equal to that of a year at the whitefishing. A small haddock boat, equipped with four nets and crewed by four men, might expect to land between 50 and 100 crans (a cran being 37½ gallons capacity, with an average of 1200 fish) of herring for the season, for which the fishermen would receive around 10s. per cran. However, a train of four nets proved more expensive than a set of lines, and would only be used for six to eight weeks of the year — these being made of hemp and somewhat bulky, before the introduction of cotton nets in the 1840's, which were but a third of the weight. Supplies, however, began to dwindle during the course of the American Civil War.

Herring boats off Aberdeen, 1890.

The means of catching herring was by drift net, of which the mesh measured one inch in order to allow enough room for young herring to escape or pass through. Nets were measured by the barrel-bulk, each barrel holding two nets, and each net being 50 yards long and 32 feet deep. Some of the larger boats carried up to a mile of nets, the drift composing of many separate nets tied together by means of a back-rope, each marked off with a buoy (sometimes a bladder, for which Collie-dogs were specifically bred). The net was sunk by means of leaden weights and fastened to the boat by a long or short trail-rope, according to the depth at which the herrings may be taken. In effect the drift net formed a huge perforated wall, and was shot immediately after sunset, floating and drifting with the tide, whereat the fish would make contact, becoming entangled in the meshes and effectively drown.

For many years Scottish fishermen stuck firmly to their belief in the open boat, but by the middle of the century fore cabins began to be introduced, a length of 40 feet commonplace for a new boat by the close of the 1860's. Full decks were being introduced, with a large open hatchway to accommodate the working of the nets; and from 1867 onwards the fashion steadily increased as the advantages became more apparent. Previously the herring fishing had been confined to inshore waters, but now fishermen began to push farther in search of the shoals, the order of the day becoming the comparative comfort and safety of a decked vessel, albeit with the additional expense. At this time Aberdeen rose to be a large herring fishery centre and from here the fishermen of the Cove would crew their larger vessels, resuming lining for whitefish at the close of the season. In 1875 the principal fishing areas for the Aberdeen fleet was the Bennachie ground, about 14 miles in a south-southeast direction and extending for 12 miles; the Shallows, lying southeast of Bennachie; the Bank, which lay around 27 miles southeast; the White Spat, 16 miles southeast of Inverbervie; and the Montrose Pits, 52 miles southeast of Aberdeen.

As in the line boats, vessels weighing many tons required to be landed at ports, rather than open beaches, and for the shareholders and crews from the fishing villages in the neighbourhood of Aberdeen, boats such as these were berthed on the south bank of the Dee in the vicinity of the Victoria Bridge, completed in 1881. At the Cove it is very probable that during the dog days of summer a cable ran from the Braedens to an anchor point to the south of the harbour, where the lobster boxes appear today. Here fishermen could tie up their vessel and go home to rest, removing the burden of having to travel to where the boat was usually berthed. Again, as in the line fishing, these large vessels were hauled up the beach at the and of the season by means of a steam traction engine. Herring fishing, nevertheless, was being pursued by smaller boats based in the Cove, and during the season, as evidenced in the school register, absenteeism was prevalent, among the boys especially.

With regard to the boats themselves, the Fifie — known as a Baldie from the famous Italian patriot Garibaldi during the Italian Wars of Independence in the 1860's — was used in both herring and line fishing. It had a frame of oak clad in pitch pine, clinker style, making the hull very strong and buoyant, tiller steered and double ended to divide the waves in a following sea. The decks were flush to the gunwales with a main hold amidships and the bunks aft, the beam made wide to carry an extensive weight of fish, the length varying from 40 to 60 feet. It carried a crew of up to eight and was propelled by 16ft. oars when there was no wind, the ballast being by way of moveable pigs of iron and blocks of granite, which could be shifted according to the weight of cargo and the course steered. The rig comprised of an unstayed main mast and mizzen, where loose-footed sails were bent on to heavy gaffs and hoisted by several men using a block and tackle; in favourable conditions it could top 10 knots. As in the whitefishing the crew were sustained by oatcakes, herring and loaf, more often supping tea to soften hard biscuits. A share in a herring boat was a complex structure, of which a third of the catch went to the boat, a third to the nets and a third to the fishermen; the boat's share apportioned out among the owners. The nets' share, however, was broken into cumbersome fractions, according to how many each fisherman owned.

As fishermen continued pushing farther out to sea, both at the herring and the line fishing, again the tendency was to increase the size of boat; the carvel build, first used in the Firth of Forth, having all but superseded the clinker in the case of first-class boats. Indeed, from 1860 there was great incentive for some fishermen to extend their working year, whereby they followed the herring round the British Isles, and from what was initially six weeks local fishing, now occupied nine to ten months of their year. Moreover, the industry developed throughout the 19th century, mainly as a result of the trade in salt herring with German and Russian ports on the North Sea and the Baltic. Though steam drifters were introduced in the latter part of that century, they made no real impact until the early 1900's. In 1907 the cost of one of these boats, including steam hauling gear, sails and other outfit, was around £700. In the coming decades smaller craft were fitted with inboard engines.

The herring fishery reached its peak in the years immediately preceding the First World War, there being three ways in which a herring was sent to market: fresh, salted, or kippered. Fresh herrings needed to reach their destination because of their perishable nature. The kipper is a fresh herring gutted on landing, then cured by hanging in the smoke of oak chips, and far superior to the common presentation of a wilted fish that has been artificially dyed. After the war attempts were made to revive the trade in cured herring, but these proved unsuccessful, the industry slipping into its protracted decline. Testament to this was one such vessel of the Cove, around 40 feet in length, which between the wars sat by the breakwater rotting away. This once great industry is remembered by way of the Herring Hole, a small inlet some 150 yards south of the harbour.

So much for fishermen and herring fishing, for this was an industry dependant on the women, of which a portion from the Cove would follow the season down the east coast of Britain, and from Shetland to Yarmouth, they'd gut and pack the 'silver darlings'. Their work, though, was coarse, dirty, hard and laborious, with long hours stood over open troughs exposed to wind and rain. It was also both tiring and dangerous owing to the foul brine in which the herrings were soaked, where even small cuts proved difficult to heal. Indeed, the hands of the women were often a mass of open sores, their only protection being a thin strip of cotton wound around their fingers and thumbs. They worked in crews of three, consisting of two gutters and a packer, making a liveable wage. In times of a herring glut they'd work long hours overtime, having little time to rest for meals. Depending on location the washing arrangements and sanitation could be somewhat primitive, with at times the only seats being the lassies' own kists. Other times they would have adequate lodgings. It was a hard life, but not altogether an unhappy one for, besides their esprit de corps, the herring girl would have Sunday off, with perhaps her own fisher lad working from the same port as she. In poetical terms it has been said that there is no voice sweeter than that of the herring girl's heart.

John Morrice (Jocky Brandy) and Robert Wood on the pier at the Cove spreading herring nets, c.1940.

Shellfishing

In the North-East shellfishing has been pursued for thousands of years, beginning with the simple task of gathering mussels, cockles, etc, at low tide; or, in the case of clawed crustaceans, looking into crevices and under heavy stones. Around 1788 a new method was introduced at the Cove for catching the edible crab, which became plentiful during the summer months. This took the form of a basket, five feet long by two feet wide, hooped, netted, and almost cylindrical, with a slatted base and a weight to sink it. The ends, or eyes, were woven inward, forming an ever-narrowing entrance for the crab, and baited with any available fish. It was attached by way of rope and a buoy and set some distance from the rocks. The same method was applied for the lobster, albeit the dimensions somewhat smaller and sunk much closer to the shoreline, where during the summer and autumn a considerable number was taken. However, at 10s. 6d. (52½p.) the cost of this new apparatus seems a little extortionate. By the end of the century, though, there was an organised fishery for lobsters in the North-East, stimulated by incoming English companies, more so for the London market. Shellfish, it appears, saved many families in the Cove from suffering the same hardships as in 1783, when the fishing had all but failed completely.

Given the cost there is no doubt that the fishermen of the Cove, and those of the North-East in general, would have realised the method in making these baskets, which, incidentally, were not much different from the present-day creel. Though widely practised, shellfishing never held the same importance as whitefishing, and at the Cove was very much the 'supporting role' until the second third of the 20th century. After the event of both World Wars, large specimens of edible crab were being taken owing to a serious lack of pursuit during the years of conflict, a case in point that, if not subjected to over-fishing, and allowing for nature to take her course, then numbers will begin to increase. At the Cove today it is still being practised, though by no more than four or five fishermen on a part-time basis, albeit a license required, with a given number of crabs and lobsters per boat. Of course, this is but the bare statistics of an industry that may be living on borrowed time, therefore necessary to expand on its operation, especially that of the creel itself.

Mending a creel at the Cove.

In earlier times the bows would be constructed from hazel, though by the early 20th century it was lightweight bamboo, in turn replaced in the late 1970's by the more endurable polyethylene-type of piping used for gas or water mains. More recently, and increasingly, the bows are being constructed from plasticized carbon steel. The rope, at first made from hemp, had a tendency to turn brittle and snap, and was superseded by polypropylene, a much lighter material with a greater elasticity, proving both stronger and more endurable. So, too, the netting, evolving from hemp to cotton to nylon, to those resolute multi-pleats available today. The buoy (especially in crab fishing) is no longer cut from cork, being replaced by tough spherical plastic floats as used in trawl nets, measuring around eight inches in diameter. The weight, usually a heavy rounded stone, is presently a portion of mixed sand and cement. Over the years, the bait, too, has become more specialised, and for the crab a more durable type is preferred, such as skate bones or cod heads; fish like saithe or haddock are quickly torn to pieces and the crab, having eaten its fill, will in turn begin to pull at the netting of the creel. The lobster, however, may be lured by oily fish such as mackerel — and not particularly fresh at that. Colour also draws its attention, as in the underside of a dab, which, coupled with a mackerel, makes for a veritable feast. It has also been known for lobsters to be attracted by means of a white porcelain plate!

In boats of up to 20ft. fishing and baiting the creels is very much weather dependent, and may be pursued on a daily basis, though three or four times per week can prove to be beneficial. It became convenient for the crab fisherman to string his creels together, rather than picking them up individually. This was termed a 'basher', and at the Cove consisted of five creels with a buoy at each end. They were shot and hauled with the tide, there being 20 fathoms between each creel and 25 fathoms on the buoy to compensate for strong tides, at which the buoys could effectively 'drown'; the dimensions of a typical 'partan creel' being 30 inches by 20 inches, with bowed hoops in the form of a D. The crab prefers mixed coarse ground, good locations being the 'Partan Crags', a little to the north of Findon, and the area between Hare Ness and the Burn of Diney. Presently a small fleet of creels may be pulled by hand, whereas a compact petrol or diesel driven winch is used for larger numbers. Each fisherman has a favoured place for the lobster, and far too numerous to mention here. Unlike the stretches of open water in crab fishing, there is real danger in lobster fishing due to the creels being in the vicinity of tidal reefs, and more so in a northerly swell, where a patch of sea may disappear in an instant, tipping the fisherman overboard. At the Cove in the past there have been several such tragedies.

On removal from the creel the claws of a lobster are tied with a rubber band, which, among other things, may be the tube of a bicycle tyre. After several trips to the creels they might number two or three dozen, being kept from the opportunist thief in wooden boxes anchored at the mouth of the harbour. Being rather an expensive commodity, lobsters are rarely eaten by the fishermen themselves, and are usually sold to contacts in Aberdeen, and in the past to the McBey family, lobster merchants based in Johnshaven. At the Cove there was a plentiful market for the edible crab, which was packed into boxes and tied to the pier, most of the sales taking place during

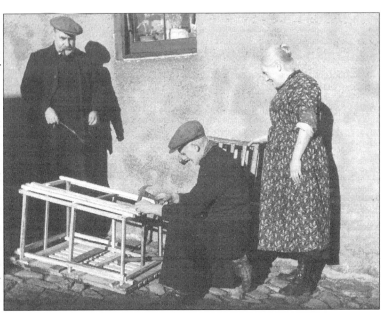

Making a box creel at the Cove, c.1945. A box creel was predominantly constructed from wooden spars, as opposed to the conventional method of being hooped and netted, albeit more susceptible to damage in storms. Another disadvantage was its overall weight, which made for a tiresome haul.

summer weekends, there at times being queues at several of the fishermen. Another method of sale was by bulk, where the crabs were picked up from the harbour by a dealer. During the 1970's Chinese restaurateurs proved particularly good for business and, heaved upon the pier an open box of partans was quite a spectacle (no little effort, a full box being quite a weight) owing to their jostling for space and fighting, which most resembled sparking wood if a carapace met with a pincer. Sometimes the fishermen themselves transported their catch to the process factory at Inverbervie. Produce as such, nevertheless, became a tempting target for thieves, it being not uncommon for the fisherman to find his box lying empty upon the pier — and sometimes smashed at that! The custom of selling crabs or, 'partans from the pier', disappeared around the early 1990's.

In regards to cuisine, the female crab is preferred for the dark red meat, having a larger body and, when in season, a shell packed with thousands of tasty orange-hued ova. The male, being generally smaller, is armed with fearsome claws and favoured for the milder tasting white meat found within. Rich in protein and nutrients, the crab is boiled for 20 minutes and can be 'dressed' in its shell upon a bed of lettuce, the meat being mixed into a paste, or separated into either half. Various additives may be applied, according to taste. In the spring and autumn they contain a greater percentage of water, being at their premium the summer; or, as any connoisseur of *Cancer pagarus* will advise, "At their best in the months without an 'r'."

Salmon Fishing

The salmon was much loved by Robert the Bruce, who made the rights to the 'reid fish' the ownership of the Crown. A most valued fish, both nutritionally and financially, salmon fishing has been pursued in the parish of Nigg since medieval times. Early methods were by drift net or sweep net, made from lengthy strands of nettle hemp, and at least from the 18th century salmon fishing was stationed at the Cove, the men having plots of ground where they cultivated vegetables to supplement their income. They were given money to purchase boots and gear, not to mention 'net money', effectively a percentage from the quantity of fish caught for the season. By the close of the century, and according to the length of time a salmon fisher was engaged (bearing in mind the success of the fishing), he could earn from £5 to £15 for the season. There was, however, the ever-present problem of the seal. On entering the net a seal will take the choicest parts of the salmon, devouring the soft underbelly and effectively destroying the entire catch within. In the late 18th century a net was devised for their capture, baited with a salmon tied to a cork — when the seal bit into the bait the cork then disappeared, at which a line was pulled by a man strategically placed upon the rocks, whereby the seal was captured.

Salmon fishers, 1920's, aboard their coble pulling on the oars.

The salmon was to the whitefishers an unlucky fish, which may stem from the heavy penalties incurred if caught with the 'reid fish' aboard their boat. Envy, even superstition, might be another factor, in that the salmon fishermen had a guaranteed wage, regardless the size of catch, or indeed the weather conditions; therefore no good would come of it. Though they fished side by side the two never mixed, as is clearly evident at the construction of the harbour: the whitefishers operated from the shingle beach, while the salmon fishers were berthed upon the rocky shore to the west of the smaller pier, their two cobles each crewed by six men and propelled by oars. In the mid 19th century a hand-operated winch drew them clear of adverse weather, and for access to operations a set of steps was cut into the steep embankment. In the summer of 1879 an additional £13 was paid for filling up and levelling the salmon fishers' location, there now being more or less a concrete barrier between the parties.

After the First World War the salmon fishers 'encroached' upon the harbour by way of a coble moored alongside the pier; the whitefishing being in serious decline. As mentioned, the nets and equipment were hoisted from the coble onto the pier by means of a wooden sheer legs, which was replaced in the mid 1950's by a substantial swivel-based and hand-cranked iron crane; the fishing gear being then transported to the bothy at the top of the cliffs by means of a Crab winch and Blondin (an aerial cableway devised by the great John Fyfe, and described in a following chapter), with a cable attached to pulleys and iron rings both on the lesser pier and atop the Berryhillock. Some years later the coble had acquired an inboard engine, and from the mid 20th century both equipment and crew were transported up Balmoral Road to the salmon bothy by means of a tractor and bogey. As for the right to the salmon fishing, from 1785 to 1863 at the Cove there were two separate leases: on the south was that of the Lands of Cove, stretching from below the inn to the Horseshoe Bridge; the other being South Loirston, from the said inn to the Black Cove inlet, a little to the north of the Poor Man rocks, and having little by way of a coastline. In 1840 three salmon fishers were resident near the Watch House, which may have been a wooden forerunner of the bothy and stores, built c.1856. At this time, too, the cellars of the shop some yards from the hotel were being utilised as a salmon fishers' bothy.

Until his death in 1843 the fishing right to the Lands of Cove was rented by John Menzies Esq., falling to advocate John Blaikie in 1848 as part of their purchase. On Whitsunday 1857 Mr. Blaikie sold the eastern part of the Lands of Cove to George Falconer Muir for £3000, excluding the rocks, braes, uncultivated land and the right to the salmon fishing, though inclusive of the ice house and bothy, of which Mr. Blaikie agreed to pay five pounds yearly for their use. The following year the commissioners of George Falconer Muir became tenants of the South Loirston fishing on a three year lease from the Crown, at an annual rent of £12 10s. John Blaikie became bankrupt in 1860, and at the end of 1862 the aforesaid rocks, braes and uncultivated land, inclusive of the rights to the salmon fishing, was disponed to George Falconer Muir for the sum of £73 10s. However, John Blaikie had still in his possession that of South Loirston, though in 1863 it was sold to Dr. Alexander Kilgour for £37 10s, effectively creating one contiguous salmon fishing station.

Salmon fishermen standing against the gable-end of present-day No. 2 Hasman Terrace, c.1895. The man second left in the back row is knocking on a barometer installed for the communal use of the fishermen, which may still be seen today.

The right to actually net the salmon was merely a form of sub-leasing, and during the 1850's Mr. John Hector was lessee of the Lands of Cove, residing at Bon Accord Cottage, his son Andrew occupying an address in the village. It appears that the boundaries were fiercely protected, for in 1855 an incident arose concerning an unlawful bolt being driven into the rocks of the adjoining station on the south (Cairnrobin), at which legal proceedings were raised to have it removed. Records indicate that the lease pertaining to netting the salmon changed frequently over the years, in the 1850's secured by Mr. Hugh Hogarth & Son, with John Hector relocating to the station at Altens. In 1861 John Hector leased the South Loirston fishings, though in the same year Hugh Hogarth held the Lands of Cove, and in 1866 both the Lands of Cove and South Loirston were leased to Mr. William Routledge, who retained the lease until 1893. Moreover, in 1883 Alexander Kilgour had purchased from the Crown the salmon fishing rights to both The Lands of Cove and South Loirston for £7,400. In 1894 they fell to John Hector; 1908 Joseph Johnston; 1918 J. Sellar and Sons. By 1936 John (Johnny) Hector had again acquired the lease, and in the following years the fishing right, the company retaining it for the following 50 years.

Left. The wooden sheer legs used to haul the salmon equipment onto the pier. In the forefront is 'Plunkie' Smith, who used to give pleasure trips in his boat. The date is c.1930. Right. The swivel-based crane in 1980, with a boat is on its slipway having recently returned from the creels.

At the close of the 19th century, however, an outlandish threat appeared in the shape of a Bill proposed to the government in 1892, requesting that licenses should be granted to fishermen for the netting of salmon in the open sea in Scotland, as was the practice was in England and Ireland. Huge opposition ensued, stating that both politically and geographically, Scotland greatly differed. Needless to say, the Bill did not go through. Of a more local interest, though, is in July of the following year melted water from the ice house was seeping into and rotting the wood of the adjoining packing house, at which a thick coat of cement was applied to the dividing wall. It was also requested by John Hector that a wooden porch be fitted to the bothy door to prevent the water encroaching into the premises when it rained. The following year a repair bill for mason work, slating, carpentry, etc, amounted to £96, which would suggest that considerable work had been done.

Cove harbour 1902. In the foreground are the winches and cables that were used to draw the salmon cobles upon the slipway, there being a set of wooden steps cut into the embankment for access.

Throughout the 20th century salmon fishing at the Cove could be described as being 'quietly pursued', with a change of crew every few years or so. In 1987 Mr. Hugh Moir had purchased the right to the fishing, working the station with his son Colin and former skipper Mr. Rob Jamieson. At the death of his father Mr. Colin Moir took over the business, albeit for an ever-decreasing seasonal catch, in turn selling to The Dee District Salmon Fishery Board on 10 May 1999. Since then salmon fishing has ceased at the Cove, the objective being to conserve the fish stocks. In September 2001, however, the pier and part of the foreshore was advertised for sale, concerns being raised that the new owners might close off the harbour to the public; or worse, fall into the hands of property developers. Fears were allayed when it was purchased locally, the objective of the new owner being mindful in regards to preserving its character.

Skipper Mr. Jimmy Hislop mending the salmon nets at Cove harbour, 1972.

Reproduced by kind permission of Aberdeen Journals Ltd.

It is uncertain if salmon fishing will return to the Cove, or indeed any of the former bag-net stations in the North-East. However, much can be said about this once-bustling commerce. The season opened on the 24 January, and began by preparing the equipment: ropes were uncoiled; nets were removed from the store; anchors; floats; weights and poles. No net or 'graith' was allowed in the water until 11 February, the official opening day of the season, the objective being (weather permitting) to land with a catch. The February mornings may be described as 'Baltic', it being not unknown for a hammer to be used in order to remove an accumulation of ice around the ropes and poles. The summer, too, was not without its peril, in the form of the jellyfish. Enticed into shallow water on hot or muggy conditions, they formed a veritable swamp, making it nigh impossible for the propeller of the coble to turn; or worse, drift into the net, accruing such a weight that it simply tore apart. The scourge of these was the Lion's Mane, or 'Libert', as it was known, a brown mass of stinging tentacles, which, on making contact with the eye, would throb for hours. A latent danger was their adhering to nets being stored for the following season, the tentacles having dried to a powder, whereat the following February the unwary salmon fisherman may be subjected to a face-full!

In the Cove the name of Hector is synonymous with salmon, and in 1827, at the age of 24, John Hector invented the bag-net. At first the nets were single, i.e. the fishing was from one side only, the objective being to catch the fish entering from the flood or the ebb. A double net to catch both ways was introduced in 1837, with another and improved model introduced in 1865. Since then there has been practically little change in the method of catching, apart from the introduction of superior materials such as cotton and nylon. Around 1820 the rent for the Bay of Nigg fishings was £10 a year, though with the introduction of bag-nets, increased rapidly. In 1839 the rent of Altens, North and South Loirston and the Cove was £71, with 150lbs. of salmon, or a monthly equivalent of 6d (2½p) a pound. Ten years later the rents had doubled. At the outbreak of WW I these same fishings were let for £1,300. Before refrigeration and the coming of the railway, by the 1830's the fish were being stored in an ice-house, then packed and readily conveyed to London by steamboat. Indeed, in the winter months, blocks were cut from the Loch of Loirston, and would persist for many months in the cool and darkened conditions. The ice house remained until the early 1950's, part of which may be seen beside the former skipper's house at No. 10 Colsea Road.

Bag-netting is an ingenious method, the net itself being somewhat triangular in shape and held in position by three vertical wooden poles, weighted down by stones or bricks. The head-pole is attached to the mooring rope and the crossbeams of the bag itself, the other two poles known as clicks, or cleeks, both flood and ebb, one of which is fixed to the rocks by means of a rope and chain, the other held fast by an anchor. The cleeks hold the ends of the bag in an open arms position, leading into the court before proceeding to a door composed of small round wooden stakes that form a ladder-like effect

Cove harbour, late 1950's, the crane on the pier having recently been installed. The coble is 'Maggie'. The hand-cranked winch in the foreground was a means of pulling the boats up the beach. As may be witnessed, they are few in number.

through which the salmon are corralled, but have great difficulty in escaping. A bag-net is positioned by first targeting a location such as a promontory, which the salmon may interpret as the mouth of a river. First the moorings are set, the head anchor keeping everything taught, and marked by a small buoy known as a 'tripper', the precise location determined by strategically placed markers above the cliffs; any slippage will result in the bag-net sinking somewhat and therefore reduce its fishing potential, at which the anchor may have to be reset. Flotation was at first by way of corks and tarred wooden barrels, in turn being replaced by polystyrene and large soft PVC buoys.

Salmon fishers at the Cove, 1926. The men have creel baskets on their backs which were used to carry the fish up the beach for onward transportation to Aberdeen. Front left is George Wood from Portlethen; front right is Jock Ritchie from the Cove.

Of the bag-nets in the Cove the most prolific were 'the Priests', two nets located opposite the mouth of the harbour, namely the 'in Priest' and 'out Priest', respectively; in fact they accounted for more than half the total catch of a season. Others by name being 'Big Mac'; 'Hare Ness'; 'the Berryman'; 'the Beattie'; 'the Pier Man'. In the mid 1970's skipper Rob Jamieson attempted to site a net at the Mutton Rock, but the tide proved far too formidable. There was also a net located hard by the rocks to the east of the pier, 'the Thief', more often than not taking cod, saithe and conger eels. Another species frequently found in the bag-nets during the summer months was the lumpfish, or paddlecock, which had a bloated appearance and a sucker on the underbelly, a means for attaching itself to seaweed and stones. Its edible roe made for highly valued caviar — the fish itself being excellent creel bait!

However, a bag-net on its own is effectively useless, and requires the salmon to be guided in by means of a leader (an exception being the aforementioned 'Thief', which, owing to its close proximity to the rocks, performed rather well without one), this being a rectangular piece of netting 38 fathoms long by 2 fathoms deep, fixed to a pole some feet from the rocks and continuing into the bag. By law the nets were prohibited from fishing between the hours of a Saturday noon and 6.a.m. on the Monday, allowing the salmon some freedom of access to the various rivers. Therefore on a Saturday morning nets were fished and the leaders removed, a process known as 'slapping'. Once ashore the leaders were spread out to dry on the ground between the breakwater and pier, being shot once more on the Monday morning. Sometimes at weekends adverse weather made it impossible to put to sea, at which the salmon fishers were basically on weather watch, known as a 'keep in', and additional to wages. Indeed, the but-and-ben of the salmon fishers' bothy became a focal point for social gatherings during the 1960's and '70's, until becoming redundant in 1987, in turn being demolished and converted into private accommodation in 1990.

Aerial view of the salmon bothy, 1985. To the left is the net store, with a bag-net hung out to dry. Only the shed with the semi-circular corrugated roof remains today. The small white square on the extreme right is the base of the lookout post erected during the Second World War.

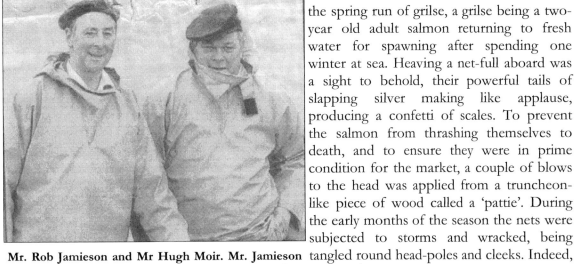

Mr. Rob Jamieson and Mr Hugh Moir. Mr. Jamieson was skipper at the Cove from 1970, and continued to work there along with Mr. Moir until 1998.

What made the Cove station successful was the spring run of grilse, a grilse being a two-year old adult salmon returning to fresh water for spawning after spending one winter at sea. Heaving a net-full aboard was a sight to behold, their powerful tails of slapping silver making like applause, producing a confetti of scales. To prevent the salmon from thrashing themselves to death, and to ensure they were in prime condition for the market, a couple of blows to the head was applied from a truncheon-like piece of wood called a 'pattie'. During the early months of the season the nets were subjected to storms and wracked, being tangled round head-poles and cleeks. Indeed, it was a regular occurrence for mooring ropes to snap and buoys to be swept away.

The nets would be hung in docks and the damage assessed, with some, or at least the more aged, beyond repair and simply burned. In the summer months a minimum of maintenance was required, but gave rise to the tedious task of 'swishing', a task performed by means of an iron hoop with a wooden handle — like a tennis racket without the strings — being swept across both leaders and nets in order to remove the clinging swards of seaweed. Of course, there was the everyday task of bailing water from the boat, manually done by the use of a deep pan resembling a wok, and known as a 'hose kelly'. The coble was moored alongside the harbour and secured at various points, the stem being attached to the mooring rope by the vulgarly named 'C**t McGregor', a rope hoop with a wooden toggle, twisted as a Spanish windlass. If the weather blew up overnight, then it was practice for the salmon fishers to be 'chappit up' and roused from their beds by the skipper, proceeding from their homes to the harbour in order to crank the three ton coble onto the pier, less it be torn from its moorings and dashed upon the rocks. It has been said that the *Maggie,* a wooden coble in use from the 1950's to 1987, was of a superior quality to the fibreglass models that followed. Up until

Cove salmon coble in mist and heavy seas.

the closure of the station the seal problem remained, though instead of a trap, the skipper had license to shoot them.

On 24 August the season ended, all nets having to be removed from the sea, with a further two weeks allowed for cleaning the equipment, the anchors having to be manually heaved aboard the stern of the boat. At the harbour the pier became a mass of kelp, mud, stones and barnacles, along with several heaps of fishing hardware — a laborious process, which involved the running of ropes and scraping from buoys beard after beard of sea growth. On 6 September the net money, or end of season bonus, was distributed among the crew, whereat a day's celebrations was had! It was then that the sea had an empty look, the buoys, ropes, poles and nets being safely stored away; the best of the year was over, and the chill in the air a harbinger for winter.

Cove harbour, mid 1990's. The salmon coble is now winched up by a mobile crane alongside the coble on the pier, the fixed iron crane having being removed in 1993 owing to it's unsafe condition.

Rock Fishing

Fishing with a baited hook is a fascinating pursuit, where, unlike hunting or shooting, in most cases the prey is unobserved; perhaps, then, the thrill lies in the unexpected, the mystery tugging at the end of the line? Until the mid 18th century there is little evidence to suggest that fishing by means of a rod, or indeed a hand line, was seriously practised in North-East fishing communities, though in the Cove small weighted lines containing around a dozen baited hooks were cast from the rocks at high tide, being collected on foot at the ebb. It is likely that salmon fishers and boys may have pursued a form of rock fishing using rudimentary equipment such as lengthy poles, the whitefishers themselves having little time for anything other than their all-consuming profession.

Rock fishing, however, proved more exciting than the hum-drum hours of back-breaking toil induced in baiting, shooting and hauling thousands of feet of line, giving rise to the rod and its development. Before the advent of glass-fibre beach-casters with multi-spinning reels, fishing from the rocks was known as 'plumping', which basically consisted of a tapered wooden pole measuring 18ft. or more, with a length of twine and a hook and sinker; more often the 'rod' being in two or three sections and heavily varnished. Such lengths were essential in order to clear the kelp line and 'bussies' (sunken reefs with a proliferation of kelp and seaweed) which bounded the rocks and yawns. The reel amounted to two metal spikes driven into the base, on which the twine was wound by hand. Though the Scarborough reel was first used around 1800 for deep water fishing, such reels in the Cove were seldom used. By 1877 the town of Kirkcaldy was the biggest producer of linoleum in the world, and a cheap and effective fishing rod could be had from the lengths of bamboo used as spines in the rolls transported to retail shops in

Aberdeen. Rods such as these were conveniently stored beneath the guttering of the house, and for a time in the Rocket Apparatus House on Loirston Road when the coastguard had vacated the premises. Such rods had an alternative purpose, however, in collecting gulls' eggs, for which a soup ladle was attached to the end of the line, making for an excellent tool of recovery, effectively removing the need to clamber up dangerous cliff ledges. A bamboo rod with hand-wound reel is the preferred means by one or two local rock fishers today.

Such was the popularity of rock fishing that in 1896 a fishing trophy was competed for by teams from the Cove, Portlethen, Newtonhill and Muchalls, along with the W. Pritchards team and the Wednesday team from Aberdeen (whose name derives from their half-day working hours). The trophy is contained in a glass dome and may be viewed at The Neuk public house in the old village of Portlethen. The competition ran until 1921 with the trophy inscribed as follows:

The Douglas Challenge Cup
Won and Presented by
Mr. Alex Douglas
To
Aberdeen Amateur
Rockfishers Association

So much for the equipment statistics. The seabed around the Cove is of coarse mixed ground, and makes for good all round fishing, saithe and cod being the predominant species. There are some excellent locations with enigmatic names. The bait is preferably the edible crab, or 'palach', which are of a size less than 4 inches across the back. Usually these are obtained from a fisherman laying aside a quantity from his creels, or a visit to the rocks at low tide and 'clicking', a method comprising of a long slim metal rod with a 90° return of about an inch at the end, the objective being to secure a hold behind the pincer of the crab and forcibly remove it from a crevice. In more fortunate times this may produce a lobster.

Like the mussel, baiting the hook is an art, and the most efficient method of preparation is to first remove the pincers! The crab is then laid on its back, and with a firm grip of the legs, while stood on the edges of the underside of the shell, the body pulled apart. A number of crabs may be readied for bait and, as an added attraction, body and pincers are crushed then cast into the water. The shell is further reduced by snapping off the undersides with the heel of the hand, followed by removing the membrane with a press of the thumb. The meat is scooped out using a knife, having the capacity for one or two baits and, being extremely soft in texture, some means is required to secure it. In the past sheep's wool, or 'oo', was gathered from fences and teased into wisps when applied to the hook, a modern and effective material being Animal Wool, as used in chiropody. Limpets, too, may be used, but do not prove so potent; nor indeed are mussels, lug, rag or sand eel. There is no doubt, that as bait for the cod, the crab is unsurpassed.

As is the rock fisher's lot, the choicest locations may only be reached at a full ebb, giving rise to limited duration before the tide encroaches, with many a good day having to be curtailed when the water is lapping at one's feet. Each fisher has a favoured spot, perhaps because of successful outings previously; or, it may be said, owing to that certain feeling. Of course, being fishermen superstition can prevail, and if a 'gunty' (similar to the bullfish) is caught, then quite simply it's a case of packing up and going home, for there would be no more fish caught that day, as though the poor creature's capture was a curse! But fishing for cod is the main objective, and luck may turn like the tide, at which the end of the rod will begin to dip, a sign that this predatory bottom-feeder is about to strike. Until the 1990's, though, every fisherman and boy had been plagued by the menace of the 'buddicks'— young saithe by the shoal, ranging from two to six inches in length, with insatiable appetites and an ability to strip the bait from the hook in seconds. Sadly, they have all but disappeared, and the number of cod being taken from the rocks has gone into steep decline. Indeed, rock fishing may require a permit in the future, as opposed to the plentiful past, when between the wars whiting were taken freely; and, more recently at locations once rich in cod and saithe, small dabs and plaice are becoming a fixture, which may be put down to global dimming, the greenhouse effect, or any other excuse which deflects the fact that the sea has been over-fished.

Four rock fishers with Elizabeth and Margaret Morrice, at present-day Craighill Terrace in the 1930's. The rough cobbled frontages of the houses remained well into the 20th century.

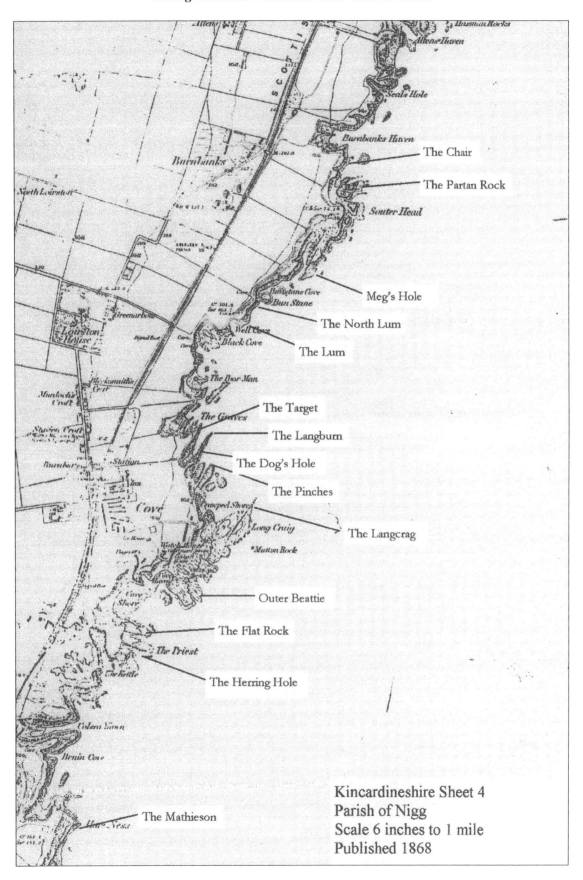

The Chair

The Partan Rock

Meg's Hole

The North Lum

The Lum

The Target

The Langburn

The Dog's Hole

The Pinches

The Langcrag

Outer Beattie

The Flat Rock

The Herring Hole

The Mathieson

Kincardineshire Sheet 4
Parish of Nigg
Scale 6 inches to 1 mile
Published 1868

Lure Fishing

At the Cove around 1840 fishing for mackerel and saithe with coloured feathers, known as flies, was seen as 'a form of amusement', or a means of catching bait. They were simple to make, requiring only a feather, or various feathers, to be whipped upon a hook. Though grey in flesh and far less appealing than the haddock, the saithe in times of adversity provided welcome sustenance for the fisherman and his family. Cod were caught by using a cylindrical piece of polished lead. This, a 'clean' type of fishing, was practised from a boat, there being few locations where it may be pursued from the rocks owing to the manifest quantities of kelp. On the North-East coast it has been christened with several names, e.g. 'the bobber' or 'the jigger'; in the Cove it is practised still, and known as 'the ripper'.

A typical 'ripper'.

Though the method is basically the same, as ever the equipment is much improved, with highly polished chrome being the order of the day, or brass and copper as suitable alternatives. To construct a lure, first a 6 inch length of ¾ inch pipe is cut, one end being flattened in a vice. A quantity of lead is heated and poured the length of the pipe. Once solidified ⅛ inch holes are drilled at either end (twice at the hook-end at 90° angles), with a split-ring and swivel attached to the flattened end, then countersunk, to prevent the gut (150lb. gauge) from chaffing, which is then looped and knotted around the drill holes before attaching the hooks. The choice of hook is the O'Shaughnessy size 6, giving rise to the aptly named 'ripper'. A further string of single lures around a fathom in length may be attached above the main lure itself, generally known as rubber eels, which at one time were red, green or black tubes of rubber sheathing, crimped upon the shank of the hook. Presently these are most likely multi-coloured plastic shapes of squid known as 'muppets', derived from the popular puppet show of the 1970's. Indeed, a number of coloured materials have sufficed in the past, from strips of oilskins to silver paper wrappers. The line attached is wound upon a piece of cork cut into the shape of an hourglass, the first few fathoms being transparent gut, the remainder consisting of multi-pleat nylon, or similar material, in order to protect the hands from the constant swish and pull of the line.

The technique is quite basic, and performed by paying out the line until the lure hits the seabed, a good sign being with a 'clunk', which indicates coarse or rocky ground. The lure is then drawn up around three to six feet from the seabed; and so begins the repetitive process of swiping the arm back and forth, at which the lure will jerk and twist, resembling a darting fish. It is essential the boat have a smooth protective covering around the gunwale to prevent the line from being chaffed away. The objective is to drift with the ebb or flow, making frequent runs over several hours, the boat propelled against the tide in order to keep the lines perpendicular, a task effortlessly performed by means of an outboard engine, but in the past could only be achieved by pulling constantly on the oars. Several hundred swipes (or more) may elapse before any fish are taken, and if a large cod or a monkfish strikes, the dead weight may feel like a stone. When the fishing is good several cod may be taken at once and, depending on size and weight, can prove to be a daunting haul. If so, great care must be taken not to allow the fish to thrash through the coils of line in the boat, which can result in a tangled mass, therefore spare lines and lures are best held in reserve, especially when fishing over wrecks. In deeper water it's common for the larger cod to buck and hiss when heaved aboard the boat. Favourable locations are the Mutton Rock, Findon Point and the Jock Hutcheon, a bouldered bank with a mean depth of 20 fathoms, located 2½ miles southeast of the Cove and stretching for a distance of around 5 miles southwards. But who was Jock Hutcheon, and why was he commemorated so? Apparently Jock Hutcheon owned a croft in the vicinity of Portlethen, and the building served as a distance marker for the outgoing boats to the aforementioned fishing ground, therefore it was christened with his name. However, the late Mr. Bill Caie, a trawlerman from the Cove, stated that he and other trawlermen recognised this particular fishing ground as 'the Granna Crags'.

Gill Netting

Gill nets are an ancient form of fishing, where any fish attempting to swim through the net are caught if large enough to allow the head to pass through the meshes, but not the rest of the body. The fish then becomes entangled by the gills as it attempts to back out of the net. The mesh size depends upon the species and size range being targeted. Gill netting for cod was introduced in the Cove during the late 1970's, its operating process very similar to that of line fishing, having buoys, anchors and tow ropes. However, instead of there being hundreds of baited hooks, the means for capture is a wall of netting around 10 feet in depth, with a length of many hundred yards. The top of the net has small floats attached, while the bottom is weighted to the seabed, effectively creating a deadly curtain; a standard cod net being around 75 yards long and 15 feet deep, with at times a two or three strung together in order to cover the length of a particular fishing ground.

This type of fishing was both inhumane and a menace to the marine environment, more so to the dolphin and porpoise, who became trapped within the netting and drowned. The gill net also caused much damage to the edible crab stocks, as once the crab became embroiled in the meshes it had no means of escape, and could only be released by snapping off the pincers along with most of the legs, rendering it physically useless. Moreover, when a net stuck fast and was cut away its fishing potential remained, there being, of course, no means of retrieving the catch. In turn gill-netting proved so effective that methods were introduced to control the number of fish caught, initially by imposing a ban on the use of single leg monofilament nets (though multi-monofilament and nylon nets were still permissible). This, too, proved inadequate, and the inshore cod stocks decreased as such that in effect this method of fishing had exhausted itself. The nets themselves, though, were not entirely responsible, the reasons being more of an accumulative nature. Thankfully, gill netting for cod is rarely practised in the North-East today.

Decreasing Numbers

By the mid nineteenth century line fishing was at its height, producing considerable catches, and in 1880 the Cove had well nigh 100 fishermen and boys, besides its recently constructed breakwater and piers. However, in 1879 the migration from coastal villages began, the fisher-folk leaving their small rocky creeks beneath the cliffs for the relative comfort of larger ports. New advances and techniques in the fishing industry were beginning to have an accumulative effect, none more so than the advent of the steam trawler. Since the inception of *Toiler* in 1882, within 30 years there were 230 steam trawlers based in Aberdeen, a time in which both the number of boats and the populations of fishing villages went into rapid decline. Torry had deeper water and a more accessible harbour, proving ideal for berthing trawlers, which none of the villages on the Kincardine coast could offer. Quite simply, it mushroomed, there being a frenzy of house building to accommodate the fishing, and in effect was absorbed as a suburb of Aberdeen in 1891. Consequently fishing families from Cowie, Muchalls, Newtonhill, Downies, Portlethen, Findon, the Cove, and Burnbanks, all made their way to 'The Land of Milk and Honey', as it was known, for the prospect of a better life and bigger wages. A number of families from the Cove went to Fittie, names such as Webster, Morrice, Guyan, Robertson and Caie.

The herring industry was at a low premium following the effects of the First World War, and by the late 1920's the fishing at the Cove was a but a shadow of its former self, the few smaller boats remaining being manned by ageing crews, the young men (and women) looking to better themselves in other industries. Indeed, a deal of dismay was felt by those hardy old souls, striving to keep their industry alive. Information reveals that there was still a good living to be made from the inshore fishing, but youth was turning to 'easier money', albeit in many cases were soon enough made redundant. The consensus among these the old fishermen was that 'the cursed dole' was the root problem of the demise of the fishing, and that it encouraged the youngsters to get something for nothing. Those cheery old men in their sea-faring jerseys, flat caps and pipes, would readily spin a yarn or two, or relate how a good price was being had for line fish, with wages being made of around £5 per week; then rail at the big houses in the suburbs of Aberdeen, built for trawler owners, and money that should have went to the line boats and fishermen of villages such as the Cove.

John Morrice by the yawl *Rival*, c.1925. On the left is a sturdy 'partan creel', comprising mostly of wooden spars, and somewhat larger than those of today. A boat as such was launched on wooden rollers. In the background is the rampart-like 'tip', constructed of granite waste from the quarries.

By now the Cove had all but forsaken fishing, though the industry, in some capacity at least, provided employment for a number at the fish meal factory. The age of wind and tide dictating wages, of being totally dependent on the sea, was over, along with the picturesque figure of the fishwife and her creel. The tables below are an indication of how the fishing at the Cove began to diminish:

1895 — 10 boats under 30ft, 10 boats over 30 ft.
1905 — 13 boats under 30ft, 2 boats over 30ft.
1914 — 10 boats under 30ft.

1900 — 12 boats under 30ft, 6 boats over 30ft.
1910 — 9 boats under 30ft, 0 boats over 30ft.
1920 — 11 boats under 30ft.

REGISTERED SAILING BOATS AT COVE, 1925

Reg	Name	Owner	Ton
A19	Cruden Bay	William Webster	1
A42	Maggie Ann Mary	James, John & Robert Craig	2
A99	That's Her	James Craig	2
A429	Be In Time	G. & D. Robertson	2
A450	Rose	James McBay	2
A543	May Flower	A. K. Stott	1
A558	Nellie	George Brand	1
A609	Rival	James Morrice	2
A644	Mary	John Wood	2
A689	Gratitude	John Morrice	3
A732	Family's Trust	William Stephen and others	3

REGISTERED SAILING BOATS AT COVE, 1930

Reg	Name	Owner	Ton
A19	Cruden Bay	F. Webster	1
A31	Golden Arrow	A. Wood	1
A42	Maggie Ann Mary	James, John & Robert Craig	2
A99	That's Her	James Craig	2
A429	Be In Time	G. & D. Robertson	2
A558	Nellie	John Ritchie	1
A609	Rival	James Morrice	2
A689	Gratitude	John Morrice	3

From 1954 — 1958 there were 2 boats remaining, both under 30ft.

Cove harbour in the mid 1940's. Salmon nets are drying in the background, though the once thriving fishing has diminished to but a clutch of boats on the shingle.

Women at Cove harbour having a break after baiting lines, 1929. Back Row: (left to right) Lena Masson, Jessie Wood, Sarah Gove. Middle: Miss Stephen. Front: Betsy Wood, Madgie Wood, Jessie Wood junior.

Mr. Walter Fraser mends his creels at the harbour, 1983.

During the middle years of the 20th century the fishing at the Cove may be described as 'existing', resigned to its lot. More recently, in the 1980's, it again came under threat from 'outsiders' who brought their boats to the harbour with a view to a 'fast buck'. At this time there were but two full-time fishermen setting creels for shellfish from spring to autumn, and shooting the 'sma line' in the winter. Mr. Walter Fraser, owner of *Girl Jean*, described that to catch the same amount of crabs as he did several years ago, 150 creels were required, as opposed to 30, adding that these 'fishermen' found it a lot more difficult than they thought. The Cove's other full-time fisherman then, Mr. Robert Sutherland, explained how they left their gill nets in longer than was necessary, whereby crabs were becoming scarce, especially in the spring, and that another season as such would seriously force him to look for alternative employment.

At present four fishermen on a part-time basis operate from the Cove in the summer months, namely Mr. William Adam, Mr. William Roberston, Mr. Ewan Adam and Mr. George Skinner. As noted, in an effort to monitor coastal stocks, the pursuit of shellfish and whitefish requires both a license and stringent safety precautions. Moreover, there have been calls for a total ban on inshore fishing altogether, with a view to allow the stocks to accumulate. Such an enterprise was implemented in the southwest of England, and within four years results had proved to be a great success. Locally, too, (especially during the war years), any length of abstinence has given rise to replenishment. However, a scarcity is found in almost every capacity, the most obvious being a lack of the 'buddicks' at the harbour during the summer months. And less than twenty years ago a 'good box' of cod could be had by means of a lure, whereas today, and in an ideal location with favourable conditions, it is not uncommon to land but a few small fish or nothing at all.

Boats at the harbour today.

Historically speaking, it was the centralisation of the fishing industry and evolving techniques which brought the demise of the rocky creeks and havens on the Kincardine coast, where larger ports such as Aberdeen and Stonehaven offered comparative comfort as opposed to the conditions in these heugh-heid hamlets, where the harsh realities were many miles removed from romantic imagery and the picturesque in books. Therefore who could blame the fishermen and women of the Cove for wishing something other than the back-breaking toil they endured to exist? With the fishing today as somewhat lamentable, perhaps a poem in the native tongue may serve to do it justice:

Auld Fisher

Syne I mind yon unco times
o codlin aff the rocks,
I'd plump aa nicht
ere it grew licht
an ca hame near a box.

Syne I mind o partan creels
poued up on simmer days,
mi fingers deid
or rinnin reid
fae barnacles an taes.

Syne I mind o baitit lines
on wunter's rimie seas,
far mait-feel gulls
shoomed roon the sculls,
skirlin oot their *Gie's!*

Syne I mind o saumon nets
as fou as rocks wi dilse,
an bugs o troot
near birstin oot
fae room fir nithing else.

Forby, I canna noo,
jist damn aal in the sea;
nae claw nor fin —
d'ye hear at, min?
Aye, fa can mind like me!

© Douglas W. Gray

Chapter 4: Access, Landscape and Coast

Getting There

Though under four miles from Aberdeen, in the 17th century the Cove was rather isolated, roads as there were being little more than tracks. Indeed, up until the early 19th century the interior of the parish of Nigg had been described as rugged and windswept, with large tracts of heath, bog and whin — sufficiently for Sir Walter Scott to make it the grim Drumthwacket Moor in his 'Legend of Montrose'.

Of course, a coastal settlement such as the Cove was removed from the main route south to Stonehaven and beyond (the present-day A90), nevertheless, some means of access did exist. As in today by the latter half of the 18th century there were three routes leading to the village. The first was the old Cove Road, which ran from the Bridge of Dee through Kincorth, turning southeast and skirting Altens Industrial Estate before continuing past Altens Community Centre and on to Langdykes Road, Loirston Road, then into the village itself. Another being the Coast Road, again running much the same as it does today, albeit the northern section leading to St. Fittick's Church being more of a well-trodden pathway. Thirdly, the Drumforskie Road, which led into the parish of Banchory Devenick, and took its name from the old Hill of Drumforskie, (Blue Hill) immediately to the west of the A90. This, of course, is the present-day Cove Road, and runs from Posties shop to the Charleston Crossroads. The name of Drumforskie (present-day Charleston) is retained by way of a farm adjacent to the northbound carriageway of the A90, opposite the Shell filling station. Moreover, the Charleston Flyover is constructed on what was known as Cove Hill. As mentioned, there was also a route by right of way, much used by the Cove fishwives on their journeys to and from Aberdeen. It began at the northern edge of the village, crossing the fields and parallel to the railway, turning northwest over the Hill of Tullos and on to the ferry crossing at Torry; there being, incidentally, the Cove Resting Cairn, located to the east of the summit, and no doubt a welcome respite on journeys between the two villages.

'Road', however, is very much different from that perceived today, the general standard in the North-East during the 18th century being considerably poor. They had been made at a time when wheeled traffic was practically unknown, and goods were transported either by pack horse or sledge. Indeed, during severe winters horses found it quite impossible to traverse such rudimentary thoroughfares, with residents in the western half of the parish being unable for many weeks to attend church upon a Sunday. Their ultimate responsibility lay with the Justices of the Peace and Commissioners of Supply, who had the power to summon the tenants and cottars in a particular county or parish to work without payment for up to six days a year. Of course, this would have proved most unsuccessful, and the roadwork done rather grudgingly. On 28 May 1795 the Turnpike Bill was passed by parliament, which effectively gave local landowners such as John Menzies Esq. of Pitfodels and the Rev. Francis Johnston of South Loirston and the Cove, the responsibility for making and administering new roads, in turn being recompensed by way of levying tolls. Up until 1800 the main route south from Aberdeen followed the Burn of Leggart, rising over Tollohill and crossing the Causey Mounth, heading towards Stonehaven.

At this time the construction of roads, more or less, involved of a load of stones being tipped in situ then rammed into the ground, sometimes covered with a layer of crushed stone and fine gravel. The tools for this simple method of engineering consisted of barrows, shovels, bars and hammers, prevailing until around 1800, when Scottish inventor John Loudon McAdam devised the method of 'macadamizing' paving by adding layers of crushed aggregate as the means to surface a road. With regards to constructions in the parish, this proved quite advantageous, the quarries at the Cove being primarily used for roadstone.

As for transportation, the first four-wheeled carriage in Aberdeen was owned by Colonel Middleton of Seaton in 1750, prior to this the means for travelling by land was either on horseback, common cart, or a rudimentary one-horse chaise with a driver in front of the vehicle. However, a Post Office was established in Aberdeen by the magistrates around the end of the 16th century, and by 1667 a regular post was appointed to run twice a week between Aberdeen and Edinburgh. The magistrates, nonetheless, were deprived of office by the government in 1674, when it was put under the direction of postmaster-general of Scotland. In 1763 two post-chaises were established for conveying travellers, and about 1770 the first stage-coach between Aberdeen and Edinburgh began — the Fly, requiring two days for the journey, resting one night at Perth. At this time it took six days for the mail to arrive from London. By 1822 it took eighteen hours by stage-coach (sixteen hours for the Royal Mail) to reach Edinburgh, there being upward of fifteen post-chaises and street coaches in Aberdeen, besides ten mail and stage coaches, plus a number of private carriages. In addition there were two manufacturers of coaches in the city, the journey to and from London now reduced to 68 hours. In 1851 there was a mail collection point in the Cove, or rudimentary Post Office, namely at the shop run by Mr. Charles Milne in the village, the railway having arrived the year before, which effectively brought an abrupt end to the days of the stage-coach. Some years later expansion and improvement was being planned, when in 1878 Alexander Kilgour wished to establish a fully operational Post Office and telegraph service.

Once the roads had been improved it opened up both the country and communication, the chaise cart becoming popular among farmers, who made day trips, or jaunts, as in today's motor car. It appears, however, that little road sense prevailed, and those on horseback and by stage or cart were 'unacquainted with what side of the road to take in case of meeting'. A high degree of maintenance was required, for the wheels of the carriages rutted the newly laid roads, which, if not at once repaired, then any further damage rapidly worsened. Stretches of roads under the control of turnpike trusts were simply known as turnpike roads, repairs being constantly carried out, and when Wellington Road was completed in 1829 it was the shortest turnpike in Kincardine, though providing a much needed route through the heart of a once rugged and difficult terrain.

When Wellington Suspension Bridge opened in 1831 it was seen as a means for the rapid expansion of the parish of Nigg, which in effect did not materialise until some years later. The total cost of construction was around £1,400, £30 of which was a contribution from John Menzies Esq., and only sufficed for making the pathway between the south end of the bridge and the road itself. The money was supplied by Dr. George Morrison, minister of the parish of Banchory Devenick, the son of James Morrison, Provost of Aberdeen at the time of the 1745 Rebellion. On 27 January 1865 a meeting of the proprietors of Nigg was held, calling for the abolition of tolls on Wellington Bridge, chaired by Sir Alexander Anderson, Lord Provost of Aberdeen. A few months later the turnpike trusts were dissolved, and in the following year the toll gates were being dismantled, the railway having secured most of the traffic from the main roads. Most of the turnpikes had crippling debts, though the Bridge of Dee turnpike managed to pay off its subscribers in full. During the diversion of the River Dee in the late 1860's and early 70's the bridge had became rather worse for wear, the question arising as to who should foot the bill, as previously the bridge trustees, using money from the tolls, had paid for its upkeep and repairs. On 26 May 1879, Kincardine County Council put the Roads and Bridges Act into effect, whereat the said trustees disclaimed all responsibility for its upkeep, though later that year proceedings arose in regards to maintaining the bridge and keeping it open.

By the turn of the century roads might be rutted, but adequate for horse and carriage; motor cars, however, would turn up huge dust clouds and send rocks flying from beneath their wheels. In 1824 asphalt was first used in Paris, taking the form of blocks, and as a method for road surfacing on the east coast of America in 1872; there being some years before its arrival in the North-East. Of a more local interest is the fact that in 1890 there were but twenty miles of roads in the parish of Nigg, two of which would be lost due to the absorption of Torry into the city of Aberdeen the following year. Nevertheless, an indication of the yearly expenditure regarding the state of the roads in the vicinity of the Cove is given in 'The Parish of Nigg Road Survey of 1853', stating that the Coast Road from the Wellington turnpike at Craiginches (Wellington Bridge) to Greenarbour, Cove, is 4 miles and 2 furlongs, with an expenditure of £9 17s. 8d; Loirston Road at 1 mile and 1 furlong (this distance is most likely between the Mains of Loirston and Posties shop), with an expenditure of £7 3s. 11d; and the Cove Road stipulated at 1.2 miles, with an expenditure of £3 5s. 10d.

Loirston Road looking south, early 1930's. The first house on the right is a former coastguard cottage, and was occupied by author and cook Janet Murray from 1958. The haystacks are now the site of present-day Catto Crescent. The field on the left was to become Cove Rangers Social Club and Allan Park; the telegraph poles having long since gone. Inset as it looks today.

In 1770 **The Cove Road** did not stretch as far as the village, therefore serving no direct purpose to the everyday affairs of the fisher-folk. It began in the grounds of the old Cove School and followed its present-day route, excepting for the bend at Rigifa Farm. At best it could be described as rudimentary, for the most part serving as the southern boundary between the Lands of Cove and South Loirston, proceeding to the lands of Drumforskie. During road improvements in the early 1800's it was extended towards the Cove Bay Hotel, where, after stopping for refreshments, perhaps, coaches would trundle up the road to the Checkbar on journeys heading south. It was, however, no stranger to repair work, as the following examples from 'Records of Commutation Roads, Minute Book of Lower Deeside', reveal:

27 May 1820 — £15 to be laid out by Messrs Duthie and Menzies (Alexander Duthie Esq. of South Loirston and John Menzies Esq. of Pitfodels) for completing the road from Cove to Drumforskie.

28 April 1829 — Repairs of £10 to the road from Cove to the turnpike at Drumforskie (the present-day Cove Road, beyond the Charleston Crossroads).

3 June 1833 — Repairs of £3 to the road from the Stonehaven turnpike (present-day A90) towards Cove (the small link road between Charleston Crossroads that leads to the Charleston Flyover).

30 July 1842 — Report by Alexander Ross, road surveyor, Stonehaven: Road from Cove to Checkbar (the present day Cove Road) on Aberdeen turnpike, £3.

The coming of the railway created additional costs, and on 24 June 1848 the sum of £28 was ordered to be paid by the Aberdeen Railway Company for damage incurred when constructing the bridge at the junction of the old Cove Road and the Drumforskie Road (Loirston Road and the present-day Cove Road). At the time, though, it would have proved more practical for the bridge to have an angular span between the Endowed School on the main street and Loirston Road itself, rather than create the double 90 degree bend which serves as a link to the hotel and harbour; not to mention the lofty retaining walls required in order to access the road. Most likely land ownership prevented this, therefore the bridge be required to straddle the boundary between South Loirston on the north and the Lands of Cove on the south, effectively continuing due east from the aforesaid Drumforskie Road. Of course, the harbour became much more accessible, unlike many other small fishing settlements, though the village itself is to this day accommodated rather poorly.

The Langdykes Road forms part of the old Cove Road leading from the village to the Bridge of Dee, effectively dividing the former North and South Loirston Estates. The name arose from the unbroken lengths of drystane dykes that stretched from the Coast Road to the Mains of Loirston. By 1785 agricultural improvements were underway, the unfavourable runrig system being discontinued, giving rise to the enclosure and drainage of the fields; the dykes having being constructed around 1800, and the huge consumption dykes to the north (still present, and regarded as having historical interest) following some years later. At the Mains of Loirston the road terminated, continuing by means of several well-tramped pathways, and was known as the Cove Crossroads (not to be confused with the Charleston Crossroads), linking up with Wellington Road. This western section, however, showed no great improvement until the latter part of the 19th century, as in 1865 it was still no more than a track, the route leading from the Mains of Loirston to Newlands Cottage on Wellington Road being of more significance. The name of Langdykes does not appear until much later, though again, repairs were much the order of the day as the following examples depict:

7 May 1822 — £10 for repairing the road from Cove to Kincorth (Alexander Duthie and John Menzies).

10 May 1828 — Repairs of £2 to the road from the Cove Road by the new church (Nigg Parish Church being under construction, and a link to Wellington Road).

31 May 1831 — A new piece of road from the new turnpike (by Newlands Cottage, Wellington Road and the Mains of Loirston) to Cove.

17 July 1845 — Repairs towards the old Cove Road leading from the Bridge of Dee along the east march of Kincorth (Farm) to Wellington Road, £8 6s.

In the late 18th and early 19th centuries parts of **The Coast Road** were merely a convenience for the fishing villages of Burnbanks and Altens, being little more than paths; even by the 1830's the section between the Bay of Nigg and Torry proved somewhat deficient. The northern section formed part of the route taken by the Cove fishwives on their way into Aberdeen to market their fish at the Green, whose name, incidentally, derives from the Gaelic 'grianan', a sunny spot, or drying place. This would most certainly have been an ancient route, in some parts at least, and a means of skirting the wild and elevated terrain which lay to the west. Indeed, prior to the construction of Nigg Parish Church in 1829, the folk of the Cove would have tramped this route to St. Fittick's Church at the Bay of Nigg. The road was much improved by the coming of the railway; though the drystane dykes could not be constructed until around eighteen months after the railway embankment had settled. As ever repair work was never far away:

13 May 1826 — Repairs to the road from the kirk of Nigg by the seaside, to Altens, £5 (this part of the Coast Road being much inferior and less journeyed than the stretch from Altens to the Cove).

29 May 1837 — Repairs to the road from kirk and Bay of Nigg to Cove by the coast, £11.

9 July 1838 — Repairs to the road from kirk and Bay of Nigg to Cove, to repay advances by Mr. Ferguson (Proprietor of North Loirston) £20 8s. 2d; and towards the completion of the same road it was resolved to recommend an allocation of £10 a year for the next three years.

30 July 1842 — Report by Alexander Ross, road surveyor, Stonehaven: Road from Bay of Nigg to the fishtown of Altens, seems to be but little used and has only recently been formed. Coast Road from fishtown of Altens to Cove, has recently been repaired, and now only wants ruts filled up, £1.

9 August 1851 — Repairs to the Coast Road from south side of Bay of Nigg through Altens and North Loirston where newly formed by Railway Company, £5 (a much improved road that ran from the Bay of Nigg to Greenarbour).

An alternative access in and out the Cove was by way of a scenic route along the cliffs, which in reality was no more than a narrow trail walked out over hundreds of years, until in 1975, and part of a local government scheme, students and unemployed youths set to work. Beginning at the southern end of the Bay of Nigg the path was widened, levelled and stepped where necessary, then given a thick layer of fine crushed gravel to accommodate drainage. On a dreich day they presented quite a sight on rounding the Soutar Heads in their multi-coloured waterproofs. The improvements stopped short of the Cove itself, reaching only as far as the path leading up to Greenarbour. It is still very much used today, albeit parts of the northern section wildly overgrown.

The cliff path today, looking south towards the Cove from the Soutar Heads.

Station to Station

In 1844 an application for the construction of a railway line from Aberdeen to Forfarshire was put before Parliament. The Royal Assent was given on 31 July 1845, and for the next few years the Aberdeen Railway Company pursued the process of planning, mapping, surveying and purchasing the necessary land. In turn embankments would need to be constructed before the railway could run through the Cove, and three bridges located within the vicinity of the village: 'Stottie's Bridge', so named after James Stott, who at the time occupied Blacksmith's Croft on the site of present-day No. 22 Loirston Road; the 'Railway Bridge', leading to the hotel and harbour; and the 'Calsay Bridge', a few hundred yards along the old quarry road, required for the transportation of granite. There was also the extensive retaining dykes on either side of present-day Loirston Place to be considered, built from the process of blasting some 200 yards to the south. Of course, once construction got underway, manual labour went into overdrive. Progress, however, was slower than anticipated, and also more costlier, the 16 mile stretch from Aberdeen to Stonehaven calculated at £14,700 per mile. For the most part the labour was done by itinerant men from the Highlands and Ireland, who followed the expansion of the railway's construction throughout Scotland and the U.K., there being little prompting for trouble between the two parties.

On 26 September 1846, civil engineer Alexander Gibb was rather optimistic in quoting: "The Works from Montrose to Aberdeen will, I have no doubt, be completed by the Spring of 1848, when the whole Line may be opened for traffic." It may well be that both financial and company pressure forced him into such a statement, for in the summer that year the company was still inviting tenders for the works between the Dee and the Cove, known as the Nigg contract. At this particular section horses were at first in great demand, but by September 1847, after a concentrated summer's effort on the earthworks, their demand was beginning to diminish. Having all but completed his portion of the work, Nigg contractor Mr. Jimmy Shanks, held a public roup of horses due to the termination of the night shifts.

The granite blocks that form the support base of the proposed railway viaduct at the Colsea Yawn. Waste from the quarries lies behind, tumbling onto the shingle below.

To the north of the Cove the land declined, for which an extensive embankment stretched as far as Burnbanks; to the south it rose, and continued into rocky moor, requiring a concentrated programme of drill and blast. Moreover, it must be taken into consideration that this was a dour and extremely hard granite. By the Colsea Yawn the stretch of track became known as 'the cutting', where the means of a viaduct was partially constructed, only to be abandoned in favour of blasting through the mass of unyielding rock. This particular section was only begun in 1849 and took over a year to complete, being described by the Aberdeen Railway Company as 'a gigantic portion of the work'. A process as such, though, was not without problem, and as in the bridge constructed by the Cove Road, much damage was done to the land adjacent to the station, most likely from the dumping of boulders from blasting operations, at which proprietor Alexander Muir sought £100 by way of compensation.

The first train ran through the Cove on 9 March 1850, carrying a party of Directors only; the objective being to test out the newly laid track that had taken so long to accomplish. For paying passengers the station officially opened as Cove Station on 1 April 1850, the return fare to Aberdeen being 4d. However, on returning to Aberdeen the train went only as far as Ferryhill, the station at Guild Street being constructed in 1867, in turn rebuilt as Aberdeen Joint Station in 1913/16. The quarries were the first to benefit, having the means of a quick transportation route on their doorstep, rather than the horse-drawn cart after cart

Boulders removed when laying the railway in 1846, as revealed at the construction of Colsea House in 2007.

of paving stones laboriously hauled to Aberdeen harbour. The railway also proved cost-effective, removing the need of the slow and cumbersome transportation by boat.

Cove Railway Station early 1900's, the building on the western platform having recently been completed. The old Mission Hall can be seen behind the 'Cove' sign. Beyond the walkway is the Railway Bridge, leading to the hotel. Local man the late Mr. George Westland was the last porter employed at the station before its closure in 1956.

It may be mentioned, though, that the comfort of the passengers was not one of the company's highest priorities, the heating being described as at best rudimentary, by means of cylinders of heated sand. The lighting, too, left a lot to be desired, the lamps having to be regularly cleaned and filled. Passenger trade was brisk albeit uneconomical, a more profitable means being by way of freight, namely fish, stone and agricultural produce. Over the years, however, day excursions to the Cove during the summer months proved very popular with folk in Aberdeen, and included leisure activities such as swimming in the harbour and the 'Beattie' (a deep rock pool some fifty yards due east of the pier), picnics on the shingle, or to simply buy a partan or two. It was common practice for the last rain to be 'stowed to the gunwales', the overspill of passengers having to make their way on foot back into Aberdeen.

Accidents and collisions were never far away, and in February 1867 the train from Edinburgh ran off the rails at 'the cutting', tearing up sixty yards of track and ploughing into a ditch on the opposite side of the line; a few of the passengers being injured in the process. To compound matters the mail train from Aberdeen was on its way, and in the few minutes left before an imminent collision, the waymen and stokers ran towards the incoming express. The driver, interpreting their actions, turned off the steam and applied the brake, in turn leaping from the train. Having escaped potential disaster most of the passengers walked to Aberdeen.

The former Calsay Bridge by the old quarry road, its heavy wooden walkway long since burned down by a spark from a steam train.

It would appear that the issue of both protection and safety had come to being, for in 1886 Alexander Kilgour wrote to the now Caledonian Railway Company wishing for sturdy barriers to be constructed on either side of the line leading from the Railway Bridge to the quarries. A spokesman for the company implied that sleeper fences were the order of the day, being cost effective owing to a plentiful supply, and that the children were unable to knock them down as they could with drystane dykes (a statement which, if nothing else, proves that community vandalism is far from a recent event). However, drystane dyking was the preferred method, and prevailed, albeit rather more expensive to construct. Moreover, the Caledonian Railway Company wished to safeguard its property, and in 1890 laid claim to a strip of land on either side of the line measuring around 12 acres, beginning at the Railway Bridge and continuing south to the parish boundary. However, the aforesaid area gave rise to much dispute, being part of the Lands of Cove as sold by John Blaikie to Dr. Kilgour in 1855. After many letters of claim and counter claim, the matter was settled when Alexander Kilgour was awarded £185 by way of compensation, including that of quantities of granite chippings removed from the quarries without his prior permission.

The first indication of any form of construction on the west side of the railway line was in 1894, by way of a proposed shelter opposite the station. It was not until 1902, however, and at a cost of just over £37, that Alexander Kilgour sold an area of land measuring 958 square yards for the purpose of extending and improving the platform accommodation there, inclusive of a fully covered premises. The first decade of the 20th century saw operations flourish, with Cove Station being renamed Cove Bay Station on 1 October 1912. On incoming trains the porter took the tickets, there being no barrier, and because of the time involved for the train to pull up to the platform, and also to process the tickets, prospective passengers could take their time on proceeding to the station.

Cove Bay Station looking east, c.1925. In the foreground is present-day Burnbutts Crescent.

Track maintenance was performed by small bands of men, each covering a 2½ mile stretch, which for the Cove lay between Blackhills Cottage and the old coastguard observatory post at Gregness, the two lines making for a 5 mile section. Tasks included gauging the thickness of the rails and replacing the wooden sleepers, which were susceptible to being charred from hot ash and cinders from steam locomotives. Indeed, on the east coast line there were prizes awarded for both the best kept station and section of line, of which the Cove was sometimes recipient. Of course, maintenance became somewhat minimal with the introduction of concrete sleepers and sundry modernisation, at which the sight of the railway gangers 'walking the line' became a thing of the past. For over 120 years the signal box held sway, but by the mid 1970's computerised systems were being introduced, therefore the end of the line for many quaint old settings; the idyllic type in Will Hay's famous comedy of the thirties', 'Oh, Mr. Porter', fast becoming extinct.

Signal box at Cove, 1974.

Reproduced by kind permission of Aberdeen Journals Ltd.

The signal box at Cove Bay Station was situated on the landward side of the railway line adjacent to present-day Burnbutts Crescent — it had no electricity or gas, being lit by a paraffin Tilley lamp, with the heating provided by a coke-burning stove; the levers worn from years of constant pulling. Becoming surplus to requirements the signal box closed in 1976. The late Mr. Norman Hinchcliffe was the station master in 1947, describing Cove Bay Station as 'neatly set, having a siding, a weighbridge, a station master's office and platforms at either side of the line'. The station closed on 11 June 1956 and was demolished in 1973. In hindsight it would have been prudent to keep the station open due to the ever expanding population of the village and its eventual absorption into Aberdeen, besides, of course, the current congestion experienced when driving in the city. There is, though (and perhaps in the immediate future), the possibility of a railway station being constructed to the east of Greenarbour.

Signal Box at Cove Bay Station, 1974. Reproduced by kind permission of Aberdeen Journals Ltd.

A Ticket to Ride

Before the advent of the motor car, transportation by road was either on foot or by horse and carriage. In 1872 horse-drawn trams were introduced in Aberdeen, followed by electrical cable trams in 1899, with public service transport arriving at the Cove in 1928 by way of bus. The service was run by W. Alexander & Son, (Northern) Ltd. Until just after World War II the bus routed down the Langdykes and along Loirston Road, then on to the terminus at 'Petrol Jean's' by the Checkbar; 'Petrol Jean' being Jane Connon, supplying motorists by way of a single hand-pulled petrol pump. The bus would then continue back along the old Wellington Road and into the Cove before proceeding to Aberdeen. Moreover, these old buses were apt to break down, and it was not uncommon for the driver to ask the male passengers to give him a hand to crank the starting handle in order to get it going again. During the war years petrol was severely rationed, at which some buses ran on coal gas, a process that incorporated pulling a custom made cart with a burning coal fire and a combustion cylinder!

The additional distance to the Checkbar proved uneconomical, however, and the terminus was relocated to the Railway Bridge by Loirston Road, where the driver performed a calculated turn in the limited space by the shop. In able to facilitate a manoeuvre as such, around 1946 the house adjacent to No. 2 Loirston Road had to be demolished, the ground being raised to a level platform. For a few years in the mid 1970's the service was re-routed into one of a circular journey in order to accommodate residents in Charleston and the surrounding area, hence, rather than turning into Langdykes Road, the bus would continue along Wellington Road and past the Loch of Loirston, before turning left down the Cove Road. The Cove bus was No. 9 and the Sunday service every 2 hours, the last bus into Aberdeen being at 21:30.p.m. Although in 1975 the Cove became Ward 42 and a suburb of the city of Aberdeen, it was not until 1981 that Aberdeen Corporation took over the service run, making for a much improved timetable. First Bus came into operation in 1998, providing two services to and from the Cove: No. 13, via Wellington Road, and No. 16, via Kincorth. In April 2008 the city bus routes were reconfigured, and the numbers changed accordingly, with No. 3 (the Purple Line) routing from the Cove to Mastrick via Aberdeen Royal Infirmary, and No. 21 (the Claret Line) from Charleston to Dyce.

The Cove bus, c.1960. Alexander's public service to the Cove ran from the Joint Station — as Aberdeen's main railway station was known — prior to the opening of the company's new bus station in 1963.

A Natural History

The rugged glory of the cliffs around the Cove is a complex geology of metamorphic and igneous rocks, their dramatic outline peppered with inlets and yawns formed by the erosion of narrow belts of softer volcanic material. Indeed, the Soutar Heads and the immediate rocks are the root of an extinct volcano. Here, too, is found the most popular climbing location in the region, with daunting routes such as the 'Mythical Wall'. At the harbour the rocks have been gouged into wave-like formations, giving rise to a pattern of niches and jagged ridges, along with a raised platform exposing andalusite, sillimanite, garnet and other various minerals. From the pier may be witnessed the horizontal sandstone strata of the Braedens, with basalt abounding the caves in the vicinity. A noted feature is the band of blush-coloured stone a little to the north of Altens Haven, known as the Red Rocks, and geologically a felsite sill. Of course, inland lies the extensive granite bedrock.

Along the cliffs the flora is both colourful and varied, crowned with springy bull grass and wind-blown heathers, the soil consisting of a layer of glacial till. Besides the often savage blasts of easterly salt, there is shelter here for the plants that thrive on lime, such as Purple Milk-vetch, Meadow Saxifrage, Burnett Rose and Cranesbill — an additional boon for plants such as these may be their sheer inaccessibility. Scurvy Grass and Lovage are present on the headlands, of which the Victorians gathered the latter for salad, albeit somewhat tart yet rich in vitamin C. Thrift may be found in more shadier locales, and a coastal fern, the Sea Spleenwort, sprouting from crevices in the rock. An interesting feature being that Lovage may be common along Scotland's rocky coasts, but is almost unknown to the south of the River Tweed, and could lay claim to being both zealous patriot and a more fitting emblem than the thistle!

Surely one of the most interesting plants that *used* to be found on the cliffs was the sumptuous Royal Fern of the Atlantic coast, which grew on steep-like rocks or by the side of a waterfall. It is believed that the vicinity of the Cove was the last hurrah of the Royal Fern in its habitat of wet or marshy inland localities, and was reported as extinct by the mid 19th century. The demise of this species was most likely due to the once fashionable hobby of fern collecting. The Royal Fern may have been sumptuous, but in no way was it unique to the Cove and surrounding area; unlike the fragile rock fern *Cystopteris dickeana,* more commonly known as Dickie's Bladder-fern. The first published reference to this plant is in Mr. Dickie's 'Flora Abredonesis' of 1838, and subsequently named in his honour. However, it quickly disappeared and was thought to be extinct, again owing to avid fern collecting at the time. The truth is, it was most certainly close to extinction, being very scarce indeed, but through the sheer inaccessibility of several clumps, somehow it survived. Now classed as an endangered species it was given legal protection under the Wildlife and Countryside act (1981), with a penalty of up to £100 for picking a specimen.

The Cove is a lure for the entomologist, too, and has attracted beetle specialists and flea collectors in the past; the earthen car park at the harbour being an SSSI (Site of Special Scientific Interest). However, it is best known for butterflies and moths, some of them blessed with poetic names as in the Feathered Gothic or the Thrift Clearwing. Such a range of wild herbs and flowers present in turn a rich diversity, but the Cove's most famous insect, the Small Blue butterfly (Britain's smallest butterfly) disappeared in

The former haunt of the small blue butterfly. Here, in the disused quarry east of the railway by the Kettle inlet, hundreds of tons of soil and rubble have been tipped into its former habitat.

1975. It's locality was the disused quarry by the Kettle inlet, not half a mile from the village, where it thrived on the abundance of Kidney Vetch. Unfortunately this was viewed as a convenient hole in the ground and an ideal dumping ground for Aberdeen and Kincardineshire Cleansing Departments, with many tons of soil and rubble being emptied into its habitat, effectively putting an end to the Small Blue's existence. By way of recompense, if not a little irony, it was adopted as part of the motif on the crest of Loirston Primary School.

Nonetheless, what is the coast and cliffs without a bird, and a rare one at that? It is possible that White-tailed Eagles were breeding in and around the Cove in medieval times. These gigantic sea birds were known locally as Ernes, though had probably deserted the area by the beginning of the seventeenth century; the last recorded specimen colliding with Girdleness Lighthouse in 1853. The name is preserved in Earnsheugh Bay, a little to the north of Findon. As opposed to Fowlsheugh, south of Stonehaven, the cliffs at the Cove do not contain massive colonies of sea birds, but rather busy little pockets. Among the ubiquitous Gulls there are Pigeons, Jackdaws, Razorbills, Kittiwakes, Cormorants, Guillemots, Terns, Puffins, Eiders, Auks and Fulmars.

Indeed, a visit by boat to the colonies during the nesting season provides both a visual and aural extravaganza. The Fulmar is a recent arrival to these shores, and is thought to have followed in the wake of trawlers and whaling ships, whilst the Arctic Skua may be seen harrying smaller seabirds in order to relieve them of any food they carry. During the winter an opportunity may arise for a rare glimpse of the Iceland Gull. However, with the fishing industry greatly diminished, the seagull has evolved to quite the opportunist thief, migrating to the roof tops of Aberdeen for rich pickings such as discarded pizzas and other assorted take-away foods. A whimsy being that before the advent of wheelie bins parts of the city centre most resembled a refuse tip, and the plastic bag was mooted as the patron saint of the seagull! Given its bad P.R., perhaps the true face of the seagull may only be seen at close quarters, as when fishing from a boat, where words like 'immaculate' and 'beauty' spring to mind.

In August 1988 the smallest wading bird in the world made a very rare appearance in Scotland — in a puddle in a field by the farm of Rigifa, around ¾ of a mile from the Cove. The Least Sandpiper had only been recorded three times in this country, previously in 1965. It was thought to be blown drastically off course while migrating down the east coast of America. Of local informational purpose is that Rigifa was once North Blackhill Farm, and christened so by a previous owner, deriving its name from a rock upon an upland moor in Caithness, situated about a mile from the coast between Duncansby Head and John o' Groats. Many species are found in Loirston Country Park and around the agricultural belt, such as Lapwing, Curlew, Magpie, Kestrel, Bunting, Partridge and Pheasant, the male of which is distinct in his brightly coloured plumage.

The Least Sandpiper.

Though sea mammals are not in any abundance, there are frequent visitors, such as the Grey Seal, the White Beaked Dolphin and the Harbour Porpoise, which, in the summer months, can make for quite a show when breaking the surface and leaping in schools of twenty or more. In the past fishermen from the Cove believed these natural spectacles were a portent for imminent gales or foul weather. Basking sharks and Whales may be sighted, too, occasionally in numbers, though have been known to fall victim to being stranded or tangled up in fishing nets. Indeed, some years ago, a basking shark was witnessed to have followed a boat from the Cove as far as the mouth of the harbour. During the 1970's there have also been some infrequent visits by 'strangers', such as a Deal Fish; a Sea Lamprey; a Sea Bass; a Bogue; and in 1974 the late Mr. Fred Cargill Sr. discovered a Ray's Bream stranded in the harbour. In addition there was believed to have been a rotting portion of Giant Squid washed up in the Crawpeel in the early 1980's, and in 2006, whilst fishing from the pier in a strong flood tide, local lad Kristofer Gray landed a Ballan Wrasse.

Meanwhile, on terra firma, Rabbit and Hare have always been plentiful, hence the headland of 'Hare Ness', though not so many are witnessed today owing to land clearance, housing development and a gravel quarry. The Fox, too, has had room to roam, though more towards the Burn of Diney and the open moor that lies to the south and west. Roe deer have been sighted in and around the Cove for a number of years, more frequently on the headland between the former grit works and the Colsea Yawn, a good vantage point being the disused reservoir west of the railway, where they can be seen to graze upon the lush vegetation. However, rarely do they number more than half a dozen at any given time. Smaller mammals like the Field Mouse, Mole, Hedgehog and Vole, are also to be found, with the Stoat and Weasel at home in a drystane dyke.

The Wrecking Coast

Between Aberdeen and the Cove the coast is teeming with rocky ledges and sunken reefs, which in the past has proved deadly to shipping. The North Sea tears into the Cove from three directions, heaving itself upon the rocks and pier, and can at times wreak the utmost damage during the winter months. But there are also more subtle dangers at work, where a full moon can induce the flood and ebb to produce powerful tidal currents; or, with the weather becalmed, give rise to 'haar', a coastal fog that can reduce visibility to virtually nil.

Shortly before six o' clock on the morning of 24 February 1873, the schooner *Victoria*, of Maryport, while on a voyage from Ullapool to Montrose with a cargo of slates, struck a sunken rock about ¾ of a mile south of the Cove and had to be abandoned, becoming a total wreck. Snow was falling heavily at the time, making it impossible for the men to see any distance from the vessel. Captain James McKay stated he was looking out for the Girdleness and did not think he was so near the land, and that the rising tide must have driven the schooner inshore. Shortly after the vessel had struck she was rapidly filling, the captain and crew of three men taking to the boat, for two hours pulling on the oars in the cold and darkness. They made the harbour at the Cove about nine o' clock, exhausted. The fishermen and Coastguard at the Cove gave every assistance available, the men being sent to Aberdeen on one of the morning trains. The master came ashore with little else he stood in, but the men, fortunately, had saved their clothes. The *Victoria* was about 56 tons register, and owned by Mr. William Crudenby of Thurso.

S.S. Countess of Aberdeen on the rocks to the east of Cove harbour, April 1894

The Aberdeen registered steamer *Countess of Aberdeen,* under the command of Captain Joss, sailed from Hull at two o'clock on the morning of 15 April 1894, bound for Aberdeen with eighteen crew, twelve passengers and a general cargo, including four horses carried on deck. Conditions were fine at first, until reaching the Kincardine coast that evening, when haar 'thick as a hedge' began to form, reducing visibility to a few yards. Unknown to the captain the strong flood tide had set the steamer inshore, and by ten o' clock was a mile distant from the Cove in the still conditions, the beat of her propeller within earshot of the Coastguard. On realising the ship was heading for the rocks they fired shot after shot of the signal gun to warn her of the impending danger. Those on the bridge apparently heard nothing, and with a grating sound the ship ran hard on the rocks some fifty yards east of the harbour, in what the *Aberdeen Journal* termed 'an accident of a serious nature'. She immediately settled, listing to starboard, and with little chance of her being refloated Captain Joss gave the order to abandon ship. Due to her listing position, moreover, the lifeboat was jammed in the davits, and on being launched immediately capsized, before righting itself and drifting round the stern. By this time the Coastguard had launched their own lifeboat, with many of those in the village having gathered on the beach to witness the proceedings. The passengers and crew were quickly transferred to both lifeboats and catered for by Mr. Coutts and staff at the Cove Hotel. However, when a muster was called, the stewardess, Miss Gordon, could not be found, and a search was conducted aboard the stricken steamer, lifeboats being rowed in all directions. After two hours searching she was feared to be drowned, possibly by fainting on deck when colliding with the rocks and falling into the water. Soon afterwards a fire broke out in the stern section — the most likely cause being one of the upturned paraffin lamps — and burned unchecked until there was nothing left but steel. Next day a heavy groundswell broke her up and she sank, a considerable amount of cargo and baggage coming ashore, the horses being lost overboard. The *Countess of Aberdeen* was built in 1878 and belonged to the Hull and Newcastle Company, being 575 tons register.

The collier and steamship *Kenilworth* lies partly submerged off Altens Haven, 1906.

On the afternoon of 30 January 1906, during a heavy shower of sleet, the coastal steamer *Kenilworth* struck the Mutton Rock while bound for Aberdeen with a cargo of coal. The reef was half-submerged in a strong flood tide which drove the steamer landwards, and was observed to stagger as if she'd run aground. Within a minute or two she was on her way. With his steamer badly holed, Captain Scorgie made for Aberdeen at full speed, but such was the extent of the damage he was forced to run her ashore on the rocks by Altens Haven before she sank. The Coastguard at the Cove were on the scene in twenty minutes with Life-saving apparatus, and a rocket with line attached fired across the steamer's bows. It was soon discovered there was no one on board and therefore supposed that the crew had taken to the small boat and made towards Aberdeen. A tugboat was despatched to search for the crew but returned to harbour without having located them. The nine-man crew had in fact left the ship, intent on rowing to Aberdeen, but owing to the high seas running on the bar, decided to land at Nigg Bay, hauling the boat up the beach in a most business-like fashion. They set off on foot into town, unaware that a full scale search was in operation, being called off only when they finally had turned up at the company's offices later that evening. The following day the scene of the wreck drew the owners, engineers, surveyors, salvage agents and not a little crowd of spectators, to witness *Kenilworth* hard on the rocks, her bow facing south-south-west and her stern low in the water. With her back practically broken the crew boarded the ship and commenced salvage operations, including the ship's log and other valuables. During the course of the afternoon she began moving in a see-saw motion, pivoting amidships, then broke up and sank during the following stormy weather. It is believed that in colliding with the Mutton Rock, the topmost part of the reef was broken off, and at a full ebb its present-day height is somewhat less than prior to the incident. *Kenilworth* was owned by C. R. Davidson an Co., coal merchants, built in 1885 and 325 tons register.

Of the ships reported foundered on the rocks around the Cove, none is more poignant, or indeed tragic, than that of *Ulster.* Five fishermen were drowned when the Aberdeen trawler was wrecked on the rocks at Earnsheugh Bay, around 1½ miles south of the Cove. The other three members of the crew scrambled onto the rocks and, after what would have been a terrifying experience, climbed their way out of danger. Two of the drowned men were married with families, one of the survivors being the father of the mate. Names have been deliberately withheld, though at the time the incident was extensively reported in the *Press & Journal.*

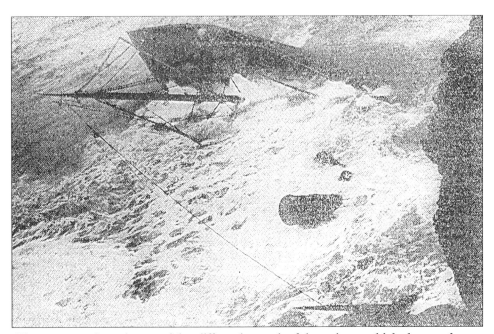

Ulster as seen from the top of the cliffs to the north of the point at which she struck.

Reproduced by kind permission of Aberdeen Journals Ltd.

Around midnight on 22 January 1925 *Ulster* left Aberdeen and was on her way to Granton for coal, a heavy mist lying on the sea, which presumably caused the loss of bearings. At two o'clock that morning one of the surviving members of the crew reported that a heavy crash rang out as the ship ran on the rocks. The skipper gave instructions for the siren to be sounded, but after only two blasts the inrushing water extinguished the fires and cut off the means of giving a distress signal. A flare was attempted to be lit by a match, but simultaneously the stern was felt to be going down, and orders given for the men to go aft, presumably to man the ship's boat. In the ensuing confusion, however, some of the men ran forward, one man tying a rope around his waist in an attempt to reach the rocks. This proved unsuccessful. A further attempt was made by another member of the crew, followed by two others, at which they scrambled to comparative safety. After covering a distance of around ten yards from the stricken trawler, the two younger men left the more senior member of the crew on a rock, which they believed was outwith the reach of the waves.

In the darkness, and in their bare feet, they scrambled across the slippery rocks, until finding themselves against the face of a precipitous cliff. It was nothing less than miraculous how they reached the top, the final sixty feet or so being almost perpendicular — an ascent for which the most experienced climber would prove difficult, even in daylight! The two men proceeded across fields of stubble to the farmhouse at Blackhills of Cairnrobin, arriving shortly after seven o'clock. There the farmer and his wife, Mr. and Mrs. George Knowles, were stunned at their condition of wet and tattered clothes, feet and hands cut and bleeding. The men stated what had taken place, that an old man was still on the rocks and in no condition to make the ascent. Word was sent to the officer in charge at the Coastguard Station at the Cove, Mr. George F. Tee, that a trawler had run aground. He in turn summoned local man Mr. John (Jock) Ritchie, a member of the voluntary lifesaving company, and together they proceeded by motor cycle and side-car to the scene of the wreck, carrying with them several life lines. There they were joined by one of the crew, sporting bandaged wounds, and the three men clambered down the cliff to a salient ledge. Sixty feet below was the old man perched on a huge boulder, at which a life-line was thrown in order he secure himself and manoeuvre into a favourable position to be pulled up. Slowly he was hoisted up the face of the cliff, but was so exhausted from the hours of exposure that he was unable to keep his body clear of obstructions, resulting in considerable bruising when brought to the top.

The three survivors were driven to the Cove Bay Hotel by Commander Wey, R. N., District Coastguard Inspector, and District Officer Morrison of Aberdeen, where they were attended to by innkeepers Mr. William and Mabel Cooper, after which they were taken to their homes and received further medical attention. None could tell what became of the other five members of the crew, the conjecture being that, as the trawler listed to the port side, they were thrown upon the rocks and rendered unconscious, then washed away by the waves. All were found to be in a state of semi-collapse, the old man stricken with grief at the loss of his son. Again, it is mere speculation how *Ulster* got into this position, foundering in a small inlet between the Red Mantle and the Partan Crags, known locally as the 'Sterlochies'. The stern of the trawler was in the mouth of a cave, her bow pointing out to sea. She lay against the rocks on her port side, and at high tide waves could be seen to be crashing over the deck, washing the gear overboard. There was a huge rock in front of her bow, very much exposed at low tide. *Ulster* must have passed over this rock, which would account for the huge dent that was visible in her stem. At exceptionally low tides it may be possible to see *Ulster's* boiler at the mouth of the cave, now known as the 'Ulster Cave'. *Ulster* was an iron trawler, built at Beverley in 1897, and was 79 tons register; she belonged to the North Star Steam Fishing Co., Ltd., Regent Road, Aberdeen.

The war years, too, took their toll, albeit for another reason than haar, tides, reefs and wind. An unidentified U-boat was sunk around four miles east of Findon Point c.1915. Having previously surfaced opposite the Cove it was witnessed by local children who had gathered on the school brae, observing what would have been an incredible spectacle. *Silverburn* was captured by a submarine and sunk by gunfire on 13 June 1917. 'British Vessels Lost at Sea 1914-18' gives the position as 4 miles southeast of Cove Bay, where she is charted as Wk PA with at least 50 metres over her in a general depth of about 60 metres. The steel screw steamship *Silverburn* was built in 1914 at Maryport, engine by Gauldie, Gillespie & Co, Glasgow. She had one deck with machinery aft, and a welldeck forward. *Trebartha* was bombed and gunned by German aircraft on 11 November 1940, while en route, in ballast, from London to Philadelphia. Four of her crew were lost. One bomb hit the port side, killing a gunner. Fire also broke out, trapping three operators in the W/T shack. The rest of the crew abandoned ship and were strafed while taking to the boats. The survivors were picked up by *S.S. Oberon* and landed at Aberdeen. 'British Vessels Lost at Sea 1939-45' gives the position as 4 miles southeast of Aberdeen, and a wreck is charted as PA with at least 50 metres of water over her in a general depth of 60 metres at 579745N, 015700W. This, however, must refer to the position of attack on the 11th when *Trebartha* was abandoned, as she did not sink until the 12th, after drifting ashore three miles south of Aberdeen, part of the flotsam consisting of crates of oranges which the local 'loons' made great salvage of. She lies in 13 metres of water close to the shore at the north end of the Cove, just below the hotel, the wreckage being widespread, inclusive of brass. *Trebartha* was built in 1920 by J. Redhead & Sons of South Shields, and was owned by the Hain Steamship Co., part of the P&O Group.

One of a series of postcards by Valentine's of Dundee, c.1950, portraying coastal locations around the Cove. The picture on the bottom right shows the Poor Man or 'Peer Man' with his 'head' attached, prior to being removed by the vibrations from explosions during salvage operations on *Trebartha*. Another derivative of the name may be from a type of candle holder, also known as a 'peer man', in which long tapered pieces of bog-fir were placed in order to illuminate the fisher-houses.

'Broonie's' Cave.

The Burn of Diney.

The Colsea Yawn.

The Kettle inlet.

Chapter 5: Religion and Education

St. Fittick's Church

Before the church came to the Cove, the Cove went to the church, and up until 1829 involved a trek to that of St. Fittick's at the Bay of Nigg in the extreme northeast of the parish. Dedicated to St. Fiacre (from whom the carriages of Paris were named), the Celtic form has been corrupted into the familiar St. Fittick. The church was founded between 1189 and 1199, of which parts are said to be contained in the existing ruins. Legend has it that a quantity of soil from Ireland, which had been blessed by St. Patrick, was sprinkled around the church in order to banish all snakes and worms from where it fell.

St. Fittick himself has an in interesting history. Born at Dunstaffnage in Argyll in the very late 6th century, in his youth he went to France, a Disciple of St. Ninian, and became a missionary, administering comfort and growing herbal plants for the benefit of the poor. He came to work in the land of the Picts, landing at the Bay of Nigg after a storm. (In a twist of fate the sailing ship *Dunstaffnage* was wrecked off Findon Ness in 1883.) After initial hostility from the local inhabitants, he founded a place of worship in the form of a rough wattle and daub construction, with the 12th century church bearing his name. St. Fittick became the patron saint of gardeners, his saint's day being on 30 August. He is also commemorated by way of St. Fittick's Well, which lay in the southeast corner of the bay and was believed to hold certain healing powers, though succumbing to sea erosion by the late 19th century. Again, legend plays its part, in that on one occasion the Virgin Mary appeared in its place, at which a statue of her was erected. Long after this statue had fallen into ruin and disappeared, a custom of making the sign of the cross persisted, including that of funeral parties from the Cove on their journey to and from the churchyard.

St Fittick's Church from the east, the west gable having been levelled to a height of that of the perimeter walls.

For almost four centuries it was under the Abbey of Arbroath, and after the reformation the church remained Episcopalian within the Church of Scotland until 1716, albeit then minister Richard Maitland deposed for praying to the Old Pretender and supporting the Jacobite cause. In 1717 James Farquhar, the first Presbyterian minister of Nigg, was appointed, but not without a near riot in which efforts were made to prevent the bell from being rung. A manse was constructed to the west of the church in 1759, and stood for over 200 years before being demolished in 1964. In the latter half of the 18th century the parish of Nigg had become quite populous through the development of farming and the opening of granite quarries, therefore the church was enlarged, the minister then being Dr. David Cruden, brother of William Cruden, twice Lord Provost of Aberdeen. On his death in 1826 Dr. Cruden left £8 sterling on behalf of the parish poor, having been minister there for an astounding 57 years, and is buried, along with his sister, by the west wall of the kirkyard, albeit the headstone completely shattered. It would be fitting, then, should it be replaced, to rightly commemorate the good he had done for the parish.

Owing to its gradual debilitation, in 1827 St. Fittick's Church was condemned by an edict from the Presbytery of Aberdeen. In the June of 1829 the church roof was pulled down, with the slates, timbers and interior furnishings sold on behalf of the parish poor. It was requested that the walls remain, the west gable end being made level with that of the side walls; the Session donating an initial two guineas towards coping and repairs. Moreover, the space within the structure of the church itself was to be used as a burial ground, a small charge being made for the benefit of the poor,

Inside the church grounds are the graves of former parish ministers and other notables pertaining to the parish.

and in time included parish ministers the Rev. Alexander Thom and the Rev. Robert Fairweather; other notable internments being salmon merchant John Hector and parish parochial schoolmaster William Barnett. In December that year a fund was initiated for a Watch-house to be built at the northeast corner of the grounds, as at that particular time medical science required a steady supply of cadavers for anatomical experimentation — grave robbers, or 'resurrectionists', were prevalent throughout the country, the infamous William Burke (though more of a serial killer) being hanged in Edinburgh in the January previously.

Nigg Parish Church

In April 1829 a meeting was held in Stonehaven and attended by the proprietors of the nine feud lots of the eastern half of the parish. Here they were reminded that each was responsible for the upkeep of the minister's manse and offices, kirk and kirkyard, dykes and schoolhouses, besides all other parochial burdens within, the cost apportioned to each as per land, rents, etc. Alexander Duthie Esq. of South Loirston and part of the Cove was liable for the sum of £225. 19s. 4d., while the number of seats allocated to each — inclusive of family — went according to their share of expenses. Nigg Parish Church opened on the first Sunday in June 1829 at a cost of £1817 18s. 4d., being located in a position of which no part of the parish was more than 2½ miles distant. The minister was Alexander Thom, who wrote a detailed description of the parish of Nigg in the Second Statistical Account of Scotland, being described as 'a little spare man who lacked flesh between the skin and the bone'. The church had seating for 900 and was built with a view to the increased population of the parish, owing to the proposition of the Wellington Suspension Bridge. Having been minister there for seventeen years in 1843 the Rev. Thom passed away and was succeeded by the Rev. Robert Fairweather. In July that year the church was broken into and a number of bibles and books stolen, a reward of £3 being offered for information that would bring the perpetrators to justice. The comfort of the parishioners, though, was somewhat slow in being recognised, for it was not until the August of 1853 that the installation of heating was mooted. The graveyard opened in 1887 and was extended in 1896, Ann Lundie, daughter of Dr. Alexander Skene of Seaview House, the Cove, the first to be interred; and in 1919 it was proposed that the Churchyard on the east be extended to incorporate a further 300 lairs. The church held sway for 171 years, closing its doors in 2000, the final service being held on Sunday 17 September that year. Presently it is a document storage facility, the entire interior and fittings having been reconfigured accordingly.

The former Nigg Parish Church looking east, 2008.

The Mission Hall

Elevation of the Mission Hall, c.1900's. Inset as seen today.

In 1858 the North East Coast Mission erected a spacious wooden hall with a capacity for 150 persons in which religious services, lectures, a Sunday School, and various social meetings were to be held. It was sited immediately east of the railway station, constructed from planking and heavily tarred, acquiring the name of the 'black kirkie'. It had no particular religious denomination and therefore welcomed all faiths. Over twenty years later, however, the building had become quite dilapidated and dangerous, requiring extensive repairs, including a leaking roof among other impediments.

A petition was presented to the directors of the Mission in 1880, signed by 95 fishermen resident in the Cove and Burnbanks, requesting their help in constructing a new hall, the existing building quite beyond repair, being neither wind nor watertight. Besides personal discomfort within the rotting hall, the petitioners had also expressed the importance of spiritual welfare by the continuing need for Bible Class, Saturday Evening Lectures and the Temperance Society, of which at least one member from each family in the village was in attendance. The Mission itself was in no position to fund the proposed new building, therefore subscriptions requested from private individuals.

There being sufficient funds raised work began in the spring of 1881, additional ground having been gifted by the Caledonian Railway Company in order to accommodate a more substantial construction. It measured 41 feet in length by 26 feet wide, having a height of 10 feet from floor to ceiling, a lean-to room 20 feet by 10 feet, a small porch at the south gable, and four lancet windows on either side. The interior was furnished with varnished pitch pine forms to accommodate 300 people, along with a raised platform, or stage, measuring 14 feet by 6 feet. Heating was by means a powerful Gill stove on the west end, and an American cooking stove in the classroom. The masonry of the building itself consisted of local granite donated by Mr. John Fyfe, lessee of the Cove Quarries at that particular time, and the ageing hall acquired by Mr. David Henderson, merchant grocer in the village. For many years it served as a henhouse, a paraffin store and other useful sundries.

The Mission Hall proved highly popular with the residents of the village, there being a short cut by right of way from between Nos. 5 and 7 on present-day Colsea Road. Over the years it was utilised for many social events, including a youth club, concerts and dances; the McKimmie family forming a band and frequently playing there. The interior, too, had a 'Cove touch', when local man Mr. Ramsay Wood painted a scenic mural upon one of the partition walls. Latterly the Mission Hall held jumble sales but was steadily falling into disrepair. In 1968 it was leased by local builder the late Mr. Fred Cargill Snr., both the interior and grounds being used as a store. Demolished in 1981, only the bell remains, there being no trace of its former location in the back gardens of present-day Nos. 1 and 2 Colsea Terrace.

St. Mary's Mission Chapel School

At the Cove during 1867 much activity arose in regards to building a place of worship and education, namely the parochial Side School and St Mary's Episcopal Church. In 1864 a Bill was passed by parliament to remove the injustice imposed upon the Scottish Church by the last of the Penal Laws in 1746 and 1792, which swept away the last restraints of Erastianism (the theory that the state should have authority over the church in ecclesiastical matters). Alexander Penrose Forbes, Bishop of Brechin, thought the Cove a most suitable place for a Mission School, which opened that year. Primarily for Episcopalian children, it was believed to have been a wooden construction and in close proximity to the southern gable of Station Croft, present-day No. 14 Loirston Road. In her book 'Schooling in the Cove', Janet Murray states that in 1876 the school had 59 boys and 72 girls on the roll (whether they all regularly attended or not is another matter, the dimensions of the building being somewhat compact), the number falling to a total of 72 pupils in 1882. The roll continued to dwindle until 1894, when the mission school finally closed. Later that year, however, the school had to temporarily take in pupils from the parochial Side School on the Cove Road, which was undergoing enlargement and repairs. By the turn of the century, though, there is no further mention of St. Mary's Mission Chapel School, nor any indication on the 1901 Ordinance Survey map of the area.

St Mary's Episcopal Church

Originally part of the diocese of Brechin, Cove Mission was first gathered in 1864. Bishop Alexander Penrose Forbes sent William Humphrey as deacon in order to establish a new church at the 'lonely village of Cove'. The foundation stone of St. Mary the Virgin, a school chapel, was laid on Saturday 3 August 1867, by the Right Rev. Bishop of Brechin, and witnessed by a considerable amount of the villagers themselves. On completion it had internal dimensions of 57 feet long by 22 feet wide, an attached porch and vestry, and built at the cost of a little over £300, with accommodation for 300 worshippers. Besides the confirmation service, and other serious moments, was then incumbent Mr. Ball being referred to as Mr. Boulder, who, incidentally, was awarded the sum of £2 5s. for the loss and damages to his crop on which the church was constructed. St. Mary's opened for worship on 30 October 1867 and was consecrated the following year. It is interesting to note that the ground on which the church stands amounts to ¼ of an acre, gifted by Dr. Alexander Kilgour, on which a school house *or* a place of worship be erected.

The church itself, though, had been originally founded by a number of fishermen, and once erected what strengthened their faith was that when the boat crews sailed to the fishing grounds they could see the church light burning within, knowing that the hopes and prayers of the entire village went with them. Indeed, in the event of a storm it provided a 'sacred lighthouse', guiding them home and to safety, and if any boat from the Cove, or from another village along the coast, was lost, then the church bell would ring to gather the congregation in order to pray for the missing men. The construction of the church had no direct bearing on the men of the coastguard and their families moving to the Cove over forty years previously, rather a proportion of the fisherman throughout Kincardine had been Episcopalian since the days of the Earls Marischal in the fifteenth century.

In 1907/8 the Cove School was being extended, and some of the pupils transferred to the church, lessons being held in the nave and screened off from the chancel by a curtain hung on a large iron frame, which still survives in the building today. In turn repairs to the church became an ongoing problem, and during the 1960's a number of whist drives, sales of work, and other fund-raising activities, was organised by former church stalwart Mrs. Isabella Adam, including Sunday school picnics, to which all other children of the Cove were invited. It became a concern that if not enough money was raised then the church might be turned into a museum, or indeed be sold for private accommodation.

The Cove required a place to reflect and pray, as the community proved on the following day of the Chinook helicopter disaster in the North Sea in 1986, when ninety persons filled the pews; and again in the days following the Piper Alpha tragedy, when the church was opened specially, and more than fifty made their way there — if the church had been removed then the village would have been spiritually empty. In 1988, however, it was depicted as one of the worst examples of church decay, and in dire need of restoration. Indeed, £20,000 would be needed to repair a badly leaking roof, crumbling stonework, broken windows, rotting timbers, and the installation of modern facilities. On the 120th anniversary of its consecration, it became rather ironic that £120,000 was the figure quoted in order to build a brand new church, and perhaps on another location. The church, in effect, would need to be saved by the efforts of the local community.

Over the years the Cargill family have gone to no little expense in putting matters right, inclusive of time and effort. Currently Mrs. Charlotte Cargill runs the church operations, and husband Fred has done sterling work to both the interior and exterior, including removal and restoration work — all of which without the church would be little more than ruinous. Moreover, in the mid 1950's the late Mr. Fred Cargill Sr. made desperate repairs to the south wall with fibreboard sheeting. The family connection with St. Mary's goes back many years, his wife Mrs. Ethel Cargill having first played the organ in the church at the age of eight-years-old! Sadly, there is no organ at present, the music being provided by means of cassette tape and CD. There has also been much in the way of private restoration work, which at times has proved rather costly.

In August 1988 acting priest at St Mary's Episcopal Church, the Rev. Lawrence Phelan (centre), is pictured after his induction by the Bishop of Aberdeen and Orkney, Fred Darwent. Also present are (left to right), the dean of the diocese, the Rev. Gerald Stranraer-Mull, and two former priests at Cove, Canon Jim Alexander, who preached the sermon, and Canon Rupert Mantle. Mr. Phelan moved to Cove from Jedburgh.

Reproduced by kind permission of Aberdeen Journals Ltd.

The panels containing Christian symbolisms on the west wall of the church, prior to their restoration.

In April 2004 improvements were again underway. During repairs to the interior of the building, then 89 year old Mrs. Ethel Cargill alerted church officials to what lay underneath. At its western end were five paintings based on Christian symbolism, and thought to be part of the original church, having previously been wallpapered, painted and covered with plywood — hidden away for over three-quarters of a century. Mrs. Cargill had remembered these paintings as a child, and was puzzled as to why the congregation wanted them covered up. Now these religious canvases hang proudly on the wall, with much being owed to the fund-raising efforts of the local community, inclusive of private donations. After £15,000 of pain-staking work in restoring them to their former glory, Rev. Andy Cowie remarked that the difference made to the church was fantastic, and that people were still making comments of how great the paintings look.

Like Onward Christian Soldiers, the church is still in use, albeit attendances somewhat small. In 1924, though, when the Cove was but a fraction of its present size, the congregation numbered 191. However, the church is beginning to flourish again by holding coffee mornings where people are encouraged to pop in, chat, and have a look around in general. St Mary's has been developed as an ecumenical church, and to be used by the whole community, there being, in event, two Services each Sunday morning — 9.30 for Episcopalians, and 11 o'clock for Congregationalists.

Rev. Andy Cowie and Mrs. Ethel Cargill.

Records indicate the first incumbent as being the Rev. William Humphrey, who was advanced to the priesthood, followed by Thomas Isaac Ball, residing at No. 5 the Cove. When St. Peter's Episcopal Church in Torry opened its doors in 1896 the Rev. Disney Innes there took over the added responsibility for the flock of St. Mary's at the Cove. Mr. Innes came to the Cove to hold Communion services once a month, though other services continued uninterruptedly through the enthusiasm of Mr. W. D. Cruickshank, a lay preacher attached to the legal firm of Butchart and Rennet. Cove Bay and Torry were transferred to the diocese of Aberdeen & Orkney in 1976. Following a long vacancy at St. Peter's, Aberdeen, Cove Bay was placed under the care of St. Mary's, Aberdeen in 1985, before returning to the care of St. Peter's, Aberdeen, in 1990. The charge was renamed St. Mary's, Cove Bay, Aberdeen, in 1998.

Incumbents at St. Mary's are as follows:

1864 — 1867 William Humphrey; 1867 — 1874 Thomas Isaac Ball; 1874 — 1875 James Jennings Dunbar; 1877 — 1878 Ulric Herbert Allen; 1879 — 1880 George Edward Jobling; 1882 — 1883 William Somerville Milne; 1884 — 1886 John Edmeades Cox Colyer; 1886 — 1896 Charge vacant (served by a lay reader); 1896 — 1985 Charge served from Torry (St. Peter's, Aberdeen); 1985 — 1990 Charge served from St. Mary's, Carden Place, Aberdeen; from 1990 the church has been more or less self-contained.

Early Schooling

A parish school is believed to have existed in 1725, and is first recorded in the Nigg Kirk Session Minutes of 1757, the schoolmaster being Mr. Andrew Bonnar. Sited at the extreme northeast of the parish, it proved difficult to access for the majority of the children in the area, being described as 'in a ruinous condition' by 1844. It was relocated to a more central position within the grounds of the new church and opened in January 1849, closing its doors some ninety years later in 1939. The first recognised school in the Cove was a long low building facing the sea, established in 1771 when Mr. George Allan converted his premises into a single classroom in order to educate the poorest of the children in the village. Its most likely location was to the immediate north of the Cove Bay Hotel, partly upon ground on which the former stables and present-day flats are constructed. At the inception of the school the Session apportioned £6 2s. 9d. (Scots money) for a box-bed to accommodate Mr. Allan, which would remain the property of the Session. Five years later, however, it was inadvertently disposed of by his widow after Mr. Allan having departed. Due to old age the service of George Allan was superseded by that of Mr. John Murray in 1775, whose fee was somewhat less at £4 12s.; and in 1779 Mr. James Ross accepted the position at a fee of £5 12s., which was to be increased to £6 if he proved suitable as a schoolmaster.

On her inheritance of the estate of South Loirston, in 1802 Miss Elizabeth Johnston gifted additional ground to accommodate the school and schoolhouse, there being, incidentally, a clause: 'that two houses occupied by John Robertson and Alexander Allan should have twelve yards square of ground to the back of them to be used for a school', as decreed in 1786 by the master of mortifications in Aberdeen and Dr. David Cruden during the division of the eastern half of the parish. Moreover, it was stated that should the need for a new school arise, its location be within 300 yards of the one existing. At this time the village children were unable to travel regularly to the parish school (discounting those provided for at the school in the Cove) because of the distance and their having to assist with the fishing by means of gathering bait, etc. What must also be considered is the given fact that a schoolmaster 'could not make bread' owing to the meagre teaching fees, which in effect was a deterrent from taking such a post. There was, however, a schoolhouse provided, albeit rudimentary. All said, the fisher-folk seemed unwilling to put their children to school, and those who did were little able to do so, hard times having fallen on the fishing.

For sixteen years the said Mr. Ross remained at the Cove, being replaced in 1795 by Mr. Alexander Scott, who in turn left some six years later. Indeed, the following twenty years saw no less than ten schoolmasters, which, owing to the remoteness of the Cove and the Spartan-like conditions, is little surprising. Some insight in regards to the surroundings is that in September 1814 a wooden partition was fitted to the back of the room to protect the children from the oncoming winter conditions. It appears that little money was spent, the only other mention being minor repairs to the school and schoolhouse in 1820, for the meagre sum of 9s. 6d. Nevertheless, religious teaching was avidly encouraged, and in the April of 1811 Robert Robertson, described as a boat carpenter in the Cove, was granted permission to open an afternoon Sunday School.

Bequests were essential towards the schoolmaster receiving an income and the children a continued education, details being as follows: in 1802 Robert Thomson willed £25 for the education of the poor; in 1809 Katherine Thomson bequeathed £15; in 1814 John Hector gifted an unknown sum; in 1817 John Menzies Esq. give five guineas towards the continuing upkeep of a schoolmaster; in 1818 Marjory Cruden gave £20, as did Dr. Cruden; in 1819 Marjory Cruden willed £30; in 1821 George Thomson gave £50 having spent happy memories in the Cove during his boyhood (as part of his epitaph in St. Fittick's churchyard suggests: 'Here lies the remains of George Thomson Esq, who departed this life on the 15th of May 1823, aged 85 years. His life sober, his life benevolent. In his last will he was mindful of the education of the children of the Cove').

In 1821 Mr. Peter Ferguson was appointed schoolmaster, and was in fact the last at that, for at the same time a considerable number of fishermen, along with several parish notables, attended a meeting regarding the proposed construction of a spacious new school and schoolhouse, inclusive of much larger accommodation for the schoolmaster. However, if one considers this building (present-day Nos. 1 and 3 Colsea Road) as being 'spacious', then what of the conditions at the former school for both schoolmaster and pupils alike?

The Endowed School

The existing school had become inadequate from being both too small and falling into overall deterioration, and with an increase in population due the development of the quarries, it became apparent that a bigger purpose-built school was required. In addition, and more importantly, was the fact that Alexander Duthie Esq. had implied that the existing school interfered with his proposed improvements to the South Loirston portion of the village, and that it be removed to another site. The new school, schoolhouse and garden was therefore to be relocated 'a little southward, and to the side of the public road more into the fishing village of the Cove', which would suggest that present-day Colsea Road had already been established as the main road of the village. Funding its construction did not present a problem, being the responsibility of the Heritors of the adjacent estates, and therefore known as the Endowed School: £20 from Alexander Crombie, proprietor of North Loirston; £40 from John Menzies Esq., whose lands included parts of the parish of Banchory Devenick and the Lands of Cove; and £60. 15s. 9d. from Alexander Duthie Esq., who demolished the existing building and retained the materials, inclusive of stones, windows, doors and partitions, making for a total of £120 15s. 9d.

The same allocation of ground was to be given the new school as that of the old, though it was accepted that 'burnside patches' were inferior, which implies that the garden stretched north to the Langburn (so named owing to it stretching from the Loch of Loirston to a termination over the cliffs), as those of Nos. 1 and 3 Colsea Road, today. In total the school, schoolhouse and garden had an area of 31 falls and one yard, a fall being a measure of 32.15 square metres, with 160 falls to a traditional Scots acre. In addition a peatstack was provided for the schoolmaster Mr. Ferguson, and at Dr. Cruden's request a sheltered privy constructed to the rear of the garden for the use of the children, 'for the sake of decency'. The new school was to be accommodated with seats and made tasteful, with the schoolhouse of a superior style, capable of receiving a large family — and even some boarders! Another indication of the extent and condition of the former school was that such a building at the time would cost but £30 to £40, as opposed to £120 15s. 9d. Moreover, then, parents were expected to pay towards their children's education.

The Endowed School opened in 1822, having a thatched roof and of a stone and lime construction; all the children being in a single room. The school and schoolhouse comprised of three rooms (incorporating a kitchen), one of which was the school itself and used for educational purposes only; any other public meetings was strictly prohibited. As mentioned, it was situated on the main street of the village, the schoolmaster's house being gable-end to the sea, with the surrounding houses interspersed to the northwest and southeast of its construction. There were, of course, repairs and expenses to be considered, the first being in December 1826 when the work amounted to 14s. Over the years the renovations included thatching, flooring, chimney tops, a back door, and a kitchen grate, besides other legal letters and transactions, inclusive of costs towards the sequestration of Alexander Duthie Esq. By the mid 1850's the running total of repairs amounted to just under £71.

Financial assistance was again required, with Dr. Cruden in 1824 giving £10 towards the insurance of the school and schoolhouse, the amount being set at 7s. 4d per annum, and in 1830 a legacy for the sum of £88 was left by a Mrs. Paterson. Nonetheless, a puzzling, if unwarranted incident occurred in 1829 when farmer Donald Sinclair, father of David Sinclair of North Loirston, complained that the part of the new school ground encroached upon that for which he was already paying rent to Mr. Duthie, and that the situation should be reviewed. In March the following year schoolmaster Mr. Ferguson was served with a charge of removal from Mr. Duthie, the Session being 'astonished', and that legal action was in order. It would appear that the matter arose from the disputed land as claimed by Donald Sinclair, though Mr. Ferguson stated he had but the precise extent of ground as allocated by Mr. Duthie himself. On behalf of Mr. Ferguson, it was stated that Mr. Duthie had 'removed the school to suit his own purposes', which no doubt incorporated an extension, or indeed the actual construction of the inn. As it happened the removal charge was dropped and Mr. Ferguson allowed to remain teaching at the school, though in the February of 1831 several march stones were purchased at a cost of 10s. and 6d., being placed between the school grounds and that as leased by Donald Sinclair.

Between the coming generation and the closure of the school lies some brief information regarding both life in the classroom and in the village itself. In October 1836 the school reopened after having undergone substantial repairs, which most likely took place during harvest time; and in April the following year a Sabbath Evening School was to commence, beginning at 4 o' clock in the afternoon. In 1839 Margaret Ferguson, daughter of schoolmaster Peter Ferguson, proposed a school for the instruction of females only, though as yet no records have been found, or indeed if it existed. On a more environmental issue was the grim affair of Mr. Ferguson having died of malignant typhoid fever in January 1841, and a replacement schoolmaster required, for which the following words describe: 'the Session would consider about a successor on a future day as it is not considered by medical men proper to convene the school at present by reason of the alarming disorder in the village of Cove particularly'. Indeed, due to the 'ravages of typhus fever', there were upwards of twenty families left fatherless in the Cove, with many — if not all — being wholly dependent on some means of assistance. One may only imagine the fear that stalked the fishtown, and it would appear that from this date onwards future schoolmasters did not reside in the schoolhouse at all. The following month saw seven suitable applicants for the post; of course, the choice as per custom was decided between the minister, prominent families in the parish, and the immediate Heritors, especially Alexander Muir, then proprietor of South Loirston, and on whose land the school was located. In May the committee chose Mr. John Forbes as schoolmaster, drawing up a list of conditions regarding his acceptance of the post. Teaching hours during summer were from 10 o' clock until noon, then from 3 o' clock until 5 o' clock in the afternoon. In winter it was one continuous session, from 9.30 in the morning until 2 o' clock in the afternoon; the harvest vacation being for a period of three weeks, without any deduction from the schoolmaster's fee. Mr. Forbes was also to attend church regularly in order to set a good moral example to both pupils and residents of the village and surrounding area.

He resigned his post in March 1844 and was succeeded by Mr. William Mitchell, who requested a salary of £20 to £25 per annum, which the Session considered reasonable. At a meeting of the Heritors in June, however, it was brought to notice that the fund was inadequate for the support of a schoolmaster at the Cove, which in turn made it difficult in securing persons suitably qualified for the position. It was therefore decided that the Heritors were each to contribute a sum towards the schoolmaster's salary, with the amount payable for each to be calculated from their respective rent values. Moreover, by the coming August Mr. Mitchell implied that he was no longer at liberty to teach at the Cove owing to other employment commitments, at which he sent a deputy in his place, a Mr. Craig, whose manner displeased the leading parishioners. In due course he proved to be inept, his behaviour described as 'unbecoming', at which the Session promptly dispensed with his services.

In the September of 1845 Mr. John Coulter was appointed schoolmaster, and in December the following year raised concerns regarding the safety of the schoolchildren due to the ongoing railway operations in the immediate proximity of the school. Indeed, as the work commenced, the western portion of the school ground and garden was needed to accommodate the railway. However, there arose some dispute as to the amount of compensation, and in June 1852, by way of arbitration, the sum of £52 was paid by the Aberdeen Railway Company, with £9 being awarded to Mr. Coulter for both the loss of part of his garden and the inconvenience caused. That the main road into the village continued to the west of the railway is evidenced by the gable-ends of No. 4 Loirston Road and No.1 Colsea Road, between them there being a small but-and-ben — though not attached — which was pulled down in 1846/7 in order to accommodate the railway track.

Under the Parochial Schoolmaster (Scotland) Act, 1803, by 1853 the school in the village was classed as a Side School, and the Heritors permitted to divide a parish between two or more teachers. Due to the expansion of the fishing and the construction of additional houses in the village, however, by this time it was realised that a new and commodious building was needed. In 1854 Mr. Coulter resigned for employment elsewhere, leaving, no less, a few wooden sheds and two chimney cans, which the Session purchased for a few shillings. His successor was to be Mr. John Scroggie, appointed in February 1855, and effectively becoming the last schoolmaster at the Endowed School.

By late 1863 the school had become dilapidated and was insufficient for the gathering numbers, the consensus of the parish Heritors being that the school be enlarged and removed to a more convenient location. The following January schoolmaster Mr. John Scroggie wrote to the authorities explaining that there were 80 pupils on the roll at the Endowed School, though fewer attended during the summer months owing to various fishing and farming duties. At this time school fees were still required to be paid, albeit miserably, with the attendance somewhat irregular, and in the last month (December 1863) one shilling only was recovered from within the whole of the fishing population, and in the preceding month a likewise sum. He stated that the fishermen had had a poor season, but as the fees were so small (no figure given) such an excuse lost much of its force, though he felt that he was quite unable to turn those away who did or could not pay, as they would then would grow up in ignorance, which, he felt, would be 'a disgrace in an age endeavouring to educate all classes'. Such affairs, he surmised, arose partly from the parents not having a sufficient education themselves, and that a teacher in a place like this would require to be almost independent, as the constant struggle for a living rather 'crippled his usefulness'. Mr. Scroggie, however, continued to teach there, even after resigning his post in April 1866, having been offered the position of schoolmaster at the new parochial Side School currently under construction.

In January 1867 the schoolmaster's house was let to salmon merchant William Routledge, albeit the parochial Side School didn't open until the following month that year. In 1869 the building lay empty, though in 1873 the old school and schoolhouse were being occupied by widow Leiper and Helen Robertson, respectively. 1881 saw both houses tenanted by Mr. James Cordiner and family, boat builders, while in 1895 the numbers were reconfigured, the old school and schoolhouse becoming houses Nos. 2 and 4. In 1898 house No. 4 had dropped 'old school' as part of its address, though house No. 2 retained it until 1950, having been occupied by Mr. John Westland from 1904. When the roads in the village were named in 1968, however, the former school and schoolhouse became Nos. 1 and Nos. 3 Colsea Road.

On the left is what was the Endowed school in the village, now presently No. 1 Colsea Road. The adjoining house of No. 3 was in fact the schoolmaster's living quarters.

Drumforskie School

In 1824 John Menzies Esq. began to build croft houses by the Hill of Drumforskie for poor and landless labourers from elsewhere in the country, predominantly from the Highlands, at which arose around 100 children. Of course, the school at the Cove was unable to accommodate such a number, therefore the Session arranged the building of a Sunday Evening School and partly financed its construction, the additional finance coming by way donations from several prominent landowners in the vicinity, besides small contributions from the fishing families in the Cove. As there was no regular minister, religious education was sought from teachers residing in Aberdeen, albeit proved difficult in regards to securing a regular service due to its isolation. The building was soon afterwards converted into a school, and in 1828 the area referred to as Charleston, including that of Charleston School. The school and schoolmaster's croft were sited directly opposite the Mains of Charleston, on what is now Charleston Cottage, there being scant details of its existence, though in 1848 the roof and thatch were severely damaged by a gale, and in 1857 the schoolmaster's croft was to be let as he was no longer resident there. By the last quarter of the 19th century the school roll had began to decline owing to the crofters leaving the vicinity, the school closing its doors by the turn of the century and the pupils attending the parochial Side School at the Cove.

The Parochial Side School

The whisperings of a proposed new school had emerged, and Mr. David Sinclair, a tenant farmer of North Loirston, became very much the driving force in regards to its establishment. In the March of 1865 he wrote to Dr. Kilgour advising him of the impracticality of the existing school and schoolhouse, and if possible to determine some permanent means of salary for a male teacher. He suggested that the larger boys should go to the parish school, though fisher-children were very unwilling to mix with those of the country; furthermore, they did not think education worth travelling for, and that the parish school was at times so full that the teacher was forced to turn scholars away.

Events, it proved, were not straightforward, for when the parish school was removed to its present locality in 1849, it was believed altogether unnecessary to have a school at the Cove conducted by a male teacher. However, the funds and the establishment of the Endowed School dictated otherwise, and stipulated a male teacher only. Dr. Kilgour disagreed, and in addition had no intention of paying the requested £10 annually towards keeping up the present school. His view was at the Cove there should be merely a school for young children and rather more grown up girls, conducted by an unmarried female teacher. He also believed that by having a suitable woman in charge she could influence mothers in regards to sending their children to school regularly, keeping them clean and neat, which a male teacher could never do. In his opinion, though, he held nothing personal against current schoolmaster Mr. Scroggie.

In an effort to remove from the parish Heritors their self-imposed subscriptions Mr. Sinclair wished for government assistance in building the school, and in paying the schoolmaster's salary. The time, he felt, was an ideal opportunity to give a good education to the fisher-children, there having been a great decrease in the fishing for the past few years (as mentioned in James Bertram's 'Harvest of the Sea'), and that the coast appeared to be overpopulated with fishermen, therefore the rising generation should look at alternative means for making a living. Apparently, the only other person of means that he'd appealed to was Mr. Robert Davidson of Balnagask, who was prepared to give £160, or more if required. Though Mr. Sinclair was but a tenant farmer, he was prepared to donate £40.

Since Dr. Kilgour had not replied, Mr. Sinclair again wrote explaining that a purpose built school at the Cove might produce someone as worthy as the Doctor himself, and that he (David Sinclair) was born and brought up in the Cove, receiving limited education at the present school. Indeed, he was more or less self-taught, having but one continuous term there between the ages of six and seven, the ensuing years consisting of a week or two during adverse weather, and long winter nights spent studying at home. In addition, he implied that the site of the proposed new school should be located to the west of the village, giving the following statistics for children in the area aged ten years or younger: the estate of South Loirston and the Lands of Cove having 194, Burnbanks village having 61, with 120 children attending the parish parochial school. These figures are surprisingly high, making for over 250 children in the vicinity, albeit some already attending the Episcopal school on Loirston Road and that at Charleston. He felt there should be both a male schoolmaster and a female teacher, proposing that the farmers in the area provide carriages to convey the children to the new school for free, being very encouraged that Mr. Ferguson and Mr. Crombie of Altens and North Loirston, respectively, were very keen to donate money for any educational purposes.

Cove School pupils by the north entrance door, 1927.

It would appear that after three letters expounding on its sundry requirements, by the spring of 1865 Dr. Kilgour still refused to support a second parochial school. A meeting was held in May that year, at which eight of the nine proprietors of the parish were in attendance, excepting Dr. Kilgour. In his absence a proposed site for the new school was discussed, there being three possible locations: adjacent to the railway bridge straddling the estates of North and South Loirston; in the field across from Greenarbour; and in the corner of the field opposite Loirston Lodge — all of which were on the estate of North Loirston and the property of Mr. Alexander Crombie. However, what the committee overlooked was the aforementioned fact that the building of a new school must be no more than 300 yards from the existing one on the main street in the village. They did, though, unanimously agree that the proposed sites were impractical, incurring quite a distance for the children resident in the Cove itself. A further meeting was called on 23 June by the now Cove Side School Committee, with again Mr. David Sinclair in the chair, a salary of £25 per annum being settled on for the schoolmaster.

A final letter was written by Mr. Sinclair to Dr. Kilgour, requesting a portion of ground on his estate for the proposed new school, and to take the existing premises in the village at its present valuation. It appears Mr. Sinclair was acting on his own initiative, and that the other members of the Committee were quite unaware of such appeals. After some consideration Dr. Kilgour agreed to an apportioned area lying to the immediate east of the burn on the Cove Road, along with a donation for the sum of £40, and with a monetary adjustment, inherited both the grounds and building of the Endowed School in the village. Though funds were in place from the existing school, a more substantial figure was needed. A subscription list and appeal was began, for which over sixty separate donations were given, ranging in sums, and from people both inside and outside of the parish, including the Rev. Robert Fairweather and George Falconer Muir.

Classes 1 and 2, 1963.

In August 1865 Mr. James Walker of Aberdeen tendered a contract to construct the masonry for the school and schoolhouse, at a cost of £219, and Mr. David Mair of Hilldowntree (to the south of present-day Leggart Terrace), the carpentry, plasterwork, slating and plumbing, for £256 2s. Though the stone on the south face of the building bears 1865 (the date in which its proposal was founded), construction did not commence until the following year, local farmer Mr. David Milne making good the school grounds by sowing grass and planting a large garden of potatoes. Heating was to be supplied by a large Gill stove, purchased for £10 18s. 6d., the coal being supplied by the bushel. The total expense for the whole school, inclusive of books, maps, writing materials, etc, amounted to £718 14s 2d, as opposed to a sum of £718 7s. 11d. raised by donations and subscriptions, including 3s. 10d. from the sale of potatoes from the old school garden, leaving a balance deficit of 6s. and 3d!

It would appear that the school was all but complete by the winter of 1866, though severe snowstorms in the coming weeks had prevented it from opening. On 2 February 1867 the parochial Side School eventually opened its doors, of all days on a Saturday afternoon, a plausible explanation being that as the event had already been delayed on several occasions, the earliest opportunity was taken to do so. The children numbered around 140 (this figure is questionable, and may have included children from other schools in the parish) and each presented with a small treat as they entered, the Rev. Robert Fairweather presiding, there being a good attendance of parents and other interested parties. Devotional exercises were also in order, along with a choir and several musical performances. After the entertainment and speeches were over, 30 or so gentlemen of note were catered for at the Cove Inn by innkeeper Mr. James Farquharson, the evening being a happy occasion, with a number of songs between each toast.

However, there appeared some conflict concerning the choice of schoolmaster or 'dominie'. Some of those who had given generously towards the new school believed that a classical master was the order of the day, and that the aforementioned Mr. John Scroggie was, to put it bluntly, 'not good enough'. An appeal, and indeed a petition, was raised in his favour, signed by farmer, fisher, and sundry occupations in between. His supporters won the day and he returned to his duties at the new parochial Side School, taking up residence and remaining there until 1886, Mr. Alexander Macdonald replacing him, an academic, and aesthete rather, who furthered the knowledge of both children and their parents alike, in turn departing in 1891. Over the years dominies came and went, each, of course, leaving his individual mark, be it one of authority, sport, or some other particularity.

The school on opening had but one classroom, with a baize screen hung the length of the room dividing the boys and girls, the headmaster and his family being accommodated at the south gable-end on which the foundation date appears. It was initially presumed that 50 boys and 50 girls would attend, which would have made for very cramped conditions. However, this proved somewhat optimistic, the roll amounting to no more than 70, and not all present at the same time either! The initial years were not without problem, though, and in August 1885 the Medical Board demanded that an additional supply of water be supplied as the school 'had no water other than a filthy ditch to supply the scholars'. Of course, there were moments of sunshine, and not all dull education. Alexander Kilgour took an active interest in the welfare of the schoolchildren, supplying a number of jubilee medals to celebrate the 50th year of Queen Victoria's reign. He was also invited to preside at a Children's Treat on 19 February 1891 at the Mission hall, tea being served at 6 o' clock and the proceedings proper commencing thirty minutes later. And in the July of 1902 the children of the parish of

School lessons, 1965.

Reproduced by kind permission of Aberdeen Journals Ltd.

Nigg attended a Coronation Picnic for King Edward VII, mustering at the schools of Kirkhill and the Cove, before marching in procession to a field at the Mains of Loirston. During the course of the afternoon games and competitions were in order, with over 350 prizes awarded, including a medal to every boy and an enamel jug to each of the girls. The children were brought through the beautiful grounds of Loirston House, Mr. Kilgour being commended for his liberal support and presence among them.

The best part of thirty years had elapsed before the presumed 100 pupils was reached, and in 1894 an extension was required to accommodate them all, some of the pupils being relocated to the school on Loirston Road during the ongoing construction work. Due to the lack of records it is uncertain exactly when the migration towards the new Side School took place, but by the mid 1870's pupils were beginning to drift away from St. Mary's Mission Chapel School. Following its closure in 1894, along with the school at Charleston around the turn of the century, it's little wonder that additional floor space became necessary.

Owing to further expansion in 1907/8 some of the schoolchildren were relocated to St. Mary's Church on Loirston Road and the Mission Hall in the village. By now the school consisted of no more than four rooms, inclusive of the headmaster's accommodation. Further extensions occurred in 1931, 1937 and 1967, until in 1977, with the roll standing at 138, two mobile classrooms were set up in the playground, these being primarily to accommodate the infants. In 1941 the schoolhouse was constructed, then schoolmaster Mr. Alexander Smith becoming the first tenant, and to the east of the playground, in 1945, a school kitchen was added, the base of which may still be seen today. Indeed, before the aforesaid addition in 1967, it was common practice for classes of differing years to be taught in the same room. By the 1950's, however, numbers began to decline, and in 1962 the school was being mooted for closure, the roll standing at a lowly 64 pupils. It's saving grace was the construction of Fittick Place and Sinclair Terrace, which boosted numbers considerably. Paradoxically, when the school closed in 1981, it had 161 pupils, and was far too small for the escalating numbers due to the ever-present housing development in the area.

With the school having closed in 1981 and the schoolhouse sold for private accommodation, another era had arrived for the ever increasing population. Because of a lack of public amenities the old school became Loirston Annexe, then Cove Community Centre and is presently Loirston Community Centre, holding diverse classes such as weight-watchers, keep-fit, a youth club and computer courses, to name but a few, managed by Educational Community Officer, Mrs. Monica McKenzie. For the best part of 113 years the school had served the Cove and surrounding area, the names of Kilgour, Crombie, Sinclair, and the Side School Parochial Board, becoming no more than a distant memory.

Cove School pupils, 1981, prior to its closure.

Some interesting extracts from the Side School log books:

1876 July 10 A number of children absent owing to the boats leaving for the herring fishing.
1884 March 10 School closed — scarlet fever.
1894 May ? Children from the Episcopal School enrolled.
1894 April 16 Children have a half-day to see steamer *(Countess of Aberdeen)* wrecked in the harbour mouth.
1895 September 20 Disagreeable odour from the Oil Factory, could not ventilate classrooms.
1898 Jan 18 Diphtheria outbreak.
1908 May 18 The infant scholars were transferred this morning from the Mission Hall where they have been since November 20 during the enlargement of the school.
1939 September 11 Trenches have been dug in the playing field for the safety of the children, all of whom carry their gas masks to school.

Of the three schools known to have existed in the Cove, (non-ecumenical) below is a listing of their respective schoolmasters.

School 1. Opened in 1771, described as a long, low building in the village, being sited immediately to the north of the Cove Bay Hotel: 1771 — 1775 Mr. George Allan; 1775 — 1779 Mr. John Murray; 1779 — 1795 Mr. James Ross; 1795 — 1801 Mr. Alexander Scott; 1801— 1802 Mr. William Milne; 1802 — 1811 Mr. Peter McEwen; 1811 — 1812 Mr. George Robertson; 1812 — 1813 Mr. James Melvin; 1813 — 1815 Mr. Alexander McRae; 1815 — 1816 Mr. William Brand; 1816 Mr. John Nicol; 1816 — 1820 Mr. John Mackray (MacRae?); 1820 — 1821; Mr. William Mackray (MacRae?); 1822 Mr. Peter Ferguson, the Endowed School opening that year.

School 2. Opened in 1822, known as the Endowed School and presently Nos. 1 and 3 Colsea Road: 1822 — 1841 Mr. Peter Ferguson; 1841 — 1844 Mr. John Forbes; 1844 Mr. Craig; 1844 — 1845 Mr. Hunter; 1845 — 1854 Mr. John Coulter; 1855 — 1867 Mr. John Scroggie, the parochial Side School opening that year.

School 3. Opened in 1867, formerly known as the parochial Side School, becoming Cove Bay Primary School before closing its doors in 1981: 1867 — 1887 Mr. John Scroggie; 1887 — 1889 Mr. Alex Macdonald; 1889 — 1896 Mr. Charles Reid; 1896 — 1897 Mr. D.M.S. Napier (Interim); 1897 — 1921 Mr. Alex J. Barclay; 1921 — 1948 Mr. Alexander Smith; 1948 — 1961 Mr. William C. Philip; 1961 (April to December) Miss Reid (Interim); 1961 — 1966 Mr. William J. Shand; 1966 — 1968 Mr. Alex Swan; 1968 — 1971 Mr. Frederick Shewan; 1971 — 1980 Mr. John T. Gibbons; 1980 — 1981 Interim teaching post.

Cove School aerial photograph, July 1973. To the right is the old library under construction, and behind the schoolhouse is the school kitchen. The two trees in the playground are also present, as is the cycle shed. At this time the school lay in relative isolation, being surrounded by open pasture. Note. By 1969 all primary seven pupils attended secondary education at Mackie Academy, Stonehaven, and gathered at the corner of Loirston Road and Sinclair Place in order to catch the morning bus.

Ringing the Changes

No school, though, is complete without a bell, and at the same time as the Society of Whitefishers in Cove was formed (May 1802), the Shore-Master, or Treasurer of Aberdeen, presented to the school at the Cove a fine bell, which in turn was transferred to the Endowed School on its construction twenty years later. And when the Cove Side School Committee formed in 1865 a separate subscription list was drawn up for a replacement bell, with a total of

£10 2s. 6d. being raised from a number of small donations. The bell was purchased from David McHardy & Son, Ironmongers, Smiths & Bellhangers, 54 Netherkirkgate, Aberdeen, at a cost of just over £8, and fitted up with plates, bushes, oak stock, lever and chain. Some years later, though, someone (believed to be then pupil David Henderson, who would in time run the shop in the village) stole the clapper and rendered it silent for over 60 years! In it's place was a small hand-bell, which for its size clattered with a 'fair dirl', even in the hands of the amateur campanologist. This bell, too, lost it's tongue, or fell out, rather, having to be fixed by a length of wire, and may be seen (albeit a replacement handle) at Loirston Primary School on request.

The bell hangs in place at Loirston Primary School.

The school bell, nonetheless, seemed to be rusting in its tower, silent and forgotten, until in 1975 Mr. David Calder, then janitor, examined it and found it to be in a hazardous condition, and that it ought to be removed. The work was carried out local men by Mr. Sandy Wood and Mr. Willie Guyan, the bell found to be a fine specimen indeed, before being refurbished and re-hung. And it still hangs today, albeit not in its original location, having been given a new home and officially 'opening' Loirston Primary School in 1981. Of course, it being no longer necessary to consider: 'that should the need for a new school arise, its location be within 300 yards of the existing one'!

In the August term that year the new school absorbed the pupils from the existing one on the Cove Road, along with the children from the surrounding housing development, the pupils being asked to design a badge that would best represent the closing of the old school and the transfer to the new, of which there were almost 450 entries. The competition was judged by Cove School headmistress Mrs. Frances Davidson and principal teacher of art at Kincorth Academy Mr. Eric Auld, the winner being Primary 6 pupil Amanda McColl, 4 Findon Ness, Altens, whose badge depicted the now extinct Small Blue butterfly imposed upon a golden bell above a symbolic blue sea. Moreover, these were the colours of the first official football strip of the Cove School in 1968, when then headmaster Mr. Frederick Shewan organised fund-raising activities for this very purpose.

Charleston Primary School opened in August 1999 in order to accommodate the expanding residential housing to the west of the Cove. It was officially opened on the 24 January 2000 by Mr. Sam Galbraith, MP, MSP and Minister for Children and Education, and at the time described as being the 'safest school in Scotland'. All said, a school at the Cove has persisted for almost quarter a millennium, from the teaching of those in workaday clothes to that of uniforms with embroidered motifs, from chalk and slate to the advent of computers, though nothing has changed in regards to the importance of a primary education.

Charleston Primary School pupils at the opening of the school in the August term of 1999.

Chapter 6: Another Business

The Quarries

By the early 1930's, and with the fishing effectively over, some alternative means had to be found in order to make a living, which in most cases involved travelling to Aberdeen seeking work. Though the fishmeal factory was still in production, it was also nearing extinction. At this time the Cove afforded little by way of a means of employment, which, over the next few decades, allowed those of a more enterprising nature the opportunity to set up in business. Of course, in earlier times, an additional pursuit in the Cove besides the fishing, was that of the opening of the quarries.

Primarily used for the construction of roadways in English cities, smooth, round stones gathered from beaches were being shipped from Torry early in the 18th century, and from the Bay of Nigg in the 1770's immense quantities were being shipped to London. Furthermore, following the destructive fire in Aberdeen in 1740, which destroyed many of the wooden houses, a more substantial building material was required. Surveys took place and quarries in the area opened up within a year, including that of Rubislaw. The potential of granite was soon realised, at which numerous other quarries appeared in the surrounding area. Being ubiquitous in the Cove, much of the original crofts and fisher-houses in the area would have consisted of stones being gathered by men collectively known as the 'boulder builders', inclusive of those built in the Cove during the 18th century.

Around 1760 Menzies of Pitfodels began consultations with civil engineers to undertake an exploration of the southern half of the parish. After what would have proved to be a successful survey several quarries were opened to the south of the Cove, the first, most likely, being that of Blackhill. Interest in the Nigg granite began to escalate, and in 1767 John Adam requested tack for the rocks and quarries from Girdleness to the Cove. Certainly, by 1780, between Hare Ness and the Cove, there were six in operation. At this time five to six hundred men were engaged at the quarries throughout the parish, decreasing rapidly after 1772, until the early 1790's when there was but seventeen local men plus a few incomers still in occupation. Numbers would increase in the next few years due to the coming of the turnpikes, and the traffic dictated by the size of stones, there being three types of finishes: nidged, puncheoned and reeled, the Cove quarries being primarily for roadstone. Dr. David Cruden, then parish minister, records that the stones were wedge-like, and that a ton could be made by a man in two days, albeit his wages too high, earning 18s. to 20s. (90p to £1) in a week, which did him no good; and that except for a few individuals, all was spent. It would be fair to presume that he meant on drink!

The granite was a mixture of blue, grey and pink, with various combinations of the three, a more detailed description being given by George F. Harris in 'Granites and Our Granite Industries', written 1888: 'The stone is very hard, and, owing to the presence of a great quantity of black mica, which occurs in minute flakes, the stone is of a dark hue, much more so than the ordinary granites of the district. A few polished examples we have seen show that it is capable of taking a fine polished surface'. Not as pleasing to the eye as the famous Rubislaw, but owing to its close-grained texture the Cove granite was, in a word, durable, being more resilient to weathering and frost. Because of this consistency it proved ideal for the insatiable demand for paving and roads, and was exported as cobblestones known as 'cassies', 'calsies' or 'causeys', to London (especially the Billingsgate area), Maidstone, Ramsgate and other English cities.

Of course, opening a quarry involved a degree of risk, there being various reasons to consider, such as the cost of preparing the site and the consequences of its location. A fault may run through the bedrock, or a seam of flint, which in effect could spell economic disaster. As in the railway, most of the clearing work was done by itinerants from the Highlands and Ireland, the owner of the land taking no part in the proceedings. Such activity brought little benefit to the fishing community, though great reward for those who worked the land, by way of lodgings for the men and the hiring of livestock and equipment. Additional employment such as blacksmiths, wheelwrights and horsemen had also been created. Indeed, from the initial surveys onwards there were numerous buildings in connection with the quarries, mostly sited to the west of the railway, though having fallen into ruin and disappearing by the mid 20th century. There is, however, remains of a small firehouse at one of the lesser worked sites, albeit very much hidden by whins and overgrowth today. Nevertheless, preparing the site was no less than brutal work, and before the advent of the JCB, or other such mechanical hydraulic apparatus, the land was cleared by hand — namely pick and shovel, the Hare Ness headland being ladled into the sea!

The quarry on the Hare Ness headland, with Cove harbour in the background. The quarry is stepped towards the sea, the floor but a few yards from sea level, which in effect would prevent any work during stormy weather.

Quarrying in the Cove at first proved economical, owing to its near proximity to the port of Aberdeen. Initially cartloads of stones would have trundled up the road to Charleston, turning north along the road to the Bridge of Dee en route to Aberdeen harbour; it is doubtful they routed along Loirston Road to the Bridge of Dee via the old Cove Road. On its construction in 1829 a more direct route was by means of the Wellington Road turnpike. In 1850 the coming of the railway proved both a great benefit and a speedy transportation route south, the quarries having their own siding. Located between the Kettle inlet and the Colsea Yawn, here the stones were loaded into wagons, as indeed they were at the station, the Aberdeen Railway Company becoming the lessees of the quarry until around 1855.

Prior to the railway, access and egress to the quarries by the cliffs was by way of a path that met with the southern end of Loirston Road, running partly along the route of the railway track itself. With the railway in situ the path was reconfigured to run parallel to the *west* of it, crossing the Calsay Bridge and leading to the quarry by the Kettle inlet. The establishment of the fish meal factory gave rise to a path on the *east* side of the railway (as seen today), with the Calsay Bridge now spanning both. By 1900, however, the western path was no longer in use, having all but disappeared, being superseded by a more substantial thoroughfare adjoining the Cove Road. The Calsay Bridge, too, has somewhat departed, its wooden walkway burned away by a spark from a passing steam train during the 1930's.

In regards to quarrying operations the process of drill and blast proved extremely hard and dangerous work, though at times a bit monotonous, being executed by hammer and drill, with three-man teams working in rotation, taking around nine hours to drill four feet. The holes were filled with gunpowder and a fuse inserted, the powder tapped down using a wooden ramrod. Unfortunately fatalities occurred, there being recorded incidents as such in the quarries at the Cove. Around 1870 much improvement arrived by the introduction of steam-driven drilling, known as the 'jumpin-dreel', where fifty feet could be drilled in six hours. Dynamite had superseded loose powder, and pneumatic drills were being introduced around 1895. At first, though, the only means of removing the blasted rock was by horse and cart (this type of work gave rise to a bigger breed of horse) until 1872, when John Fyfe invented the 'Blondin', an aerial cable-way carrier, so named after Charles Blondin, the famous French tightrope-walker. The idea for this invention arose while travelling Deeside, where he saw an ingenious method employed by the local postman for pulling his mailbag back and forth the river; thus, with a few moderations, the 'Blondin' came to pass. Legend has it that he deliberated on its finer points while sitting in church, visualising the gallery and the pulpit as anchor points. The Blondin transporter allowed quarrying operations to go much deeper in search of better quality stone.

Obviously John Fyfe was not the initial lessee of the quarries, though in the mid 19th century they were being worked by John Gibb. In 1863 the Manuelle brothers, Alexander and Frederick, secured that of the Kettle inlet. In this case, and other leases which followed, the agreement was to keep the quarries free of rubbish and to blend in with the landscape as far as was possible, concealing all excavations with granite waste and soil. However, in 1870 loose stones were being removed from the Cove Farm land by unsolicited individuals, being dressed and shaped for making causeways, or simply for use as ballast; many having been removed from an extensive cairn. The tenant farmer Mr. Masson accepted responsibility, though he was entirely unaware of the extent of the situation. Nevertheless, all stones sold had to be accounted for, and a list made out to estate owner Dr. Kilgour. In the immediate vicinity were two houses known as 'the Calsies', and Calsay Croft, which was in existence until around 1860 before being absorbed into part of the Cove Farm land.

A sectional drill line in the quarry at Hare Ness. A number of these, and the drill holes themselves, may be witnessed on the tumbling rock face.

The quarry by the Kettle inlet. On the skyline in the background are the lofty constructions at Blackhills Quarry (initially Blackhill), currently in operation.

Moreover, in 1870 the quarries at the Cove were advertised in the press for lease, being described as 'these famous granite quarries'. On the east side of the railway the Manuelle brothers appeared to have prevailed, though they sub-leased in 1871 to master quarriers from Kincorth, the Reid brothers, albeit with stipulations: they were not to open a quarry on arable land; fill up the old quarry holes with waste granite from ongoing quarrying operations; or permitted to discard their waste granite over the 'rubbish hill' into the Kettle inlet below. As it was, they but lasted a year. John Fyfe, however, had already written to Dr. Kilgour regarding a possible further lease of the quarries, stating that those on the east side of the railway (most likely at Hare Ness) were very much interlaced with unworkable rock, parts of which could be seen protruding from the waste of former operations. He added that the stone was of a very marketable quality, and could best be accessed at a level of around sixty feet below the old workings, though as the good rock was so much interlaced with bad, he did not consider it viable. However, being both forward thinking and business-minded, he noted that the quarry on the west side, 'may, if properly opened up, stand good for a long period, but not until properly prospected'.

It would appear he held such speculation worthwhile, for the following year he had secured the lease for the whole of the quarries, both east and west of the railway, there being extensive constructions forthwith. In 1875 he wrote to Alexander Kilgour of his intentions to pull down and re-erect a smiddy, offices, and a stable by the quarries on the Cove Farm land, which was an indication of the work envisaged in the coming years. John Fyfe was the sole lessee until after the turn of the century, supplying many thousands of tons of stones, a typical invoice reading: Cove Quarries, Near Aberdeen. By 1891, however, plans were afoot in regards to fencing or encircling the quarries with a drystane dyke, there being little requirement for the Cove stones at present, albeit unknown what the short term future might develop. Indeed, John Fyfe had been working the quarries at a loss for a considerable period, though held the lease until after the turn of the century, passing away in 1903, aged 73 years.

The huge stone counterweights as used by the crane sit stacked upon the quarry floor. The large crack in the bottom lintel has been caused by various fires being kindled beneath it over the years.

As for the quarries themselves, a few had but brief working lives, amounting to no more than shallow holes in the ground and covering little area. Hare Ness was more extensive, though not continuously in operation, a smithy being located to the southwest of the headland, traces of which may be seen today. The quarry was leased as recently as 1902 and believed to have been abandoned around 1920. In 1908, however, the theft of a quantity of brass bearings from the engine room at the main quarry put fifty men temporarily out of work. By the Kettle inlet work persisted, and around 1900 a crusher was constructed, giving rise to 'the tip', a huge ramp of earth and stone which led to the roof of the works. Here granite waste would be hurled over the cliff, landing on the shingle a fearsome distance below. At the same time a tall brick chimney was constructed at the northeast corner, from which a steam-powered Blondin transported rock to the crusher above. Around 1960 the demise of this chimney provided exciting entertainment when it was demolished by the Army Territorials, who used so much explosives that, on detonation, the bricks flew for proverbial miles — along with the decibels and dust! The huge stone counterweights for the crane are still present, being neatly stacked in the centre of the quarry floor, which, incidentally, has quite an extensive sea cave running underneath it, along with some interesting carvings on the rock face.

The largest and most extensively worked area, however, was situated some 400 yards southwest of the Cove Farm buildings, and concentrated into two huge holes; other surrounding locations having been abandoned soon after initial exploration, or deemed not viable to be continued. Operations began at the first of these during the early 1800's, the workforce being housed in temporary wooden sheds, and by the middle of the century became the primary location for granite in the area. Apart from the initial clearing operations it did not consist of an extensive workforce, the principal exit route being a track which led to the Cove Road, a little to the west of the old Cove School, a portion of which is now asphalt and remains a right of way. As mentioned, an additional access route ran parallel to the railway, commencing at the south end of Loirston Road. During the last quarter of the 19th century the second of these huge holes was beginning to be developed, the former being all worked out by 1900. At the turn of the century there appears to have been a great demand for roadstone, as by 1923 this particular quarry had quadrupled in size, with operations by the Kettle inlet also expanded during this period. In 1902, however, John McAdam & Sons had gained the lease of the quarries at Hare Ness and the Cove. It may be that the passing of John Fyfe led to the lease being lost (or indeed surrendered), before the company regained it six years later, retaining it until 1952, when the quarries began to be utilised by Aberdeen City Council as a municipal rubbish dump.

By the late 1920's the quarries on both the Cove Farm lands and to the east of the railway were all but finished, though in their day the roads would have 'fair dirled' with horse and cart on their way to Aberdeen with paving stones; or indeed the line, from wagon after wagon heading south by rail. During the Second World War even the waste had a use, as foundation for the airstrip at Fourdon; and in 1974 the retaining walls of the crusher works themselves (some 200 yards along the old quarry road) were carted off as in-fill for the quay when Aberdeen Fish Market was undergoing extension. Remains of quarries may be seen both at the Hare Ness and either side of the railway, though only the tips of the numerous steel ventilation shafts are an indication of their two main locations, as if the land itself had never been disturbed.

The Coast Guard

The British Coast Guard was established just after the Napoleonic Wars for the purpose of preventing smuggling, under the heading of the Preventative Water Guard. When the Coast Guard Act of 1856 put this task under the direction of the admiralty it was reorganised to perform coast-watching and lifesaving duties, and became known as the Coast Guard. The Cove proved an ideal site for a station, being within striking distance from the port of Aberdeen. In 1820 the Scottish Customs Board met in Edinburgh to discuss the draft proposal of Watch House, Boat House and cottages, all of which were taken on a 38 year lease in September that year, the land being owned by John Menzies Esq. and Alexander Duthie Esq., respectively. The Watch House and cottages were constructed using local granite and had slated roofs, as opposed to being thatched; the Boat House at the harbour consisting of quarried portions from the rocks in the vicinity of the Crawpeel. The following year the buildings were inspected and the station became fully operational.

There were seven Coastguard cottages plus the Head Coastguard's cottage strung along Loirston Road — four to the east and four to the west, including that of the Head Coastguard (presently No. 15, 'Grahmor'), which is of larger dimensions and structurally differs. They were numbered from one to eight, beginning at the northern end of Loirston Road, with the odds to the west side and the evens to the east. The seven smaller cottages were rather distinct from the neighbouring crofts on the road owing to their gothic style windows, six of which may be seen today, as Nos. 9, 25, 31, 2, 8, and 16 Loirston Road. The other cottage being present-day No. 20, whose frontage was completely altered in the mid 1940's, and the walls raised to incorporate a second floor. In 1859, however, after the initial 38 year lease, it was proposed that one be taken out of commission and used to accommodate a civilian pensioner. There was the Flagstaff, too, located some seventy yards to the

A typical Coastguard cottage with gothic-style windows, as may seen on Loirston Road.

southwest of the Watch House, behind the old salmon fishers' bothy (presently No. 12 Colsea Road). This was essentially a semaphore station, and had a small, neat fence surrounding it, flags being hoisted to inform of the weather and other maritime business, or on special occasions such as remembrance days. A flag was last raised there on the wedding day of Mr. Albert Ross and the late Jane Ross of 2 Springhill Terrace, on 20 November 1945. Regrettably the Flagstaff fell prey to local vandalism, being cut down in 1960. Further to operational purposes a Flagstaff was also placed upon the Berryhillock.

'At Cove', 1861, by James Cassie. The Watch House stands like a sentinel over the harbour. The thatched roofs of Balmoral Place are seen to the left, while some men are stood by a boat. On the extreme right of the picture is the Flagstaff, which stood behind present-day No. 12 Colsea Road. In the foreground appears a croft by the cliffs, and may be for cosmetic purposes only, as at this time there is no indication of any construction to the east of the inn on the Ordinance Survey map of the area.

The duties of these men had little to do with the crofters and the fisher-folk of the village, and probable that the bulk of their work included weights and measures, along with the inspection of vessels arriving at Aberdeen. They were said to be methodical and tidy, both in appearance and the way they went about their business, as may well be expected from men with a naval background. A short-term posting was the order of the day, the men being frequently assigned to other locations, and unlikely that a man be posted to his own town or village. The personnel at the Cove came from places such as Portsmouth, Banff, Lerwick, and even Wales, to name but a few.

The old Coastguard Boat Shed by the harbour.

Unlike villages along the Buchan coast, the Cove wasn't noted for smuggling, and very little evidence supports any large-scale operations. There was, of course, the odd incident, as in July 1788 when a Cove boat fell prize to a customs vessel while making for the harbour, there being 49 ankers (a liquid measure of 6½ gallons) of spirits and two mats of tobacco found aboard. Moreover, there is a tidal hollow adjacent to the Poor Man rocks known as the Gin Cave, though unlikely used for smuggling purposes. Therefore it appears unreasonable as to why such a large contingent of personnel were initially employed at the Cove, though in 1874 two of the cottages were purchased by station member Captain G. Garner (besides another being privately rented), one of which he subsequently leased. The Boat House was of course essential to operations, at all times there being a boat in situ, or if repairs were in order then a replacement was immediately at hand. However, it too fell out of use when the station was relocated, and in 1925 became the property of Mr. J. Sellar & Sons, and used for storing salmon fishing equipment.

In 1860 the Board of Trade provided and funded both the rescue and life saving equipment, including the part time wages of local bodies of men known as the C.L.S.C., the Coast Life Saving Company, whose duties were assisting the Coastguards during rescue operations. In earlier times the rescue equipment was stored at the hotel, until construction of the Rocket Apparatus House in September 1867, whereat the adjacent Coastguard cottage lost part of its garden, the tenant being a Mrs. Colville, whose husband was stationed at the Cove. When vacated in 1923, for several years it became a store for the rods and lines belonging to local fishermen, then later as a hall for various purposes, including that of war-time dances organised by local nurse Miss Robina Reid. In 1947 it became a chip shop and restaurant before being converted into private accommodation in 1955. Presently it is No. 7 Loirston Road. In 1892, though, and for sanitary purposes, Station Officer Mr. Alexander Boyd wished to erect a washing house for each of the five remaining cottages in service. However, both legal and financial technicalities between the Admiralty and Alexander Kilgour dictated otherwise.

By 1896 there were twenty men from the Cove involved in the C.L.S.C., there being on each quarter of the year a full exercise utilising the equipment, with a stipulation that at least one of these had to take place on a dark night! To ensure that the men were proficient the Board held competitions to see who could hurl the 'throwing cane' (a weighted stick with a rope attached) the furthest, the winner receiving a monetary prize. However, accidents at sea are not particular in regards to their location, and if the boat was unable to be launched from the harbour then the lifesaving equipment would be trundled to the scene in a cart or 'hurley'. This could prove a difficult operation, which in most cases meant having to negotiate drystane dykes, broom, whins and tangles of bramble in an effort to get a life-line aboard a stricken vessel. Many hours were spent in practice around the cliffs in the vicinity of the harbour, and if a distress signal went up, then most of the village would be on hand to observe or to help with the proceedings. If a fishing boat from Torry or Burnbanks was making heavy weather, it would be forced to put into the Cove and 'guided in', at which a Coastguard Officer would climb the Berryhillock in order to get a clear view of events, shouting directions when to come on as per wind and waves allowed, a process known as 'smaain awa'. By the mid 1870's, however, the foundation of the Boat House was being constantly undermined by the inrush of seawater during storms, albeit the construction of the main breakwater prevented any further damage.

Still, apart from the infrequent rescue operations, the life of a Coastguard rarely strayed from a daily routine where age-old methods applied. Communication, though, was greatly hastened in the August of 1893 when a telegraph line was constructed between the Coastguard Station at the Cove, the Cove Post Office by the Railway Bridge, and Girdleness Lighthouse. On seeing its advantage Alexander Kilgour wished for the line to be extended to the village, but given it was a private concern there was little chance of his request. The following year there arose more consternation. In May 1894 Station Officer Boyd complained to Mr. Kilgour that the fishermen were not leaving enough space on the beach for the lifeboat to be launched when required. It was then proposed that davits be constructed on the pier from which the boat could be launched directly into the harbour. This the admiralty was not prepared to do, as it would incur a great deal of expense, and in effect make redundant a structurally sound and fully operational Boat House.

By 1923 the Coastguards had left their cottages, with only the Watch House being occupied by Mr. George F. Tee, who was later to conduct operations when the trawler *Ulster* ran aground. A station had been established at Findon, albeit of a lesser capacity, consisting of three cottages only; the primary reason for departing the Cove being one of economics. After the end of the First World War the Royal Navy were being forced to cut costs, and on 1 April 1923 an Act of Parliament was

The single building dwelling of the Watch House in the 1930's. A large wooden shed is adjacent to the south face of the building. Inset: the Watch House today.

passed which took the Coastguards out of naval hands. Understandably they were reluctant to give over their land and property to an outside influence, therefore in certain places the need for relocation arose. Though less substantial than that of the Cove, the station at Findon was more an observational post, affording a more panoramic view of the seascape — from the Soutar Heads to the north, and as far south as the cliffs at Fowlsheugh, some twenty miles distant. In 1927 the Watch House, too, was vacated, the last station officer being Mr. Charles G. Davis. It was in turn occupied by several tenants before being purchased for private accommodation, becoming fully modernised and greatly extended in the early 1980's.

In 1959 Mr. Joe Mennie, 'Auld Joe' to his friends, retired after fifty years service as an L.S.A. (Life Saving Apparatus) man, and was honoured for his services. His career began with the Cove Bay C.L.S.C. in 1908, and when it disbanded he joined the Findon Company, from which he retired, aged 72 years. Mr. Mennie was reserved in regards to memories of his service, but among those he recalled were *Ulster* and *Kenilworth*. He also assisted at numerous cliff accidents in the vicinity, having an outstanding and unique record of never missing a drill. This part of operations was the Cliff Rescue Service, and staffed by local volunteers, the rescue equipment again being stored at the hotel. At the end of World War II gull's eggs were being actively pursued, more so by the youth of Aberdeen, with incidents at the cliffs becoming more frequent. If someone was reported as having fallen, or being stranded on the face of a cliff, then Mr. Mennie would be summoned and hasten to the scene, with volunteers from the Cove running to assist, leaving their everyday jobs at an instant. At the top of the cliffs a wicker basket was placed upon Mr. Mennie's head in order to prevent any injury from falling rocks, and a thick Manila rope wound about his body. He was then lowered down to the stricken individual, who most likely suffered from vertigo or panic and, once secured, a signal was given for both to be hauled to safety, there at times being more than a dozen men at the rope. Today, of course, Fast Rescue Craft, or indeed helicopters from further afield, have the capability of arriving on scene within minutes.

Boat Building

Besides the various methods of fishing, there was also the profession of boat building, which is first mentioned at the Cove in 1811, namely Robert Robertson, 'boat carpenter', who was again noted in the 1841 census records and described as a 'boat builder'. There is not, however, any location of a yard or premises given. On 30 November 1860 a lease was signed by Andrew Forbes for the construction of a boat shop on land belonging to the Inn Croft, then leased by Murdoch McLeod from proprietor George Falconer Muir. This took the form of a large wooden shed, situated opposite present-day Balmoral Terrace, and in the following year Andrew Forbes described as a 'master boat builder'. The boats were 'clinker built', where each plank or planks, overlapped the one below, giving rise to the 'clinking' sound they made on contact with the water, a technique developed in northern Europe and successfully used by the Vikings. They proved ideal for tidal harbours and rocky inlets, being easily manoeuvred and having manageable dimensions, ranging from around 15 to 25 ft. in length. As per custom a new boat built and launched at the Cove would have provided quite a ceremony, incurring much toasting to good catches, with perhaps a fiddler and a piper supplying music to accompany the well-wishing.

A sketch of the boat shop, c.1877.

At the death of his father 1869 it appears that Andrew Forbes did not wish to continue the business, and in January 1870 John Lewis — who was to rise to fame from his shipyard in Torry — was considering the lease of the boat shop, besides accommodation at No. 6 the Cove, recently vacated by merchant grocer Mrs. Barbara Craib. However, he described the house as being in a dilapidated condition, with much repairs to be done before he considered taking the lease, his address at the time being No. 262 George Street, Aberdeen. Thus done, the lease began on Whitsunday that year. In 1873 he relocated to the newly constructed No. 87 'Loirston Road', (present-day No. 15 Stoneyhill Terrace).

Workforce at Cordiner's boat shop, c.1885. The company founder Mr. James Cordiner is on the extreme left of the picture.

In December 1877 James Cordiner occupied 87 'Loirston Road' and took over the business of boat building in the Cove, moving into the old Endowed School on Main Street around 1880, and given a further lease the following year. However, the improvement to Balmoral Road in December that year included raising the bend opposite the boat shop, at which he was unable to manipulate any large vessels into the harbour until the road was lowered to its former level; smaller boats, though, were launched directly into the Crawpeel (where a specially deepened pool may be witnessed at low tide). He had also intimated to Alexander Kilgour that he was 'feeling the pinch like others', and at the time had an order for a large boat which, owing to the height of the road, could not be built inside the boat shop, therefore the work required to be done outside, even in the depth of winter.

The Cordiner family were deeply religious, at times preaching at the hotel of a Sunday evening; or, in the summer, held gatherings below the high retaining railway dyke at 'the danders'. In the summer of 1885 the boat shop is recorded as being 'shut up', albeit temporary, with an employee by the name of Mr. Carmichael undertaking the carpentry repairs of the village, and at the time residing at Balmoral Place. In the July of 1890 James Cordiner, owing to illness, was obliged to leave the Cove, being unable to regularly climb the brae from the boat shop to his house. He had lately been suffering rheumatism in his leg, at which he proposed to relocate to Torry, the boat shop being his property, costing £60 when he first took the lease of the ground, and remaining in good order throughout. He stated it would be advantageous for the fishers to have a boat builder in the village, and was prepared to sell the boat shop to Alexander Kilgour, or indeed any subsequent tenant. If no purchaser was forthcoming, he would then remove the boat shop to his new premises and advertise it in the local press.

Due to the trawler boom, however, and the harbour being insufficient for larger vessels, boat building in the Cove proved uneconomical and was no more, the boat shop ground being leased to Mr. John Valentine of the Cove Farm. What remains of this once important business is but a small portion of concrete slipway on which the boats were launched into the Crawpeel. Over the years the foreground became a dump for old building materials, and has since been levelled into a car park, affording panoramic views of the sea. As mentioned, there are rare herbs and insects here, the area being noted as a site of special scientific interest.

ST's PETER & ANDREW A153 (scale model)

Built at Cordiner's new premises by the River Dee in 1902, for 80 years this scale model yawl hung in the nave of St Peter's Church, Torry. It was given to St Peter's, Fraserburgh in 1983.

The letter 'A' is the registration letter for the Port of Aberdeen and number 153 the number of fish caught in the Miraculous Draught.

Length: 12 ft 9 in	Beam: 4 ft 2 in	Height of Main mast: 10 ft 10 in

John 21:1,11 King James version. Describing the Miraculous Draft of Fishes: *Simon Peter went up, and drew the net to land full of great fishes, a hundred and fifty and three: for all there were so many, yet was not the net broken.*

'The Stinker'

Towards the end of the 19th century there was little by way of occupation in the Cove other than being governed by wind, weather and tide. In the late 1840's the coming of the railway provided plentiful, albeit temporary employment, with only a handful of jobs when it became fully operational in 1850, and much the same may be said of the quarries. However, things were about to change.

In March 1894 the newly formed Aberdeen Fish Manure and Oil Company Ltd. opened a state-of-the-art factory at the edge of the cliffs on the north side of the Colsea Yawn, about a half a mile south of the Cove. The total cost of buildings, machinery, etc, amounted to £5,300, with a prospectus for the setting up of the factory explaining how much capital the company had, inclusive of 12,000 shares at £1 each; Alexander Kilgour being tempted to invest. The opening ceremony was conducted within the factory premises, with around one hundred persons attending and largely composed of businessmen from Aberdeen connected with the fishing industry. Food and drinks were provided by Mr. John Coutts, mine host at the Cove Hotel, where glasses were raised to the factory's success — which became locally known as 'the stinker'.

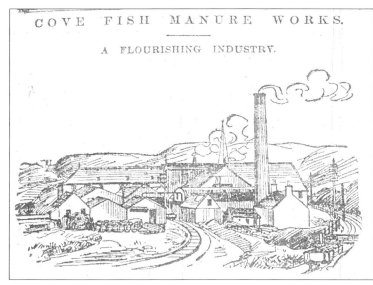

A sketch of the factory in 1904.

Reproduced by kind permission of Aberdeen Journals Ltd.

For quite some time the company had been scouring the countryside in order to secure a suitable location for the proposed premises, making journeys to similar factories in Hull and Grimsby, and taking note of the processing methods in place. Having purchased the necessary land from Mr. Kilgour, the works setting proved ideal, being geographically economic in the fact that Aberdeen was a major fishing port, offering an almost unlimited supply of fish offal. The factory itself was bright and spacious, with a concrete floor and ample drainage; a small donkey-house being constructed to supply power by way of wire rope traction for loading and offloading purposes. The premises had also the railway at its door, along with a siding which ran into the processing heart of the operations, providing a quick transportation route south.

There were four coal-fired boilers supplying steam, the coals arriving in wagons alongside the offal and second grade fish. At the height of the factory's operations 80 to 100 wagons of offal and coal could be seen being shunted through the Cove, at times slipping on the incline of the rails. Moreover, a special train was despatched from the fish market in Aberdeen to the factory works. The boilers were cleaned out every Sunday morning — 'murder' being the optimum word to describe the conditions within. It was estimated that 40 tons of raw material would be dealt with every day, the factory requiring copious quantities of water, and supplied by the Coldsea Burn, diverted to flow through the ground now occupied by the building. In addition, a powerful steam pump was installed to draw water directly from the sea some 200 feet below.

Two commodities were produced: guano, an excellent fertiliser; and oil, which was processed from fish livers and herring refuse. Wagon after wagon shunted into the work place, and the fish offal removed, in turn the wagons filled with outgoing first class fertiliser. Certain types of fish were too big for barrels, such as skate or squid, and had to be manually pitch-forked; others, like the sea perch, were prickly and poisonous, and on contact with the skin induced severe swelling on the hands and arms. The barrels were rolled out onto a concrete platform and emptied, the offal being placed in

Viewed from the west, the Aberdeen Fish Manure and Oil Company factory works, 1920's. In the background are the quarry buildings and the slope of 'the tip', where sundry waste and granite cuttings were thrown into the Kettle inlet.

large steam driers. White fish was cooked for seven hours in giant pans, each pan with a capacity for sixteen barrels of fish. A rather quirky part of operations was 'fishing out' hooks and other metal objects, where a man would stand above the steaming pans with rod, line and magnet! From the driers the manure — containing at least ten per cent of ammonia — was riddled, the bones being separated and sent to the 'devil', a powerful disintegrating or crushing machine, then subsequently remixed with other manure to form a compound of great agricultural value. Moreover, the spacious storage accommodation on the upper storey was at times severely crowded, there being bags of fertiliser piled one upon the other throughout the entire area.

Viewed from the east, the sheer scale of work operations at the factory is evident. The date is again from the 1920's.

A special department of operations was the manufacture of fish oil from the fish livers, which were forwarded in barrels, there being a cooperage connected to the factory to ensure that the barrels were kept in prime condition. The livers were placed in a steam tank, known as a liver kettle, in which they were first boiled then put into a steam pan and squeezed under hydraulic pressure. Oil being extracted from herring refuse in much the same way. Once the oil had been separated from the residue and vapours it was placed directly into a store tank, the said residue being mixed with guano. Nothing was wasted. There was a good market for this oil in regards to lubrication and many other purposes, one of the chief destinations being Rotterdam.

The handling of the finished products required little manpower due to ingenious methods of hatches, pulleys, engines, and an overall accessibility. By a special arrangement of pipes the gases were drawn off from the tanks and driers, then led through a spacious dam, thus reducing to a minimum of smell. The directors were aware of the pungent odour produced in the process of fish manure, and had 'adopted the latest scientific methods of destroying smell'. They also proposed that the prevalent westerly winds would blow it out to sea; or, if borne on an easterly wind, then any disagreeable smell would dissipate over agricultural land where there were very few houses. School records indicate otherwise, and on a few occasions refer to the rooms being unable to be ventilated because of the overpowering odour.

By 1904 the factory provided employment for 25 men, most being resident in the Cove. Although the nature of the work was unattractive, the industry itself was the means for bringing a good deal of money to the district — not to mention a steady wage. Indeed, the factory proved a profitable enterprise, with a market for its produce coming from many countries. Other companies such as the Aberdeen Commercial Company, the Aberdeen Lime Company and the Northern Agricultural Company, were using considerable amounts of guano for mixing purposes, compounding it with other materials and exporting enormous quantities to Kent for use in the hop fields, to the vineyards in France and to the beetroot farms in Germany. Moreover, America had developed a market for this type of manure, which could scarcely be satisfied. Owing to the great demand which existed, as well as for the purpose of preventing waste in the driers from cooling down, the machinery in the factory was kept going night and day. This also enabled an abundant supply of electric light to be generated, giving rise to the premises being brilliantly lit up at night.

Workers at the Aberdeen Fish Manure and Oil Company, April 1923.

In general, the process was a proverbial hive of industry, not only from men and machines — gulls flocked to this free for all, screeching, diving, and 'skittering' everywhere. Rats, too, abounded, a mongoose being kept within the factory in order to keep their numbers down. In addition the Cove residents had access to 'clinkers', or 'danders', a cinder-like residue from the coal-fired boilers, being utilised for drainage and filling in potholes in pathways and roads. Because of this practice the western end of Spark Terrace is locally known as 'the danders', and the road leading to the factory itself more or less consisted of them. A congealed hillock or two of these may still be seen today, located by the cliffs to the east of the site of the premises.

Mr. Charles Catto.

The success of the company was largely down to the rapid development of the fishing industry, especially that of trawling. Indeed, such was the prosperity that it was calculated at the turn of the century the value of fish landed at Aberdeen was around a million pounds per annum. The company expanded, too, and had for some time been anxious to secure an extensive water supply, especially for the drought in summer, the existing reservoir on the factory roof proving somewhat inadequate. In January 1909 the building of a huge retaining wall was completed, located 300 yards to the west of the factory on a natural basin between two hills, the construction under the supervision of Mr. Charles Catto, works manager, and gave employment to twenty men over a twelve month period. Some 5,000 tons of granite was used, with a capability of storing 100,000 tons of water. Underneath the foundation stone there is supposedly a steel casket containing newspaper clippings of the day, along with coins of denominations ranging from farthing to guinea. After the opening ceremony had been performed the directors added a finishing touch by adjourning to the Cove Hotel for a cake and wine banquet. The 'pond' or 'dam woody', as it came to be known, was later stocked with trout and required a permit to be fished; furthermore, at the northwest and southwest corners there remains the rusting metal stands of plaques which read 'No Fishing'. Presently the dam is structurally sound, though no water is retained, only the aforesaid Coldsea Burn, seeping through the marshy ground and sluiced out by means of a narrow channel.

The reservoir today.

On the death of Mr. Kilgour in 1921, the following year the company acquired the estate of South Loirston and the Lands of Cove, including commercial properties and housing, works manager Mr. Jock Catto taking up residence at Loirston House in 1923, though returning to Burnbutts Croft some four years later. At this time the company had over eighty employees, having relocated their offices from Commercial Road to No. 14 Bon Accord Square, Aberdeen, in turn becoming the Aberdeen Fish Meal Company Ltd. on 5 July 1928. Such prosperity was not to last, however, and after a downturn in demand for guano and oil the company went into voluntary liquidation on 15 July 1937, selling off its properties and assets.

Mr. John (Jock) Catto is centre right. First left is Mr. John Morrice, known as Jocky Brandy, next is District Nurse Miss Robina Reid. The others are not known. The photograph is c.1940.

The remaining portion of the Fish Meal Factory, viewed from the northeast across the Colsea Yawn.

Looking south. The flat roof was a small reservoir used for cooling and cleaning purposes. It is presently used as a store by current owner Mr. Robert Sutherland.

For 43 years the factory held sway, from the first works manager Mr. D. L. Crombie, to Mr. William Ritchie, the last, who lived at 'Grahmor' on Loirston Road. Though having fallen victim to demolition, part of the process works remained, being purchased by John Hector, salmon merchant, and used for storing the fishing equipment. In 1952 he leased it to Mr. James Adams, who utilised the premises both as a hen run and a piggery, and could be seen around the village collecting food refuse in his van. By 1980 'the piggery' lay empty before becoming the property of current owner Mr. Robert Sutherland. As evidenced today, this once thriving industry amounts to no more than a crumbling building, along with some partial walls and drains. Nevertheless, if the fish meal factory, or 'the stinker', is all but gone, and its rocky plateau now the domain of seagulls, something still lingers other than a smell, in the form of a parody, a song made famous (or infamous) by Aberdeen's Harry Gordon, that inimitable Aberdeen music hall entertainer. Many thanks to Mr. Callum Stewart at the Culter Heritage Society for reproducing the lyrics. 'A Song of Cove' was on the Beltona Label No. 1370 and written by Forbes Hazelwood.

A SONG OF COVE

Some may sing o Tennessee and some o Alabam'
But I've nae ees for places that ye canna get a dram,
They can keep their Salt Lake City and their Ohio
For gin I need a change o air — I ken the spot tae go,

Aye, take me back tae Cove,
Tak me back tae Cove
Far the air is as strong as can be,
For ye'll only need one guff
To feel ye've had enough
By the side o the silvery sea.

Some are keen on Banchory and others on Braemar
For they say the Westren air's the healthiest by far,
But that's fit maks me stick to my resort wi greater zest
For aye fin I gin sooth tae Cove I feel I'm aye gan west.

So, tak me back tae Cove,
Tak me back tae Cove
Far the air is as strong as can be,
Even if yer wife is dumb
in yon effluvium
By the side o the silvery sea.

Tak me back tae Cove,
Tak me back tae Cove
Far the air is as strong as can be,
A skunk that passed that way
Drapped doon deid o jealousy
By the side o the silvery sea.

Nae sae very lang ago I dreamt that I was deid
And Auld Nick cam tae meet me wi the horns upon his heid,
He says, "We've been expectin ye, jist come awa inside,"
But fin I saw my rooms I said, "If that's far I've tae bide..."

Oh, tak me back tae Cove,
Tak me back tae Cove
Far the air is as strong as can be,
Auld Nick says, "Please yersel,
But I couldna stand yon smell
By the side o the silvery sea."

Tak me back tae Cove,
Tak me back tae Cove
Far the air is as strong as can be,
Fin the folk oot there need cheese
They cut bitties aff the breeze
By the side o the silvery sea.

The Cove Bay Hotel

In the North-East during the latter half of the 18th century the selling of alcohol could best be described as a free for all. In October 1788, however, Ale Licenses had to be approved by the magistrates of Aberdeen, and those requesting a license were to attend the Town House on the 25th of the month, or face prosecution if they did not. This went some way to curtailing spirits being smuggled into the country, especially quantities of gin from Holland. At the turn of the century, though, there were eight or nine alehouses in the parish — and not all licensed at that!

The Cove Bay Hotel is a substantial construction compared to the houses in the village, and was previously a coaching inn, a staging post on the road between Aberdeen and county journeys southwards. The lower portion of the building was most likely constructed c.1823 by Alexander Duthie Esq., proprietor of the South Loirston estate, as the Kirk Session Minutes refer to his intended 'improvements to the town' (the Fishtown of Cove), which included the demolition of the existing school and the construction of what was to be the Endowed School on present-day Colsea Road. However, a letter written to Alexander Kilgour in 1880 refers to an inn being present some seventy years previously. It is probable that some form of ale house existed beforehand, albeit not in the present location; or, if so, had been demolished and replaced by the aforementioned masonry as seen today. After 1835 it was known by the name of the Muir-Arms' Inn, the proprietor then being Alexander Muir, though by 1850 referred to as the Cove Inn. As a coaching inn there was land attached, albeit at first a smallish area, where a field led down to the edge of the cliffs. It was bordered by the Langburn on the north, and to the south by a line of march stones continuing due east of present-day Spark Terrace, effectively dividing the estates of South Loirston and that of the Lands of Cove.

Of course, the inn was not only leased as a hostelry but also as an agricultural venture, which went by the name of Inn Croft and remained — in name at least — until 1929, and was in fact a part of the inn itself, the aforementioned fields being for crops such as turnips and barley. The modern flats alongside were formerly stables for the horses when the coach pulled in with passengers and mail. A few yards north of these was a large stone drain for the purpose of cleaning down the coach, the water in turn being sluiced down the Langburn. However, the Cove was off the beaten track in regards to Edinburgh and places farther south, and would have served on journeys more of a local purpose. When the railway arrived in 1850 the Royal Mail coaches fell quickly out of favour, and with the station less than a hundred yards away, travellers were afforded easier access to a dram! The stables, however, were still very much in operation, being used by gentlemen making visits to the inn by means of private horse and carriage, a practice still very much in place some twenty years later, as written by proprietor Dr. Alexander Kilgour: 'a good stable is much needed for gentlemen's horses, and a good shed and coach house to keep their vehicles from rain'.

Early tenant landlords were Mr. James Craib from c.1830, and Mr. Richard Maitland by 1851. On Whitsunday 1857 George Falconer Muir leased the Cove Inn, inclusive of houses, garden and 7½ acres of arable land, to Mr. Murdoch McLeod, the cost of the lease being £29 for the inn and £31 for the land, payable by two yearly instalments, namely Whitsunday and Martinmas. At that time the masonry of the inn was composed of a centre building with two lower wings, the accommodation comprising of kitchen, dining room and bedroom on the ground floor, with a passage leading to a large room and a hall (though not the present-day Smuggler's Cove) which formed the south wing. The kitchen had attached to it another kitchen built to the north gable of the house. Upstairs were two further rooms, two bedrooms, and a small room at the top of the stairs which coupled as parlour and bedroom. Thus there were five apartments to let, but of these both the rooms at the top of the stair and the bedrooms were somewhat compact.

In addition, two small attics were used as lumber rooms only. The premises, though, had a slated roof, as opposed to the thatch of the fisher-houses.

In July 1863 the Cove Inn became the property of Dr. Alexander Kilgour, with the land pertaining to the inn extended (the eastern portion of the Lands of Cove having been acquired from George Falconer Muir) and stretching from Balmoral Road to the old Station Master's house, though the field to the north of the Langburn was never recognised as belonging to the inn itself. The following year brought a noted event to the Cove, when in July 1864 one of Aberdeen's recognised Institutions, namely 'The Royal Salmon Dinner', was hosted by then innkeeper Mr. Murdoch McLeod, the occasion having been stated with regard to James Cassie's canvas entitled 'At Cove' (1861): 'if you choose to look out (from the inn) you have peeps of such fine sea effects as Cassie delights to put so beautifully upon canvas'. After extensive interior repairs, including plumbing work, carpentry and redecoration, along with improvement to the pavement, the Cove Inn was leased to Captain James Farquharson in 1865, who in addition ran the Post Office and shop some 50 yards down the road. The term was for seven years, though in his fifth year he drew up a Renunciation of Lease, and was in 1870 succeeded by Mr. John Leslie, for a yearly rent of £58. At the time of entry, though, Dr. Kilgour placed a clause regarding proposed extensive alterations, whereat Mr. Leslie and his family would be required to vacate the premises without warning. The Cove Inn was about to undergo massive renovation, with a sum in excess of £500 in regards to enlargement and improvement, Mr. Leslie being obliged to remove and relay the kitchen floor with wooden sleepers. By the close of 1870 the work had begun, though extension and upgrade to the stables had been completed in October that year. At this time an indication of the cost of living may be had in the form of a bill presented by innkeeper Leslie to Dr. Kilgour, for lodgings provided while a workman repaired the houses in the village, amounting to six nights at a cost of 1s. per night and nineteen meals at 9d. each, making for a grand total of £1 and 3d.

Cove Bay Hotel, c. 1910's, from a postcard series of the village, possibly by Valentine's of Dundee. On the right are the original fisher-houses, now present-day Colsea Square. It was in 1899 that then tenant landlord Mr. David Haig installed gas lighting, as supplied by the Bon Accord Gas Co. in Aberdeen, the rooms having previously been illuminated by means of a paraffin lamp, the fuel being stored in an outhouse to the rear of the hotel.
Note. Three corners of the photograph are missing.

Dr. Kilgour had wished to 'smarten things up' and make the Cove Inn more fashionable, including more rooms in order to accommodate parties requesting overnight accommodation. The wings were raised to correspond with the centre building and the attics made into spacious bedrooms, in effect giving the property three separate floors. A staircase was to be added in the centre of the house leading to the attics, and among other sundry alterations was a room constructed for the innkeeper and his family. However, no additions were to be made to the rear of the building, which would restrict the view to the sea. The garden walls were rebuilt further to the east, enlarging the area, and the entrance pavement made up of pebbles set in concrete. Dr. Kilgour instructed the exterior be given much character and style, though at a moderate cost, hence the uniform blocks of local granite composing the entire frontage of the hotel today. As opposed to that of the surrounding houses the masonry is of a superior quality, albeit the rear walls composed from mostly rubble. Thus the outside appearance as present, excepting the aforesaid Smuggler's Cove, and initially the dance hall.

However, the selling of alcohol is not without incident, and in 1874 there was stiff resistance to the 'demon drink' from much of the parish teetotallers, as this document suggests.

GENERAL RULES
(Excerpt)

I.   The Society shall be designated "THE COVE TEMPERANCE SOCIETY."

II   The object of the Society shall be to discountenance and suppress drunkenness, and all degrees of intemperance in drinking, and also to be a mutual *moral* benefit.

III   The means to be employed shall be holding Weekly Meetings, or, as often as expedient, delivery of Lectures, circulating Temperance Literature, and adopting such other plans as may be deemed most effectual for enlightening the people in regard to the nature and injurious effects of Alcoholic Liquors, when used as beverages and luxuries...

IX   If any member of the Society his or her promise, or obligation, a fine of Two and Sixpence will be imposed for the first infringement, Five Shillings for the second, and Seven and Sixpence for the third; and afterwards their names shall be erased from the roll.

With the interim of the lease pertaining to John Leslie removed, the aforementioned Richard Hallglen became innkeeper on 1 September 1876, and soon after the premises known as the Cove Hotel. Though fully licensed, trouble was not far away. In 1880 a letter of concern had been written by the Chief Constable in Stonehaven regarding the number of current hotel licenses in the district, wishing to remove the Cove Hotel License and restrict it to that of a Public House. It appears that the hotel itself, or indeed the landlord, was not in question, but rather the trouble that followed due to the drunken behaviour of those heading home on the road to Aberdeen on Sundays. It was stated that parties proceeded to the hotel in an orderly manner but returned quarrelsome and fighting, using the most foul oaths, which very much disturbed the residents of Nigg; one of the more descriptive being 'swaggering Aberdeenwards'. Of course, Alexander Kilgour had strong objections and defended its character stoutly, a petition being raised opposing the withdrawal of the Hotel License, with around 140 names from the Cove and surrounding area. Points of issue being that the only other hotel between Aberdeen and Stonehaven was over eight miles away in Muchalls; that the Cove in the summer months had over one thousand visitors from Aberdeen in the course of a week, the hotel being used by many for food and refreshments; that the hotel was frequented by farmers and others in the surrounding district for the purpose of holding public dinners and social meetings, there being no other place in the vicinity; that on occasions of storms, as had happened recently, the hotel was used during the night by travellers and fishermen for necessary food and refreshment; that the withdrawal of the Hotel License would be severely injurious regarding the interests of the village of Cove and the surrounding district, therefore a Public House License would be insufficient for the requirements of the place. All told, if the fishing and farming communities held socially apart, then the hotel brought them very much together! Nevertheless, after much campaigning and ballyhoo, the Sunday license was indeed revoked.

It appears that a Hotel License had been reinstated in the mid 1880's, though the Chief Constable held other ideas, and in the September of 1887 placed a watch on the premises on Sundays. What compounded matters was that drink was being bought and consumed from licensed grocer Mr. James Farquharson some yards down the road, at which patrons were entering the hotel already intoxicated, there having been trouble as such before. Therefore in April 1888, at a hearing at Stonehaven, it was stated that the privileges of selling drink to bona fide travellers on a Sunday had been greatly abused, and that 'batches of intoxicated young men had behaved in a lawless and indecent manner', who on many occasions had damaged property on their way back into Aberdeen. Furthermore, that the Cove was in no way convenient for travellers between Aberdeen and Stonehaven, being fully a mile from the main road, yet as many as 50 persons within the opening hour were believed to be entering the premises on Sundays, the hotel in turn being characterised as 'a crying nuisance to the county of Kincardine'. Support for the License came by alluding to the requirements of the district, and that the 71 objectors who signed a petition was but a mere fraction of the 1100 inhabitants of the parish. In addition, certain names included were unaware of its very existence! After some deliberation an application for the renewal of a Hotel License was refused, though once again the bench was in favour of granting that of a Public House.

Even in the face of strong appeal, and a petition signed by many notable gentlemen in Aberdeen (no doubt influenced by Alexander Kilgour) could the initial decision be swayed, which only served to further fuel the animosity between innkeeper Hallglen and Mr. Kilgour, the former demanding a rent reduction as the hotel was obliged to close on Sundays. Mr. Hallglen, it would appear, was given to deceit, and had in fact the tenancy of a public house elsewhere, which in effect caused a great deal of embarrassment to Mr. Kilgour, who wished to relieve him of his tenancy. As previously mentioned, it is no surprise that by the following year he had gone.

In the early 1890's further renovations were carried out, both internally and externally, including a striking drystane dyke with rounded coping, stretching 130 yards from the old Post Office bounds to the top of Balmoral Road, though giving way to the construction of the modern houses on Colsea Road in 1971. A large new sign reading Cove Hotel in block capital letters was erected above the entrance in 1894, remaining in place for many years to come. At this time innkeeper Coutts had personal letterheads reading, 'John Coutts, Proprietor, Cove'. It would appear that subsequent tenant landlords ran the business as a public house or hotel only, and discontinued that of an agricultural enterprise.

A Hotel License again came to the fore — albeit ironically — when in 1900 innkeeper Mr. David Haig, a former Chief Constable, stated that many people came to visit the Cove Hotel at the weekend, wishing to stay over the Sunday, but were unable to do so as there was no Sunday license. Alexander Kilgour was again in favour, being party to a recommendation signed by several gentlemen of high standing in Aberdeen, who had remarked that they would benefit from such a license. Even the Rev. Mutch, an Episcopal minister, gave his support. As ever, there was opposition, with a petition raised and signed by 152 out of 250 parishioners. The objections, it may be said, contained both hyperbole and déjà vu: 'the license was desired simply in order to induce people to come out to the place to drink; and that instead of only one policeman, they would require to provide ten or fourteen, when ten, twenty, or thirty thousand people rushed across the border from Aberdeen to be supplied with strong drink.' Serious stuff! Mr. Haig was denied his license, but could provide light refreshments on Sunday, such as tea, coffee and milk, on the understanding there would be no 'suspicious dealing'.

COVE BAY HOTEL, 4 MILES FROM ABERDEEN, IS FAMED FOR SALMON AND OTHER FISH TEAS. MAGNIFICENT SEA VIEW. BOATING AND FISHING. PICNIC PARTIES CATERED FOR. SUITABLE FIELD, HALL, ETC. CHARGES MODERATE   **L.S. ADAMS, LESSEE.**

Advertisement, June 1903. Reproduced by kind permission of Aberdeen Journals Ltd.

The above indicates 'Cove Bay Hotel', as opposed to 'Cove Hotel', which would suggest that the addition (as the village then was known) occurred on the lease of Mr. Lewis Adams. An opportunity for increasing trade was by way of entertainment, and around 1903 a dance hall was added to the main part of the building (presently Smuggler's Cove), though no access gained from the hotel itself, there being a separate door some yards to the south. Though the masonry is somewhat inferior, the dance hall had a sturdy wooden floor with seating arranged around its perimeter. Founded prior to the First World War the Cove String Band became regular entertainers, the players being Helen Henderson and Charlie Sangster on the fiddles, with Harvey Sangster on piano. Of course, an audience could be drawn from elsewhere than the Cove, the railway station being but a few yards away. In due course a Hotel License was restored, the hall becoming popular for local club dances, weddings, meetings, etc.

The first private ownership of the hotel (other than the proprietor of the estate) was acquired in 1939 by Mrs. Ruby Spark from the liquidation of the Aberdeen Fish Meal Company, including the portion of ground containing present-day Colsea Square. She served for thirteen years as the Representative for Nigg and District on Kincardine County Council, and was responsible for many improvements in the area, having also worked for numerous public bodies, including the Royal Workshop for the Blind. She died in 1966.

The old bar, c. 1955. Mrs. Ruby Spark pours a beer as Mr. George Wood and Mr. Joe Mennie look on.

Mine Hosts the Prestons in the new lounge bar, 1973.

At this time the adjoining house was known as 'Chequers', so named after Winston Churchill's country retreat in Buckinghamshire, and may have been built at the same time as the inn, if not before. In 1973 the old hostelry was given a new look, courtesy of Mr. and Mrs. Raymond Preston. After building an extension to the bar four years previously, the old counter was replaced and arranged in order to present back-to-back serving facilities, the lounge becoming the lounge bar. The woodwork was ash and teak, with Mrs. Preston's collection of glasses from all over the world taking pride of place in the public bar. The old beer pumps were retained for ornamental purpose, along with a ship's plate and lamp, while the seating was completely rearranged in order that the patrons may look out of the huge bay windows and enjoy a panoramic view of the sea. The dance hall was named the Crawpeel Lounge, inclusive of a serving bar and live music at the weekends. As a result of the extensive renovations, customers had for the first time entry to the dance hall by way of a corridor leading from the lounge bar, including access to the hotel from the car park at the rear. At this time the hotel had an unusual mascot in the form of a three-legged terrier called Patch, belonging to Mr. and Mrs. Preston's son Andrew. Patch had the misfortune to have been hit by a train, and was carried home in the arms of her master. After extensive treatment miraculously she survived, hopping around the premises and subject to second glances, from which one less leg may have been put down to one too many!

To the east of the premises the land had all but gone, the greater part being purchased by Mr. Alexander Strachan of the Cove Farm, with the remainder going to Cove Bay Nurseries. The former stables and the entrance car park were sold in the early 1990's, leaving only the means to an access and car parking facilities at the rear. History has proven, though, that the hotel not only served beer, wine and spirits, but in addition provided a meeting place for issues that concerned the welfare of the village, being a focal point for the locals to have a pint and a blether, going some way to strengthening the character within the community. In the ensuing years various forms of entertainment was provided at weekends, including live bands, big screen football matches and discos. More recently its monopoly has been lost, and a drink may be had at the Cove Rangers Social Club, which opened in August 1984, or the Snooty Fox in 1985, re-named The Langdykes in 1998. Today it is teeming with 'new' Cove faces, specialising in lunches and dinners, with a reputation for serving high quality fare. In itself this may be construed as a fitting tribute, for until the mid 1990's there was fixed a light blue wooden plaque above the main entrance, adorned with a crest, two mermaids and 'messis ab alto' — food from the sea, which was precisely what the fishing yielded to the village.

Mine Hosts over the years being as follows: c.1811 — c.1830 unknown; c.1830 — 1840 (Muir-Arms' Inn, 1835) Mr. James Craib; 1840 — c.1846 Mrs. Barbara Craib; c.1846 (the Cove Inn) Mr. Richard Maitland; 1857 Mr. Murdoch McLeod; 1865 Capt. James Farquharson; 1870 Mr. John Leslie; 1876 (the Cove Hotel c.1878) Mr. Richard Hallglen; 1889 Mr. John Coutts; 1894 Mr. Alex McDonald; 1898 Mr. David Haig; 1902 (Cove Bay Hotel) Mr. Lewis Adams, 1904 Mrs. Margaret Stewart Adams; 1924 Mr. William and Mabel Cooper; 1929 Mr. John Cowie; 1930 Mr. T.C. Bisset; 1936 Mrs. Ruby Spark (proprietor in 1939); 1962 Mr. Raymond and Helen Preston (c/o Mrs. Janet 'Jenny' Patterson, deceased 1973); 1975 Mr. William and Edith Dewar; 1978 Mr. Jack and Elizabeth Pillow; 1984 Mr. Hamish and Helen McCallum; 1990 Mr. Hugh Thom; 1994 Mr. Alistair Gray; 1995 — 2008 Mr. George Clark & Partners.

The 'Shoppies'

There appears no record of a shop or 'shoppie' in the Cove before 1840, though in a document dated 1852 there is mention of a feu being granted around this time by John Menzies Esq. in regards to a commercial premises. Goods may have been obtained from the inn, but for the most part food, and every day essentials, would have been 'home grown'. The census records of 1851, however, indicate there were two in operation: grocer and spirit dealer Mr. Charles Milne, located a few yards south of the inn, and No. 6 the Cove, a terraced house on present-day Colsea Road, run by widow Mrs. Barbara Craib. It is possible that Mrs. Craib set up in business c.1846, resigning her lease of the inn (Richard Maitland taking over). As mentioned, her husband had also been tenant landlord there, with son George Craib described as a butler, which suggests he was employed at Loirston House. Both of these shops were tenancies, the properties belonging to George Falconer Muir. A reason, perhaps, for the presence of two shops, may be the coming of the railway, which provided a much needed transportation link, along with a means of delivering goods for commerce.

Henderson's shop, c.1950

In 1854 Captain James Farquharson took over the premises from Mrs. Agnes Milne, an indication of the death of her husband Charles. In 1862 another shop appears — albeit briefly — at No. 77 the Cove (present-day No.4 Loirston Road), the tenant being Murdoch McLeod. At this time it would appear that being keeper of a shop and inn appeared to go hand in hand. Sadly, Captain Farquharson's wife Jane died in 1869, aged 26 years, his sister Penelope, or 'Peenie', helping him run the business until 1889, when Mr. David and Christian Henderson took on the tenancy. In turn their son David became proprietor in 1921, leaving his parents to look after the premises. Mr. Colin Simpson, a relative, described how it was the order of the day to see groceries being trundled from the Cove Station to the shop in a barrow. In 1930 daughters Mary and Cathy ran the family business, including the Post Office franchise, until its closure in 1972. The shop had been in the family for 83 years, the building being converted into flatted accommodation in 1984.

In addition Mary and Cathy Henderson owned two other 'shops'. The first being a wooden shed with a drop leaf serving hatch, located a few yards south of present-day No. 25 Loirston Road. It was erected in 1936 and owned by Mr. Hugh Milne of No. 10 the Cove, and in the following year by Mr. Andrew Milne, an engineer, of Tullos House, Nigg. The shop lay vacant for a couple of years until 1940 when Mary and Cathy became proprietors, selling cigarettes, confectionery and various small household items, a number of their customers coming

The small wooden shed located at the harbour, which during the summer months was a rudimentary shop.

from the newly constructed Catto Crescent. This was soon replaced by a large green hut with a walk in facility and serving counter, again selling stationery and general groceries. The original small wooden shed was relocated to the harbour some yards from the breakwater, opening for business during weekends of the summer months only. On occasion it could be found afloat during stormy weather! It proved none too successful, though, being acquired by local builder Mr. Fred Cargill Sr., and used as a petrol store during the war years. The large green hut on Loirston Road ceased trading in 1966.

From 1959 to 1963 there existed the 'Braeheid Shoppie', owned by Aberdeen man Mr. Alexander McKay of Spa Street, and managed by local woman Mrs. Gertie Simondson. It was situated between Stonecraft Fireplaces on Balmoral Road and the footpath to the harbour, opening at weekends and holidays only, selling confectionery, soft drinks, tea and sandwiches. No more than a ramshackle wooden construction, it fell into much disrepair, being recorded as uninhabitable by 1966 and the property of a Mr. Bowden of Midlothian. It was eventually demolished in 1969.

Loirston Stores in the mid 1950's. Inset as seen today.

With Catto Crescent already established and the construction of Sinclair Crescent in 1948/9, there appeared the opportunity to provide an outlet for trade to a swelling population. Loirston Stores opened for business in 1950, owned by Anthony Marcello, known as 'Tony' to his customers. The shop proved extremely popular and did a brisk trade, boosted by the house building programme during the 1960's. It served those in the vicinity well, providing cold meats, confectionary, groceries and a paper delivery service, besides having Christmas and firework clubs for the youngsters. It briefly held the Post Office franchise in 1970, and was, like other shops in such-like villages, known as a 'Johnny a'thing'. The shop became vacant in 2001 and was subsequently demolished, being developed into flats by Grampian Housing in 2005.

Previous owners: 1950 — 1953 Mr. Anthony 'Tony' Marcello; 1953 — 1954 Mrs. Isabel Anderson; 1954 — 1958 Mr. William J. Shand; 1958 — 1971 Mr. and Mrs. John Thompson; 1971 — 1972 Mr. and Mrs. Brian Macdonald Kerr; 1972 — 1978 Mr. James and Yvonne Jack; 1978 — 1984 Mr. Douglas and Sylvia Sharp; 1984 — 1990 Wia (Willie) Nang Lam; 1990 — 1991 Mr. James A. Davidson; 1991 — 1995 Mr. Joseph W. Ellis; 1995 — 2001 Mr. Brian and Marilyn Samshor (then known as Anna Marie's).

Posties is a much frequented shop, present owner Mr. Terry Kennedy proving a popular figure among his customers. It was completed in April 1869, after having been financed in stages by Dr. Alexander Kilgour as the work progressed, incorporating cellars and an attached living quarters known as Railway Cottage. At the time of construction his intention was to license the shop to sell liquor, at which Captain Farquharson (who already held a liquor license) wrote to him outlining that it would not be recommended to do so, as the new shop was on the road to the hotel, therefore prove detrimental to each of their trades. Dr. Kilgour in his wisdom took heed of this advice. The first tenant shopkeeper was Mrs. Helen Begg, previously assistant to Mrs. Barbara Craib at No. 6 the Cove, commencing on 4 June 1869, the lease being for nine years, though Mrs. Begg had indicated she wished to retire within the term of the lease, and that the tenancy be given over to a Mr. John Currie, which was agreed by proprietor Dr. Kilgour. Mr. Currie's time as shopkeeper was somewhat brief, for in 1878 Mr. Robert Thomson is recorded as being tenant. In 1889 the Post Office operated from here, though in December that year Mr. Thomson requested a rent reduction from Alexander Kilgour owing to a decrease in the population of the village, which in turn had a serious effect on his business. It seems rather odd, then, that in March 1892 a Mrs. Beattie wished to open a shop on Seaview Terrace, her husband being a quarry worker. Mr. Kilgour, however, was having none of it.

The location by the Railway Bridge has proved ideal, serving both the old village and the housing to the west of Loirston Road. It became licensed to sell alcohol in 1915, and during the 1950's and 60's had outdoor facilities, such as a petrol pump and a chewing gum machine — on which an excessive thump of the fist could dislodge a packet or two! In 1970 then proprietor Mr. John Leven feared the worst when the quarry holes a few hundred yards away were being in-filled with top soil after having served as a municipal rubbish dump for the past eighteen years. On displacement from their lairs it was thought that a plague of rats would invade the area, and a number scurry into the shop. Fortunately this did not materialise, although contaminated water seeped into the drains in the village. Having held the Post Office franchise since 1971 Posties continues to flourish, trading for almost 140 years, bearing witness to three centuries and many changes, but with a thriving community and well-stocked shelves, business may be described as 'pretty steady'.

Mathieson's Shop by the Railway Bridge, looking north up Loirston Road. The house on the right was demolished to make way for the bus stop. The date is believed to be the early 1940's. Inset: Posties as seen today.

Shopkeepers over the years: 1869 — 1877 Mrs. Helen Begg; 1877 — 1878 Mr. John Currie; 1878 — 1903 Mr. Robert Thomson; 1903 — 1915 Mr. John Mowatt; 1915 — 1930 Mr. William K. Mowatt (licensed); 1930 — 1950 Mr. William Mathieson (proprietor in 1939); 1950 — 1967 Mrs. Agnes W. Mathieson (widow); 1967 — 1974 Mr. John Leven; 1974 — 1979 Mr. Thomas A. Mennie; 1979 — 1982 Mr. Harold & Margaret Darcey; 1982 — 1988 Mrs. Marie Morrison; 1988 and presently Mr. Terry Kennedy.

Cove Bay Nurseries

Mr. Jimmy Penny with his father in the foreground, setting up their stall at the Green, 1955. Cove Bay Nurseries continue to trade there today.

The Penny family have been selling flowers, shrubs and vegetables at the Green since 1947. Mr. Jimmy Penny left school two years previously at the age of fourteen, finding work in the Cove as a market gardener with Mr. John Ellis in the grounds of Loirston House. During the winter of 1946/7 it snowed for 54 days, blotting out Langdykes Road, at which work became rather scarce. He was advised to seek out other employment, at which his father introduced him to the owner of Cherrybank Nurseries in the Hardgate. However, Jimmy's fledgling career almost came to an abrupt end, the owner having looked askance at his 15 years, remarking that he wanted, "A man, nae a loon!" He was, of course, persuaded to give Jimmy a trial, and the rest, as it happens, is history.

Cove Bay Nurseries began with an acre of ground behind the hotel when Jimmy and his father (who retired as a joiner due to ill health) built cold frames and greenhouses, applying to the Town House for a license to sell their produce at the Green. They in turn rented part of the old stables adjacent to the Cove Bay Hotel, which for many years was used for storing crates and bottles. Here they stored cut flowers, keeping their dahlias and seed potatoes in the cellar beneath the dance hall of the hotel itself. His parents stayed at No. 37 the Cove (present-day No. 7 Hasman Terrace), and when first married Jimmy and wife Mary stayed at the 'red houses', situated at Peterseat in Altens, where he adapted a windmill to power the electric in their tumbledown house — including a nine-inch television set! They later moved to council property in Fittick Place, and as the business expanded built 'Langburn' in 1968, where they still reside today.

Mr. Jimmy Penny Sr., c.1949, at the east entrance to the former stables belonging of the Cove Bay Hotel.

Son David now runs the family business, and has done so since 1996. He, too, has built a house on what is now 10 acres of land, in turn his son Ian showing a keen interest in affairs. Jimmy described this way of life as being peaceful, natural, and of course... down to earth.

Stonecraft Fireplaces

Beneath a surface of concrete lies a small cobblestone square which has been in existence from at least the mid 19th century. As noted beforehand, here Alexander Kilgour employed a handyman for carrying out repairs to the housing stock in the village, including a joiner's workshop, a communal midden, and the village privies. During the 1950's it became a chicken run, followed by a wood preservation store from which the powerful smell of creosote pervaded the village.

1965, and Mr. David Steven enters Cove harbour with his yawl laden with baskets of sea-washed stones, ready to be shaped into fireplaces.

Mr. Fred Cargill Jr. acquired the premises in 1962, and began to manufacture fireplaces with an initial staff of five after being inspired by the colourful stones that lay on the beach at the Burn of Diney, about 1½ miles south of the Cove. Moreover, it's a bit 'Crazy' how the business came about. He said that he drew his inspiration from that old Patsy Cline favourite — not so much the song, rather the striking backdrop of a floor to ceiling chimney breast clad with rounded stones! He began to export fireplaces with sea-washed faces the length and breadth of Britain, incorporating large chunks of mica schist and sandstone for added effect, which were split and

Mr. Fred Cargill cuts a large piece of mica schist, 1972.

rounded into an attractive finish by the friction of sand and grit in a pan mill. The fireplaces were built to specification, each being made with a particular type of stone, such as limestone, quartzite, sandstone, etc, brought to his yard and fashioned into custom-built fireplaces, which at times involved trips to Buckie and Keith in order to quarry the raw material. During the 1970's the snow-white Skye marble was in great demand, the mantelpiece and hearth being mostly constructed from polished Westmoreland slate or riven-faced Caithness flagstones.

The late Mr. Willie Westland, 1972.

When the government introduced smokeless zones it was never a concern that the end was nigh for the building of fireplaces — interior tastes had began to change, and wooden mantles with marble inserts proved popular in the modern living room. Today most of the work is indeed of a polished marble design, and since 1999 Mr. Cargill's son Ewen has been managing the day to day affairs of the business, though old habits die hard and Mr. Cargill still 'tinkers' a couple of days a week. For almost as long as the Stonecraft has been in existence Mr. Cargill has been aided by Mr. David Steven, who retired last year. The flowers and neatly kept garden were for some years tended by the late Mr. Willie Westland, a retired railway worker.

Further Sundries

From late 18th to the mid 19th century professions that were not directly related to land or sea were mostly one-man operations, such as in 1840 when James Angus was a barber and Charles Couper a shoemaker. Ten years later William Allan inherited this profession, in turn his son John carrying on the family business from Burnbutts Croft in 1870. In 1850 Agnes Catto was a lace knitter, Mary Leiper a spinner of twine. There is little doubt that diverse occupations existed in the Cove at this time, which, before the coming of the railway, held a rather insular status, being more or less self-sufficient regarding everyday necessities. The railway, of course, opened up a fast and efficient commuter service in and out of Aberdeen, and with means of an access to such a population density it would therefore have an impact on any local businesses.

The Aberdeen Fish Meal Company Ltd. was the last employer of any real consequence, and by the late 1920's the people of the village began to look elsewhere for employment opportunities. From the early 1930's to 1940, Mr. James Valentine and another man, locally known as 'Troupie', ran their joinery business from a large wooden shed. It was located by present-day Nos. 5 and 7 Spark Terrace, then known as 'the Den'. After the Second World War opportunities arose, and in 1945 restaurateur Mr. Thomas Angus sold chips from a shed outside of No. 77, which the following year became the property of Mr. Jonathan Manson. As noted, this particular address in the Cove has proved somewhat significant, both by way of occupants and its position within the village itself. By 1947 the chip shop had relocated to the old Rocket Apparatus House across the road, Mr. Fred McDonald taking over in 1951, at which a 'local loon' suggested that the chips were fried in whale oil! By 1953 the restaurant had closed and was turned into private accommodation, becoming No. 7 Loirston Road. The school, too, provided additional employment for three cooks and a janitor on the construction of the kitchen in 1945; so, too, the old library located some yards away, erected as a 'temporary' means in 1973 before moving to its present location in 2005.

Situated by the Horseshoe Bridge at the extreme edge of the parish boundary was the melting plant of Mowatt's Pioneer Iron Grit Company Ltd. — 'the gritter', constructed in 1951, the head office being at 15 Holland Street, Aberdeen. Here crushed cars and all forms of scrap metal were picked up by means of a crane with an electric magnet attachment, then dropped into the furnace to be made into various sizes of grit for shot blasting purposes. Though it did not offer extensive employment for men of the village, for the most part the work was regular. The premises was vacated by 1984 and acquired by David Stewart Metals, before being demolished in 1996. An interesting footnote being that in the late 19th century the establishment of the company was very much encouraged by John Fyfe, who recognised the potential of iron grit as a means of abrasive in the process of cutting granite.

A taxi came into service in the 1950's, and continued until the early 1960's, operated by Mr. Matt Sutherland, the said vehicle being a large Buick. When not is service the taxi was garaged at the rear of Burnbutts Croft. Another business began in the 1970's, known as Cove Taxis, the operator being Mr. Charlie McDonald of No. 8 Loirston Road.

The late Mr. Fred Cargill Sr. set up a refractory business for repairing and renewing the brickwork in industrial heating boilers, having two full time employees. He branched into house building and redevelopment during the 1960's, including the modernisation of Nos. 1 to 5 Bunstane Terrace in 1966, constructing Nos. 25 to 47 Colsea Road and Balmoral Terrace down by the harbour. Latterly his store became the disused Mission Hall east of the railway, until its eventual demolition.

From the mid 1950's to early 1970's Mr. John Torrie supplied pink paraffin to the Cove and Aberdeen from a huge cylindrical tank, mounted on a lofty stand with a gravity feed. His premises were on the Cove Road, next to present-day Charleston Road, of which the house may still be seen on Charlestown Circle (spelling varies as per addresses), albeit fully modernised and absorbed into the surrounding development. Paraffin, then, was a cheap and plentiful supply for portable household stoves, before central heating became standard as today. Local men such as Mr. Bob Law, Mr. Billy Beattie, Mr. Norman Penny and Mr. Jimmy Kerr, established individual rounds in the suburbs of Aberdeen, competing against city drivers selling 'Esso Blue'. During winter weekends trade was more brisk, and assistance provided by a local teenager, who besides earning a small wage, received an abundance of gratuities from customers for carrying a gallon or two to their door, especially over the festive season. By the mid 1970's demand for paraffin was on the wane, and in 1976 Bruce Plant opened up a sand pit to the rear of where the tank was located, the land in turn being redeveloped for housing.

At No. 14 Loirston Road, formerly Station Croft, Mr. Ronnie Winram installed facilities for making window blinds in 1969, part of which was rented by Mr. Bob Dempster and turned into a joiner's workshop. Mr. Dempster relocated to the Cove Road in 1973, his premises replacing a large wooden hut belonging to the 12th Kincardineshire Boy Scout Group, which, having fallen into disrepair, was removed two years previously. In 1979 the premises became an auto spray and repair workshop, owned by Mr. Leonard Parker, followed by Mr. Derek Allan in 1989. Since 1996 it has operated as Cove Auto Centre. Further up road is the popular children's nursery Oranges and Lemons, which began as Braehead Nursery in 1992. In 1987 No. 14 Loirston Road was the premises for a veterinary surgery, before being developed into the present-day Henhouse Studio and Art Gallery.

Today there are sundry occupations pursued in the Cove, from dog roomer to nail technician, from driving instructor to gardener, besides, of course, computer repairs and website design — there is even a private detective agency!

The much maligned row of retail outlets which currently serve the Cove and Altens area. Currently there are plans being mooted for the provision of additional shops between Whitehills and the Loch of Loirston.

Chapter 7: Some Folk

The Last of a Kind

Isie Caie at Aberdeen Fish Market in 1958, heading back to her stance with the day's fish.

In both their everyday lives and special occasions, much has been lost to antiquity concerning persons local, therefore more recent events have taken precedence. Isabella Caie, known as Isie, was the last of the fishwives in the Cove, and one of the remaining few in the North-East area. Isie sold fish at Aberdeen Market and the Green for a number of years, being a 'weel kent' face to many, latterly collecting fish at Aberdeen Market and selling them on at the Green, there being no longer the option for her to supply fish directly from the Cove. On the whole it may be said that the fishwife had to sell her wares for the family to survive; unfortunately there were those who were only too aware of this, and would exploit these women in their attempts to make an honest living. Such individuals were known as the 'poor man's friend', who bought unsold fish from the fishwife at a nominal cost; or, if on occasion she had an abundance of partans, then a whole creel might fetch the price of a loaf! Isie also polished and cleaned the fittings and interior of St Mary's Church on Loirston Road. For most of her life she lived at No. 64 the Cove (diagonally opposite of Seaview Terrace), its gothic style windows similar to those of the coastguard cottages, moving to No. 51 in 1959 when her house became uninhabitable and subsequently demolished. Though small in stature she cut a distinctive appearance with her roomy apron and oblong wicker basket, both on the service bus into Aberdeen and trudging round the market seeking fish. On occasion she carried a spacious creel. Isie disliked her photograph being taken and discouraged inquisitive conversation. She had, though, many loyal customers, including in her own words several 'high quality ladies'. Having passed away in May 1966 at Arduthie Hospital, Stonehaven, she was buried in Nigg Churchyard, and may well have been described as a window to a bygone era.

A Happy New Year

Until the early 20th century Christmas Day was not so much celebrated on 25 December in the Cove and other fishing villages in Kincardine, rather 'Aul Eel' (Old Yule), which fell on 5 January. The fishermen went from house to house the length and breadth of the village, feasting on plain fare such as bannocks, oatcakes, fish, cheese and biscuits, complemented by liberal doses of drams! The wives, too, joined in the celebrations, as did the children, who for their efforts would be granted a glass of ginger ale. Everyone had to perform at least a song or a poem. On 31 December children of the Cove would go knocking on village doors during the course of the evening, reciting a poem in the local dialect. They went in pairs, or in groups of three or four, calling out how many stood upon the step awaiting a reward of sweets, fruit or a small amount of money, it being the custom for the housewife to refrain from opening the door until the recital was over, therefore presenting the appropriate number of 'goodies'. The concept was similar to that of the present-day 'trick or treat' at Halloween, and in no way particular to the Cove, being performed in several locations on the east coast of Scotland; in fact it was an old Edinburgh guising song. A similar poem was recited on Hogmanay morning in the Fraserburgh and Peterhead areas around 1900, with the closing couplet as follows:

"We sing for breid, we sing for breid,
We sing for aa your orra bawbies."

There is no definitive version due to regional variations, and over the years certain lines have been altered or deleted accordingly, with additional parts most likely having been lost. The same may be said of that of the Cove, where the tradition died out around 1970:

"Rise up guid wife an shak yer feathers,
Dinna think that we're beggars,
We're only wee bairnies cam oot tae play,
Rise up an gie's wir Hogmanay.

The day will come fan I'll be deid
An winna care for milk nor breid,
So tak the gully by the hand
An rin tae the meal stand.

Dinna cut it thick nor thin,
Gie's a piece an let's aa rin.

A coagie fu o brandy,
A coagie fu o beer,
We wish ye,
We bless ye,
A Happy New Year."

shak: shake, rouse.
gully: a large cutting or sawing knife.
coagie: a wooden container made of staves; a pail or bowl.

Footnote. No title exists, in living memory at least.

Dance Dance Dance!

In a bid to beat the British record of 54 hours non-stop dancing, at 6.30pm on Friday 7 February 1970, Cove Youth Club staged a marathon dance session in the pavilion belonging to Cove Thistle at Recreation Park, the title being held by a YMCA in Glasgow. Each of the eleven members taking part were sponsored, with over £200 raised to provide coal and groceries for the Cove pensioners. Initially the dance was to be held under floodlights on the football pitch, but icy winds dictated otherwise.

So off they went with a table-load of food and black coffee to keep them going, a record player and tape recorder churning out tune after tune, the first time anyone had ever attempted such a feat by dancing two-hour stints with half-hour breaks; the teams from Glasgow taking it in turns to rest. One by one the dancers dropped out, though at 1.30am on Monday morning they had done it, albeit only two of them remaining — Mary Still (17) and Derek Stirton (18) danced on until 3.30, breaking the previous record by a couple of hours. And how did the teenagers feel? Well, just tired!

Broadcasting from Home

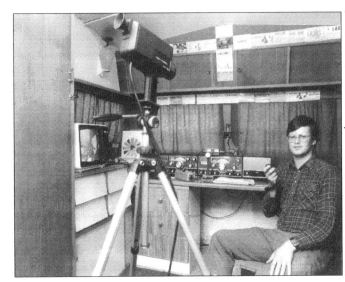

James with his equipment.

Reproduced by kind permission of Aberdeen Journals Ltd.

The Cove had another record, albeit in a different form, when in May 1982 the first successful sound and vision link was made between amateur television buffs in Scotland and Holland, thanks to the pioneering work of local man Mr. James Penny, then aged 26 years and founder of Cove Bay Television. Broadcasting House was a tiny caravan at the back of his father's nurseries, and the pictures were as clear — if not better — than the commercial television signal from the Durris transmitter. The fact that most didn't speak very good English was more than compensated when James was afforded several views of Amsterdam, his Dutch counterparts panning their cameras across the city from high-rise windows.

James, a chemist, had been a radio ham for three years before dabbling with amateur television broadcasts, having already managed to pick up Russian and eastern European television. His main problem was atmospherics, conditions being favourable once every couple of months or so, as signals travelled better over sea than on land. At the time he gave a demonstration of colour pictures with sound, beamed live from the country of... Northfield. James emigrated to Australia not long after, but intermittently pops across to visit his parents at the Cove.

James with 'Broadcasting House' in the background.

Reproduced by kind permission of Aberdeen Journals Ltd.

The War Years

During the first two years of the war several of the Cove womenfolk organised the village Spitfire Fund, which was part of a nationwide effort to raise money to build the now legendary fighter aircraft. For the purpose of donations, concerts were held in the dance hall of the Cove Bay Hotel, the school piano being commandeered for the activities; performances may be described as being delivered with gusto.

Mr. Jimmy Penny remembers the terrific explosions and smoke in the action that took place on 9 February 1940, some 2½ miles southeast of Girdleness, when two converted trawlers performing minesweeping duties were sunk by a German aircraft. In 1976 these wrecks were dived and thought to be *Fort Royal* and *Robert Bowen,* there being a twisted mass of aluminium fuselage on the stern of the former.

The Luftwaffe attempted to blow up parts of the railway in an effort to cut supplies in and out of Aberdeen, a bomb exploding by the side of the line to the south of the village of Burnbanks. The precise location is determined by a section of wooden fencing a few yards from the access bridge, the drystane dyke having never been rebuilt. The dimensions of the impact would suggest it was part of a cluster bomb. On another occasion a bomb exploded in the vicinity of the quarries to the west of the railway. Aimed at the mail train, it detonated around 3 o' clock of a morning, shaking the whole of the village, there being a strange smell, though not of gas. Local lad Joe Wood came back next day with a piece of metal from the bomb itself, to be told in no uncertain terms by his mother, "Dinna put that bliddy German thing on my dyke!" There was also witnessed a direct attack on the Cove, a German fighter pilot strafing the road to the south of the hotel.

At the southern edge of Whitehills was a raised platform on which a searchlight and machine gun post were positioned. Mrs. Rosemary Gray recalls that on occasion the Luftwaffe would make a low approach from the south, at which one of the soldiers stationed there would be heard to shout, "Fire! Fire!" to the gunner. And Mrs. Muriel Wood remembers convoys heading south from Aberdeen, under air attack, at which the bullets from the said machine gun post would whizz over the village and 'rattle the lums'.

Anti-tank blocks located to the east of Balmoral Terrace.

Gone but not Forgotten

Besides the weekend concert and dance, or any other organised activity, in the post war days folk had to provide their own entertainment. Of course, money was in short supply, and simple walks round the Loch of Loirston became a popular pastime on Sunday afternoons, with, perhaps, a visit to McHardie's shop by the Charleston Crossroads in order to buy some boiled sweets or lemonade. In 1950 there was outrage at the 'massive inflation', when the penny soda drinks were raised to tuppence!

As a means of acquiring 'a few bob', clandestine card schools on Sunday evenings were organised by the men and took place at Stotties Bridge, with a look-out posted to give warning if the local bobby had been tipped off and was seen to approach. In addition to supplementing their income a few grew their own vegetables, creating plots at the top of the cliffs in order to cultivate potatoes; evidence of these may be seen by the Kettle inlet, in the form of low turf embankments dug out for the purpose of enclosure.

A method of passing the time before the advent of television, and even when television became established, was for groups of mainly older men to gather at focal points in and around the village, such as 'the tip', overlooking the harbour and the old quarries, the drystane dyke outside the Post Office next to the hotel and at the Railway Bridge by Posties, where on the coping may be evidenced a smooth hollow from the sharpening of their pocket knives. And up until the mid 1960's local teenagers created their own diversion by conjuring up a hide and seek affair known as 'huntie', where the whole village and surrounding area became the boundary for two teams to catch each other by way of a short length or rope; the objective being for a 'victim' to be encircled, in turn becoming part of the chasing team. Indeed, due to there being little traffic various games were invented that could be practiced by utilising the road, inclusive of a quiet amble to the village of Burnbanks (at that time there being no pavement).

With the Cove now having two regular bus services, and most households having a car for access to the shops and supermarkets, those mobile traders from the mid 20th century have simply disappeared. Indeed, it used to be a thrill to hear the ice cream van make nightly and weekend visits to the village, with a few sharp blasts of the horn, or perhaps in the form of some musical chimes. The same applies to the baker's van, by way of Strathdee or Mitchell and Muil, where a 'fine piece' or a big cream bun was a weekly treat to savour. In the 1960's the Co-operative Society, or the Co-opie milk lorry, would make its way round the village, at which local lads would assist the driver and the 'milk quines' with their deliveries, receiving at times a free pint of milk or a few pence from the women themselves. Moreover, goodness knows what the Health and Safety Executive would have made of youngsters jumping on and off the back of a moving lorry! At this time, too, there existed the enormous form of the Co-operative Society's grocer van, a veritable supermarket on wheels, which again held stances throughout the village.

Regarding the above were occurrences which gave rise to some humour, as when the steam powered coal lorry made its way round the village during the late 40's and early 50's, known as 'the brookie pot', owing to its rather smoky chimney protruding from the front of the cab; or the rag man and his wife who did their rounds in a horse and cart, whereby a balloon or whistle would be given in exchange for a number of items of disused clothing, albeit their accompanied by a devious monkey who was apt to grab anything edible out of one's hand, or indeed as much as 'steal a piece from the mouth of a bairn'!

There was, of course, the potato holidays, or going to 'the tatties', when farmer Mr. William Simpson of Altens used to wait by Loirston Road to collect the squad in his tractor and bogey, the floor of the bogey being strewn with straw for a rudimentary comfort. The actual picking consisting of a complete drill being marked out by strides — and a day of back-breaking work. However, for the village children a wedding proved great entertainment, giving rise to a 'scramble', where handfuls of coins were dropped from vehicles conveying the bride and groom to church, at which a free for all ensued. With reference to a relic of the village itself is that the last known site of paraffin-fuelled street lighting was to the outside of No. 8 Loirston Road, in the form of a wooden post on which a metal frame was constructed and a wick contained within, though no longer in functional condition, and having disappeared by the mid 1950's.

On the following pages are pictures capturing the focus of the village in the mid 20th century:

Looking north up Colsea Road towards the hotel, c.1940. To the right is the once striking wall with its rounded coping — very much leaned on for rest and conversation — built by Alexander Kilgour in 1892, and stretching as far as Balmoral Road. A small portion of the above remains today.

Top. A saunter up Stoneyhill terrace. Bottom left. Two local children walking Bunstane Terrace. Bottom right. Looking east down Hasman Terrace. The date is 1955.

Reproduced by kind permission of Aberdeen Journals Ltd.

Left. Down the cobbled length of Craighill Terrace comes the late Mr. John Mutch with his next door neighbour, six years old Donald Hadden, collecting a hurl in his barrow, Right. Mr. John Leven, county councillor and Cove Bay's post-master, bringing home the milk, 1972.

Profile of the village from the southeast, 1965. In the foreground are present-day Nos. 11a and 15 Stoneyhill Terrace, the newer houses seen today are more than a decade away. The stepped to slope profile of Craighill Terrace is apparent in the background, complete with outhouses. On the far left is the gable-end of No. 6 Seaview Terrace. As mentioned on the page previous, the striking stone wall that ran from Henderson's Shop to Balmoral Road may be seen on the extreme right of the picture.

Aerial view of Burnbutts Croft on Loirston Road, 1967.

Aerial view of the Cove looking east, 1974.

Aerial view with Falkland Avenue in the foreground, 1986.

The Beautiful Game

When a small village in the mid 1950's the Cove could boast not one, but two amateur football teams: Cove Rangers and Cove Thistle. Cove Rangers were established around 1900, and for many years played their matches in a field behind the old school, on what is now Earnsheugh Circle. In 1922 they joined the Aberdeen Juvenile League and were technically 'founded'.

COVE RANGERS F. C. 1906.
Sat on the extreme left is Mr. Charles Catto, Works Manager at the Fishmeal Factory.
The name of the hotel lessee, Mr. Lewis Adams, is lettered above the doorway.

COVE RANGERS F. C. 1920

Back Row: A. Watt (Sec), J. Stephen, C. Stewart, G. Still (Capt), W. Thom, J. Westland,
H. Stephen, R, Cruickshank, Wm. Mowatt.
Second Row: P. Lamb (President), G. Valentine, Wm. Adams, G. Wood, Wm. Webster.
Front Row: A. Barclay, D. Fiddes, D. Tarbert, R. Wood, G. Westland.
Wm. Mowatt ran present-day Posties, and A. Barclay was the schoolmaster.

In 1928 the booming Aberdeen Fishmeal Company Ltd. donated a piece of land for the benefit of the people of the village, including Cove Rangers F.C. The ground was dug over and constructed into a football pitch, the trustee being then schoolmaster Mr. Alexander Smith, and known as Recreation Park. What is all but forgotten is that in the mid 19th century this was the eastern portion of four acres of land known as 'Fowlis Bank', most likely derived from Fowl's Bank, and the means of keeping poultry. Moreover, between the football pitch and the Rocket Apparatus House a large

The opening game at Allan Park, 1950

wooden pavilion was constructed, along with a tennis court and bowling green; most of the carpentry work being carried out by local man Mr. Charlie Sangster. Funding came by way of concerts in the Mission Hall, organised by shop owner Miss Mary Henderson. Interest in the tennis court fluctuated over the years, it eventually falling into neglect and disappearing by 1960. The pavilion was reconstructed into private accommodation in 1951, being demolished and rebuilt in 1982, in turn becoming the present-day Oranges and Lemons nursery.

COVE RANGERS F.C. 1923, the old school playground.

Back Row: J. Harrison, J. Westland, R. Wood, W. Lamb, G. Cheyne (*Secretary*)
Second Row: J. Harrison Jr., J. Guyan, A. Shaw, J. Silver, J. Morrice, R. Cruickshank
A. Smith, (*President*), A. Cowie (*Trainer*), J. Catto.
Front Row: C. Stewart, A. Turner, D. Tarbett (*Captain*), W. Guyan,
G. Westland (*Treasurer*), G. Stewart, J. Johnston.

Having purchased a piece of land in 1948 from local farmer Mr. William Allan, Cove Rangers F.C. shared the privileges of the field and pavilion until moving to their present location at Allan Park in 1950, becoming the first amateur football team in Aberdeen to acquire their own ground. The opening game was a challenge match against Culter F.C. — Mrs. Allan officially kicking off proceedings — a fixture which, over the years, provided many fine games, the two clubs becoming great rivals. At first the trappings were rather meagre, the changing rooms or 'sports pavilion' being no more than a rough wooden hut. This was superseded a few years later by a more substantial bricks and mortar construction. Cove Rangers became a formidable team, proving difficult to defeat on the compact Allan Park, winning many league championships and trophies. But as irony would have it, their crowning achievement was in fact a defeat. In the 1953/4 season they reached the final of the Scottish Amateur Cup, losing 0-1 to the Royal Technical College, the team captain being Mr. Kenny Campbell, originally from Dumbarton, who had married and settled in the Cove. There was a train load of supporters from the Cove that day, and legend has it that the village was half empty! Notable secretaries during the amateur era were Mr. John Thom and Mr. James Stewart.

The Cove Rangers Social Club was opened in August 1984 by Sir Alex Ferguson, then manager of Aberdeen F.C., and followed by a 'friendly' between Cove Rangers and Aberdeen — even then Fergie was livid at several decisions, and didn't take things lightly! This was another impressive achievement, becoming the first amateur football club in Aberdeen to own their own social club. In 1985 Cove Rangers left amateur football and joined the Junior ranks, winning the Second Division title in their first season. The following year they joined the Highland League, which they eventually won in the 2001/2 season. However, after playing the first ever Scottish Cup tie at Allan park, losing 1-2 to Cowdenbeath in season 1990/1, they missed out on a trip to Ibrox Park to take on the mighty Glasgow Rangers. Even though, their semi-professional standing makes for an impressive c.v., winning the Highland League Cup on three occasions, including a match against a star-studded Manchester United XI in 1992, which officially opened the Executive Lounge and the switching on of the floodlights. Their most recent achievement is winning the Highland League championship in the 2007/8 season.

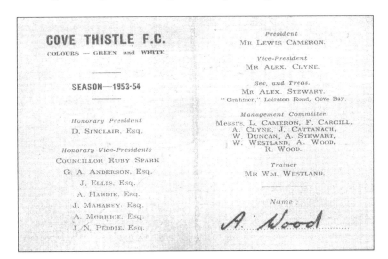 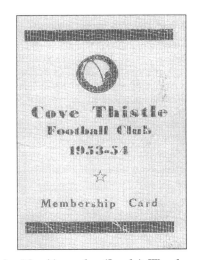

Cove Thistle Membership Card for the first full season, as signed by Mr. Alexander (Sandy) Wood. Some notable names appear, including Mr. David Sinclair, proprietor of North Loirston Estate, John Ellis of Loirston House and Councillor Ruby Spark, owner of the Cove Bay Hotel.

Though not as illustrious as their neighbours, Cove Thistle was founded in 1952, Cove Rangers having vacated Recreation Park. The primary reason for another football team in the village was that the latter began to overlook local talent in favour of introducing 'outsiders' from Aberdeen (which in itself was a measure of the ambition at the club). At this particular time Recreation Park was more like a building site, the trenches still in place where schoolchildren used to take precautionary shelter during the Second World War. In the post war years they had filled with water, having to be drained and levelled over with soil; local lads such as Willie Guyan and Tony Still, to name but two, set to task and, after no little effort, a playing surface was accomplished, complete with the famous Cove Road slope.

Cove Thistle at Recreation Park, 1954.

Kincardine County Council took over the ownership of Recreation Park in 1956, Cove Thistle acquiring a pavilion of their own, followed by a smaller store for equipment such as lime, flags, nets and assorted football accoutrements. The first secretary of the club was Mr. Alexander Stewart, followed by Mr. John Leven and Mr. Alexander (Sandy) Wood, who for many years was the mainstay of the team. Indeed, the supporting voice of Sandy carried far across the village during home games on a Saturday afternoon, with hollers such as "How'zee, ref!" ('How is he, ref', at which he meant an opposing player was in a position of being offside) or, "Haud yer tongues, lads", when tempers got frayed, in order to prevent his players from receiving a caution or getting booked for dissent. The Thistle couldn't boast the same success as the Rangers, but still won a number of trophies and honours. To say they were rivals may be classed as an understatement, for when these two met the local derby gave rise to many bookings, sending-offs, and heated arguments! Their surroundings, too, might not have been so plush, the 'grandstand' at Recreation Park consisting of a raised concrete platform known as the 'troch', with seating provided by a short supporting wall. Indeed, for many years a trough, or 'troch', was sited here, and up until the mid 1970's the Cove Farm cattle would drink from it on being herded from field to field.

Though Cove Thistle F.C. remain at Recreation Park — renamed Catto Park by Aberdeen City Council, after Charles and Jock Catto, former works managers at the Aberdeen Fish Meal Company, and officially opened by Mrs. Renee Parkinson, great granddaughter of the latter, on 8 Feb 1996 — the changing pavilion and store fell into disrepair and were demolished in 1981, the club having made arrangements to change in the Cove Bay Hotel. It presented quite a sight, not to mention sound, on witnessing both teams clomping up the road in their football boots and strips, heading towards the pitch! In the 1981/2 season Cove Thistle met Cove Rangers in the North of

Mr. John Leven, Mr. John Matthews and Mr. Alexander Wood at a trophy presentation dinner.

Scotland Amateur Cup, which the latter won by a goal to nil. A new management team was installed the following season, with Mr. Alan Braik holding the position as secretary until the year 2000. Purchased in 1986, the current pavilion is the old telephone exchange to the rear of Cove Auto Centre, for which the club received a grant of almost £14,000 from the National Lottery via the Scottish Sports Council in 1995 in order to upgrade the changing facilities and showers. The current secretary is Mr. Graeme MacPherson, their most recent success being winners of the North of Scotland Amateur Cup in season 2007/8.

Football, however, is not only confined to men, and Cove Primary School may also lay claim to a bit of success. In the 1968/69 term they won the Kincardineshie (East) League Championship and reached the final of the McLean Cup, being defeated 2-0 by Laurencekirk. They repeated this feat in the 1972/3 term, winning the League Cup by defeating Arduthie 1-0 in a play-off, and losing 4-2 in the Maclean Cup final to Fettercairn & Luthermuir.

Back Row: Graham Stewart, Bobby Scott, Steven Wait, Alistair Davidson, Stuart Gray, Richard Kuczynski, Steven Beattie.
Front : Steven Kuczynski, Ian Harrison, Stewart McKimmie, Stuart Hay, Ian Stephen.
Stewart McKimmie, of course, went on to play for Aberdeen F.C. and Scotland.

The ladies, too, got into the act, and in the 1970's Cove Ladies played a host of friendly matches against various other pub and district ladies' football teams. Presently there is Cove Rangers Ladies, managed by Mr. Eric Reid, who compete in the Scottish Women's Premier League.

Cove Ladies F.C. at Allan Park 1972.

Reproduced by kind permission of Aberdeen Journals Ltd.

Mr. John (Jock) Ritchie, 1965. Jock was the skipper at the Cove salmon fishing and was known by all in the village, residing at No. 50.

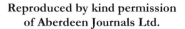

Reproduced by kind permission of Aberdeen Journals Ltd.

Mr. Jimmy Morrice, c. 1955. Mr. Morrice was locally known as 'Mosh', and lived at No. 45 the Cove. A deeply religious man, on Sundays he would make the trek from the Cove to Nigg Parish Church, regardless of the weather.

Mr. Robert Wood with two fine specimens of salmon, c. 1963. Mr. Wood was born in 1900 and given the by-name of 'Stormy Morning', owing to there being a terrific gale at the time, causing much damage to both the boats and the harbour.

Mrs. Jean Watt and Mrs. Ann Still, c. 1958. The picture is taken by the garden shed at No. 6 at Catto Crescent, the women being next door neighbours, previously residing with their husbands and families at Nos. 57 and 55 the Cove, respectively, now present-day Bunstane Terrace. Mrs. Still was locally known as 'Deem' (Dame) and her husband as 'Auld Pope'.

Chapter 8: Salvation or Damnation?

The Coming of the Council

Until 1939 the Cove, in essence, lay to the east of the railway, apart from the coastguard cottages, the church, and a few crofts either side of Loirston Road. The previous year Kincardine County Council bought the fields to the immediate south of Loirston House and began to construct Catto Crescent, of which the houses were the first in the Cove with modern facilities. This provided much-needed accommodation for local families due to the dilapidation and overcrowding of the houses in the old part of the village, several of whom being allocated a 'new hoose'. Further council development ensued, and 1947 saw 'temporary' accommodation in the form of four prefabricated houses on the west side of Loirston Road, named Tarran Place. Though at first a welcome abode, in the ensuing years they proved both damp and of extreme temperatures during the summer and winter months. They stood for 39 years before being demolished and replaced by the present-day row of modern houses in 1986, in turn their addresses being absorbed into Nos. 17 — 23 Loirston Road. In 1948 Sinclair Crescent was begun, named after the Sinclair family of North Loirston, and in 1952 six small detached houses were built on the south side of the brae leading to the railway bridge known as 'Stottie's Brig', from James Stott who occupied Blacksmith's Croft on Loirston Road during the construction of the railway. As private houses their address at first was Accommodation Way, becoming Loirston Place in 1957; the first of the four larger houses opposite being constructed in 1955.

It became apparent there was insufficient housing to suit demand, and in 1960 Kincardine County Council purchased four acres of land from farmer Mr. William Allan. Three years later phase one of Fittick Place was completed, (named after the old parish church of St. Fittick) with phase two following a year later, which, on occupation, the westernmost houses were being plagued by field mice at harvesting time. Still more was needed, and 1967/8 saw a flurry of construction: Sinclair Terrace, Sinclair Place, Burnbutts Crescent and Catto Walk, along with nine small council houses sited around the older part of the village; in addition was the redevelopment and improvement to others. As mentioned, at this time roads in the old village were individually named, though for many years after Bunstane Terrace was still referred to as 'quarry raw'. The largest housing project, however, was that of Altens (which is geographically incorrect, the land being that of the North Loirston estate), initially a private development, but latterly funded by Aberdeen City Council and constructed in two phases, beginning in 1976/7. Excepting the fourteen affordable homes built by Grampian Housing in 2004/5, Altens became the last council house development of any significance in the area.

Private Development

By now the Cove was a sizeable place, both in population and area, with the first private development of any consequence coming in 1975 by way of the Scandinavian-type houses in the field pertaining to Burnbutts Croft. Moreover, for the older folk of the village the show house interior must have seemed like another world. Thus 'Grampian Land', as it was known, paved the way for the massive housing projects that followed. Beginning in the fields immediately south of Langdykes Road, in 1981 Barratt and Wimpey began construction between present-day Loirston Primary School and the Mains of Loirston, with Loirston Manor already underway. The following years saw addresses such as Clashrodney and Earnsheugh, with Falklands Avenue appearing in 1984. Development pressed ever west, the latter part of the decade bearing witness to the construction of addresses such as Allison, Dunlin, Cassie, Tern, Cormorant, etc, the housing having stretched as far as the road through Whitehills.

The terraced rows of the village today:

Colsea Road.

Spark Terrace.

Hasman Terrace.

Springhill Terrace.

Bunstane Terrace.

Craighill Terrace.

Stoneyhill Terrace.

Seaview Terrace.

Development continued on the south side of the Cove Road, and in 1992 Wimpey Homes acquired a piece land extending to around 4.4 hectares belonging to the Cove Farm. The initial phase began with the construction of Cove Circle, Gardens, Crescent, Wynd, etc; the second phase consisting of Creel Place, Creel Walk, etc, and completed in 1994. By the millennium construction had drawn parallel with Charleston Primary School, the first phase of 'Woodlands' having been completed. Today the Lochinch and Charleston addresses sit no distance from the Loch of Loirston itself, with the once beautiful Charlestown Wood and open stretches of pasture having long since disappeared.

The Post-war Years

Behind the statistics, though, lies a distinctive unfolding of the village, and after the voluntary liquidation of the Aberdeen Fish Meal Company in 1937, its assets were sold off piece by piece, with, as mentioned, Mr. Charles G. Kennaway acquiring the housing stock in the old part of the village. As a landlord he did little in the way of repairs, the tenants being given the option of purchasing their property at a nominal price owing to the onset of decay. By 1951 more than half of the housing stock was privately owned, which, in many cases, involved houses being purchased for between £60 to £100. At present market value the cost of a single house today would be enough to have purchased the entire village then — several times over! Lady Marjory Bell became proprietor in 1953, there now being only two houses occupied on Balmoral Place, while in 1958 the ownership of the remaining houses in the village fell to Kincardine County Council. In 1948, however, Loirston Road began to be populated by houses other than former crofts and coastguard cottages, Murdoch's Croft being redeveloped, becoming Breezy Neuk that year, followed by Maryville and Ollaberry. In the coming years both new and named residences would appear: Murraybank; Keonord Cottage; Rose Cottage; Jesmond; Shangri La; Langcrag; Hillsea Cottage and Ardron, among others.

Mrs. Duncan and Mrs. Webster of the Cove drawing on one of the pumps located at the top of present-day Craighill Terrace.

Reproduced by kind permission of Aberdeen Journals Ltd.

The Cove post-war was no more than a sleepy residence, far removed from its former glory, there being a number of ruinous and dilapidated houses. Though electric had arrived in 1930, most did not as yet have piped water. By the early 1950's there were seventy houses, mostly but-and-ben with cobblestone or concrete frontages, and apart from a few householders most drew their water from six pumps sited around the village. At times the flow was such that it took an hour to fill a pail, and in times of drought the villagers were forced to go to the hotel for supplies, it being 1962 before the houses to the east of the railway had hot and cold running water. There was in addition a collective frustration, as the Cove Farm controlled the flow to the aforementioned pumps, and when a plentiful amount was required for dairy purposes, etc, then the farmer had the means of cutting off the supply to the village.

In 1955, however, an ambitious redevelopment plan was proposed by the aforesaid Mr. Alistair J. Sturrock, which would lead to the creation of a model village yet retaining its characteristics. The cost of this project was to be just under £100,000, which would allow for the retention of some of the buildings, albeit with alterations. Others would have to be demolished, with a proposed construction of 28 new houses and 14 garages, most of which would be on the cleared areas. Sewers and water mains would cost an additional £10,000. Mr. Sturrock had stated that he was appalled at the general approach made by some local Scottish authorities towards old properties, for they did not realise their potentialities, therefore by pulling them down the building heritage of many towns and villages was lost. Indeed, the Cove is indebted to the work of this man, for if the planners had their way a very different picture of the village would be seen today, most likely by way of unsightly constructions and a blight upon its character.

During this time it may be said that the Cove was but a dormitory for those with occupations in the city of Aberdeen, with almost no work afforded in the village itself, the majority of the fishermen and their families having long relocated during the days of the trawler boom. Indeed, from the 1940's, to the onset of the oil boom, there evolved an air of resignation. For a long time the school roll decreased, and by 1959 there were but 82 pupils, whereby the education authorities decided to cut the teaching staff to three. Hard times had hit the Cove, of which the house-building programme of the 1960's would begin to appease.

Between the period of World War II and the early 1960's, the Cove had doubled in size, albeit not in population, which in 1961 amounted to 529, increasing to around 1000 at the beginning of the 1970's. As mentioned, any redevelopment had to be kept in character with the existing houses in the old village, of which 60 were original fisher-cottages, along with some 150 houses west of the railway. However, sweeping changes were about to take place, the first of which was the acquisition of the estate of North Loirston and Redmoss Farm in 1966 by Aberdeen City Council, the grounds of the latter containing present-day Wellington Circle and the wholesale outlet of 'makro'. In fact, in 1968 Aberdeen was to extend its city boundaries by almost 1300 acres, stopping at the Langdykes Road, the pressure to build on this area clearly evidenced by the rising population of the village itself. The former estates of Altens and North Loirston were considered to be of particular importance, not only for housing needs, but also for industrial development. The Royal Assent was given to the boundary extent in 1970 and hopes expressed that a new industrial estate might be realised and would, perhaps, produce a continuous line of industrial

Mr. John Leven, 1972

development extending from Aberdeen City to the fringes of the Cove. Moreover, during the mid 1970's Aberdeen was the most rapidly growing urban area in Britain, and at this time suggested that a whole new chapter in the history of the Cove lay waiting for the first page to be turned.

Like Harry Gordon's parody of the fish meal factory with its chorus line of "Tak me back tae Cove", in 1968 there was one man who literally was taking folk back to the Cove in order to prevent it from becoming a residence of strangers. County Councillor, the late Mr. John Leven, then owner of present-day Posties's, made it his prime objective that some of the recently constructed council houses to the west of the old village were rented to young people with families, who some years ago on getting married, had been forced to leave the village of their parents and grandparents in order to secure accommodation elsewhere; the impetus for his actions being that many of the houses in the old part of the village were purchased by harassed city dwellers, and offered 'balm to the soul', with the Cove being ideal for commuting to Aberdeen. Mr. Leven also feared that the old village would be seen as an attractive dormitory and weekend home for outsiders, and that eventually they would outnumber the established residents. There was also the fact that the policy in Kincardine was to let houses to people from all over the county, which in one respect was forward thinking, as it introduced new blood into the towns and villages, therefore preventing communities from becoming somewhat insular. Furthermore, with the Cove now literally on the doorstep of Aberdeen, the consensus of the village was reflected by Mr. Leven in that it wished to refrain from becoming part of the city, but if so, then for the next five to ten years the people pay only County rates, which at the time were so much less than that of the City. In the course of events that followed the collective voice of the Cove and Mr. Leven appears optimistically prophetic: "We don't want to become part of Aberdeen, and I don't think it will happen."

Cove Bay's Fight is Over

Mr. Robert Noble addresses the public protest meeting at Cove Bay Hotel in 1972. Also in the picture is Mr. John Lawson (left).

Reproduced by kind permission of Aberdeen Journals Ltd.

For a number of years the planners of Aberdeen City Council had cast their eyes beyond the green belt south of Tullos to the surrounding area of the Cove. In 1971 a plan was revealed for massive housing development, inclusive of an industrial estate at Altens, which, in no uncertain terms, produced outrage and uproar throughout the village. A meeting was called and an Action Committee formed to counter this proposal. A roar of sheer dissent rose from a packed hall at the Cove Bay Hotel when Kincardine County Council officials forecast that nothing could stop the area going into the new Aberdeen district. Spurred on by the enthusiasm which saw the parishes of Maryculter and Banchory Devenick 'save' themselves from being absorbed into the Aberdeen district, after losing the boundary battle the Cove decided to fight all the way in order retain a green belt between the village and the city. They put up an amazing show, swinging M.P.'s and even ministers towards an understanding of their views, producing a professional study of the area, inclusive of facts and figures.

The crunch came on the evening on 24 April 1972 when the Action Committee laid it squarely on the line, that a fighting fund of £3,000 would need to be raised in order to counter the proposed plans for industrial and housing development, which would simply swamp the village. However, 'houses, factories and jobs', was the consensus from the hall, and that the working man should not have to be standing at the 'buroo' (job centre). Such an

Some of the audience who attended the meeting. Local author Janet Murray is first right in the front row.

Reproduced by kind permission of Aberdeen Journals Ltd.

attitude, or change of heart, must have felt like a bolt from the blue, for after all their intensive efforts this impassioned plea fell on the ears of under 50 villagers, where less than a year before stood a packed audience, 90% of which had signed a petition against such a plan. The Action Committee heard the vote — eight to press on with the fight and fourteen to surrender, the rest all having abstained. They stepped from the platform, leaving chairman Mr. Raymond Preston to follow the wishes of the meeting, the prospect of a better economic future having won hands down against a gallant bid to preserve the village. Heads bowed they faded out, deciding instead to reform an amenities committee for such tasks as cleaning up the beach, a scant reward for their years of endeavour, and little consolation!

Propositions, Preservation and Amenities

By the 1970's the frontage of Craighill Terrace had badly deteriorated, and remains in a poor condition today.

By the mid 1960's Balmoral Road was in great disrepair, whereby the older folk of the village were unable to safely access the harbour, therefore a continuous stretch from Stoneyhill Terrace to the pier was macadamized by Kincardine County Council. However, with the sewer laid along the centre of the road, the rather inferior surface was soon torn loose when it rained and frequently overflowed, having to be resurfaced with a material of superior quality. During this time the car park at Balmoral Terrace was constructed from money raised by the villagers themselves, a grand total of £1,500 no less, in order to provide parking to facilitate the harbour. In 1974 there appeared posters throughout the village which gravely stated 'The Fate of Cove' regarding its absorption into Aberdeen City limits, though a proposal was put forward in 1976 by the district director of planning in Aberdeen that the village (now a suburb) be designated as a conservation area, the Cove and Fittie being the only remaining examples of fishing settlements within the city since the disappearance of Old Torry due to the oil boom. The harbour and the cliffs were looked upon as of outstanding scenic interest, and that the distinctive appearance of the Cove as a sea-town should be preserved, while the area east of the railway between the Poor Man and the Kettle inlet be made into a conservation area. Although the but-and-ben rows of the fisher-folk hold historical interest, concerns were raised regarding the condition of the 'roads' between them, especially that of ambulance access, the majority of residents being elderly.

At the same time other former fishing villages along the Kincardineshire coast were battling to preserve their identity amid the ever-increasing demand for commuter housing, Portlethen and Newtonhill having expanded almost beyond recognition. The Cove was about to do so, and the watchdogs of Cove Bay Village Council, while accepting expansion at the Cove as inevitable, were hoping that more would be done to build amenities in concurrence with the housing, though plans for a secondary school might not materialise. During this deliberative year there were no community facilities in the village, only the adaptation of existing buildings such as the hotel, the school or the church.

In 1977 the draft plan proposal over the next ten years was to increase the population five-fold, with a projected housing figure of 1,700, and that these developments should be no nearer than a quarter of a mile from the A956 in order to maintain the concept that the main road into Aberdeen passes through a 'green corridor', and to achieve the principle of contained communities surrounded by open space. Among the traffic proposals in the plan was the intention to discourage motorists from using the Coast Road between the Cove and Balnagask, and that the public bus system operated by Grampian Region for the city should be extended to provide an adequate service for both Altens Industrial Estate and the Cove. For a quick and alternative route into Aberdeen it was suggested that Grampian Regional Council consider approaching British Rail on the possibility of re-opening the former railway station as an unmanned halt, and that it might be feasible to convert the old primary school and part of the farm buildings at North Loirston for use as nursery schools, serving the south and north areas, respectively. With the city centre a little over three miles away, the planners felt it would be uneconomical to provide a full range of shopping facilities in the Cove, and for a projected population of 5250 a range of around 8,000 to 10,000 square feet should lend adequate provision. The plan recommended plenty of green space and that 120 acres to the west of the proposed housing areas be set aside for the construction of a golf course, along with the possible relocation of the library, whose present situation in the extreme south of the village would be inconveniently off-centre.

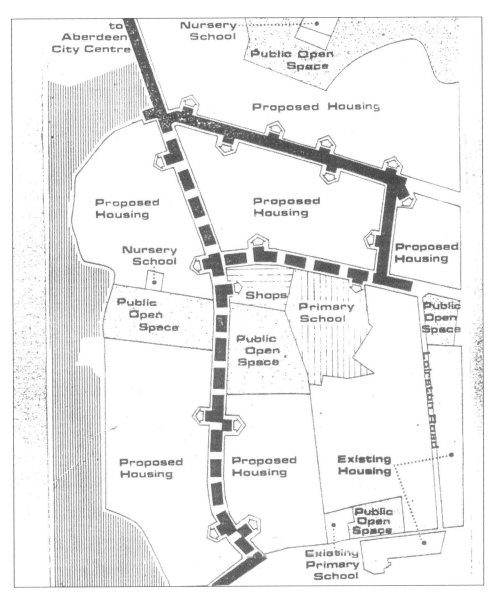

The draft plan for Cove Bay, 1977 — one of five local plans being prepared by Aberdeen District Council for development in the district.

In March 1980 the residents of the Cove were fighting for better facilities and battling to put the spirit back in the community. They requested a £100,000 plan for a purpose-built community centre, besides a place where teenagers were welcome in a bid to prevent correlated boredom and vandalism, given that in the 1960's the decaying Mission Hall doubled as a youth club and had fifty active members. The old folks, too, were being denied, the Cove and Altens Pensioners Club being crammed into a damp prefab on Loirston Road, their meeting place for playing bingo, having 'a natter', and

Cove and Altens Pensioners' Club in their cramped prefab on Loirston Road, September 1980. The Club was later relocated to Altens Community Centre.

Reproduced by kind permission of Aberdeen Journals Ltd.

other social entertainments. A community centre management committee was formed, seeking permission for a new centre to be built behind the existing school on the Cove Road; the pensioners, however, were relocated to North Loirston House, which of course became Altens Community Centre.

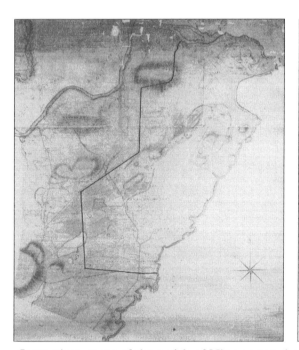
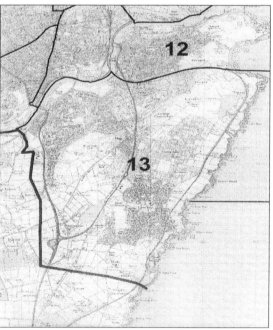

Comparison maps of the parish of Nigg as per the division east and west, 1785, and an Ordinance Survey of the area, 2006. Cove Bay is centrally placed in what is now Aberdeen City Council Area, Electoral Arrangements, Ward 13, Kincorth/Loirston. As may be seen of the original parish boundaries, to the west lies suburb of Kincorth, and to the east the vastly expanded Cove Bay and Torry. Much has been built on by way of housing and industrial estates. However, both the Balnagask headland and Loirston Country Park remain undeveloped, while to the south and west of the Loch of Loirston is mostly that of an agricultural enterprise.

Reproduced by kind permission of Aberdeen City Archives.
©Crown Copyright. Local Government Boundary Commission for Scotland.

In 1983 it was admitted the Cove was a mess and the village overdeveloped, an Aberdeen councillor describing it as being a 'disaster area', and that care should be taken to ensure the mistakes that blighted the village were not repeated when developing the Bridge of Don. Furthermore, the following decades bore witness to an unrelenting housing programme, which, from a suitable vantage point, appears as a sea of roofs, with little by way of amenities; and indeed remains so today.

Nevertheless, from 1986 the area was to be championed when Cove and Altens Community Council was formed, their 21st anniversary being held in the Cove Rangers Social Club in August 2007. Presently there are plans afoot for further development between Whitehills and the Loch of Loirston, inclusive of open spaces and additional roads and pathways, not to mention the possible redevelopment of the existing block of commercial outlets by Earnsheugh Road. Cove Bay Health Centre opened its doors in 2007, and there is also planned the construction of the multi-purpose Henderson Complex in 2009, so named after the late Mrs. Sally Henderson, whose tireless endeavours brought many benefits, inclusive of community magazine the Cove Chronicle, which continues to flourish on a bi-monthly basis through the efforts of Mr. Andy Finlayson and Mrs. Michele McPartlin, among others. Of course, as a village the Cove no longer exists, and indeed is a dormitory suburb of Aberdeen, though its history cannot be denied; and whichever direction progress may take, the true identity of the Cove remains in the form of terraced houses on the slopes above the harbour.

Satellite image portraying the massive expansion and development, 1996.

Reproduced by kind permission of Aberdeen City Archives.

Summary

Having covered most aspects of existence during earlier times it may clearly be seen that life today is incomparable to that of the 18th and 19th centuries, routine issues being very much taken for granted, such as running water and electricity, while communication and transport are all too readily available. Indeed, our standard of living has been so improved — for the younger generation at least — that those far off days cannot be fully comprehended. In addition, if the fisher-folk of yesterday lived in modern Cove Bay it would be most unlikely if they hungered for the old ways, and to think anything otherwise is merely drifting into the unreality of a romantic 'auld lang syne'.

However, it would be folly to forget the past in order to understand the future; indeed, one has only to look east of the railway to see where it all began, then west to acknowledge the contrast in architecture and surroundings, and witness a village very much of two parts. Land, of course, has had the biggest impact, and within a century the parish of Nigg has completely disappeared, being no more than a suburb of Aberdeen (a glance at the comparison maps on page 172 bears witness to the extent of development during the process of industrialisation and urbanisation). The City Limits are spreading ever southwards, and may soon reach Findon, eventually encapsulating the town of Stonehaven — such is the need for expansion.

The Cove, in turn, has lost many of its scenic locations, including Charlestown Wood and huge tracts of open pasture, while the slow but surely deterioration of the harbour persists, where, in but a few years time, the pier may be deemed as unsafe. Of course, the picturesque cliff-scape and the panoramic views of the sea will ever remain a feature. The granite quarries and the oil works, too, have long since closed, the Coastguard long departed, albeit the fishing continues on a very small scale. Furthermore, much of the former estates of North Loirston and Altens have been given over to industrial estate, with an additional 45 acres currently being developed by the Charleston Crossroads.

Owing to the huge rise in population green space and public facilities appear to have taken second place, though a community spirit survives, and is greatly encouraged by the Cove and Altens Community Council, inclusive of a summer gala which has been in existence for more than thirty years. The fact is that Cove Bay proves an ideal base for those with occupations in and around Aberdeen — and an attractive one at that — with properties in the area being very desirable. East of the railway, though, the 'fishtown' remains relatively the same, a few houses having been demolished and modern versions constructed, all of the original but-and-bens being privately owned with the exception of no more than half a dozen; the hotel, moreover, is subject to many visitors, albeit the thoroughfares between the rows of houses could be vastly upgraded and improved.

Finally, from 'le Coyf' in the 16th century, to present-day Cove Bay, there have been manifold changes, much of the area being unrecognisable and its sundry characters all but forgotten, it is hoped, therefore, that in the preceding pages some light has been shed on the history of both a unique and fascinating place.

Event Chronology

1170	Barony of Torrie gifted to the monks of Arbroath Abbey by King William I (the Lion).
1411	'Knicht of Lawriston' mentioned in a poem lamenting the Battle of Harlaw.
1527	First recorded mention of the Cove, as 'le Coyf'.
1580	Murder of Alexander Menzies at the Cairn of Loirston.
1581	Halymanis–coif (Cove Bay) first mentioned in the Great Seal.
1607	Isobel Smith of the Cove charged with witchcraft.
1647	Gilbert Menzies acquires a half share in the barony of Torrie.
1647	Cove is described as Coiff.
1667	Regular Post Office established between Aberdeen and Edinburgh.
1704	The Town of Aberdeen purchase an undivided half of the barony of Torrie.
1709	Two Cove fishermen obtain a tack agreement to fish from Cove harbour.
1746	Birth of Rev. Dr. David Cruden, Nigg Parish Minister.
1750	First four-wheeled carriage in Aberdeen.
1759	Manse at St. Fittick's Church constructed.
176?	First surveys of the Cove Quarries undertaken.
1768	Five fishermen lost off the Cove.
1770	First stage-coach between Aberdeen and Edinburgh.
1771	First school established at the Cove.
1777	Survey of the land of the barony of Torrie completed.
1784	Severe storm recorded at the Cove.
1785	Division of the parish between the Town of Aberdeen and John Menzies Esq.
1786	Eastern half of the parish belonging to the Town of Aberdeen apportioned into nine lots and feud.
1787	Three fishermen lost off the Cove.
1788	Estate of South Loirston and parts of the Cove acquired by William Matthew in April.
1788	Creel fishing introduced in the Cove.
1788	Estate of South Loirston and parts of the Cove acquired by the Rev. Francis Johnston in September.
1788	Cove boat captured smuggling by a customs vessel.
1790	Six fishermen lost off the Cove.
1791	First Scottish Statistical Account written (1791-1799).
1793	Birth of Alexander Muir.
1795	Turnpike Bill passed by Parliament.
1800	John Louden McAdam invents 'macadamizing'.
1802	Estate of South Loirston and parts of the Cove acquired by Miss Elizabeth Johnston.
1802	The Society of Whitefishers in Cove founded.
1803	Birth of Dr. Alexander Kilgour.
1803	Cove fisherman drowned.
1810	Estate of South Loirston and parts of the Cove acquired by James Hector.
1811	First mention of boat building in the Cove.
1816	Estate of South Loirston and parts of the Cove acquired by Alexander Duthie Esq.
1821	Coast Guard station established at the Cove.
1822	Endowed School constructed.
1822	Construction of the inn on present location.
1824	Drumforskie (Charleston) School constructed.
182?	Initial layout of terraced rows in the village as part of the estate of South Loirston.
182?	Initial layout of terraced rows in the village as part of the Lands of Cove.
1826	Death of Rev. Dr. David Cruden, Nigg Parish Minister.
1827	The Society of Whitefishers in Cove disbanded.
1827	John Menzies Esq. gifts the mansion house and estate of Blairs to the Bishop of Aberdeen.
1828	John Hector invents the bag-net.
1828	Drumforskie recognised as Charleston.
1829	Wellington Road completed.
1829	Closure of St. Fittick's Church.
1829	Nigg Parish Church opened.
1831	Wellington Suspension Bridge completed.
1834	Estate of South Loirston and parts of the Cove acquired by Alexander Muir.
1836	Birth of George Falconer Muir.
1839	Two Cove fishermen drowned.
1841	Typhoid fever present in the Cove.

1842	Loirston House constructed.
1842	Five Cove fishermen lost off Burnbanks.
1843	Death of John Menzies Esq.
1848	The Lands of Cove acquired by John Blaikie.
1848	Severe storm hits the east coast of Scotland, sinking 124 fishing boats.
1848	Two fishermen drowned off Cove harbour.
1849	Construction of the new parish school at Nigg.
1850	Death of Alexander Muir.
1850	Cove Station opened, train service running from Ferryhill.
1851	Post Office established at the Cove.
1851	Janet Sinclair is tenant farmer at North Loirston.
1851	First recorded mention of a shop in the village.
1852	Birth of Alexander Kilgour Jr.
1853	Bunstane Terrace constructed.
1853	Last recorded species of an Erne.
1854	Western portion of the Lands of Cove acquired by Dr. Alexander Kilgour.
1855	Estate of South Loirston and parts of the Cove inherited by George Falconer Muir.
1855	Seaview House constructed.
1856	Balmoral Terrace (then Street) constructed.
1856	Salmon bothy and stores constructed.
1857	Eastern portion of the Lands of Cove acquired by George Falconer Muir.
1858	North East Coast Mission Hall erected (wooden construction).
1860	Boat shop constructed on Balmoral Road by Andrew Forbes.
1863	Estate of South Loirston and the eastern portion of the Lands of Cove acquired by Dr. Alexander Kilgour.
1863	Lands of Cove and South Loirston become one contiguous salmon fishing station.
1864	Initial construction of houses in the village (thirteen in total) by Dr. Alexander Kilgour.
1864	St. Mary's Mission Chapel School opened.
1865	Turnpike Trusts dissolved.
1866	Loirston House greatly extended and improved.
1866	Westerton Farm House at Whitehills constructed.
1866	Death of Janet Sinclair.
1867	Passenger train derailed at 'the cutting'.
1867	Construction of the Rocket Apparatus House (No. 7 Loirston Road).
1867	St. Mary's Episcopal Church constructed.
1867	Parochial Side School (Cove Bay Primary) opened.
1869	Present-day Posties shop opened.
1870	John Lewis takes over as boat builder in the Cove.
1870	Cove Inn extended to its present-day proportions.
1870	North Loirston House (Altens Community Centre) constructed.
1872	Horse-drawn trams introduced in Aberdeen.
1872	John Fyfe invents an aerial carriageway known as the Blondin
1873	South row of Springhill Terrace constructed (three houses only).
1873	North row of Stoneyhill Terrace constructed (two houses only).
1873	The schooner *Victoria* sinks.
1874	Death of Dr. Alexander Kilgour.
1877	James Cordiner takes over as boat builder in the Cove.
1878	Initial constructions at the harbour completed.
1879	Seaview Terrace constructed.
1880	Sanitation in the village condemned.
1881	David Sinclair I proprietor of North Loirston and Altens.
1881	Victoria Bridge completed.
1881	North East Coast Mission Hall erected (masonry construction).
1883	Commission of Enquiry set up in Aberdeen for damage incurred to line boats by trawlers.
1883	Alexander Kilgour purchases the salmon rights to the Lands of Cove and South Loirston.
1883	Extensions and additional constructions at the harbour.
1883	*Dunstaffnage* wrecked off Findon Ness.
1887	Graveyard at Nigg Church commenced.
1890	Cove Farm tenanted by John Valentine.
1890	Migration to Torry has seriously decreased the village population.
1890	Boat building in the Cove is no more.
1891	First sewer laid in the village.

1891   Absorption of Torry into Aberdeen City.
1892   Spur breakwater added to the main pier.
1893   Telegraph line constructed by the Coast Guard for operational purposes.
1894   Establishment of the Aberdeen Fish Manure and Oil Company Ltd.
1894   Death of Mary Elizabeth Kilgour.
1894   The steamer *Countess of Aberdeen* sinks.
1894   Closure of St. Mary's Mission Chapel School.
1894   Initial extension of the parochial Side School.
1896   Graveyard extended at Nigg Parish Church.
1899   Electrical cable trams introduced in Aberdeen.
1900   Severe storm recorded at the Cove.
1900   Cove Rangers F. C. founded.
1902   Station premises constructed on the west side of the railway line.
1903   Death of John Fyfe, granite merchant.
1904   Alexander Kilgour Jr. admitted to Elmhill House, Loirston House now vacant.
1905   Birth of David Sinclair II.
1906   The steamer *Kenilworth* sank.
1909   Reservoir completed by The Aberdeen Fish Manure and Oil Co. Ltd.
1911   Death of David Sinclair I.
1912   Cove Station renamed Cove Bay Station.
1914   Greenarbour tenanted by Miss Mary Marr.
1915   U-boat sunk off Findon Ness.
1917   The steamship *Silverburn* sunk by gunfire.
1919   Nigg Churchyard grounds further extended.
1921   Death of Alexander Kilgour Jr.
1922   Estate of South Loirston and the Lands of Cove acquired by The Aberdeen Fish Manure and Oil Co. Ltd.
1922   Cove Rangers F. C. join the Aberdeen Juvenile League.
1923   Loirston House occupied by John (Jock) Catto.
1923   Coast Guards vacate the station at Cove.
1925   The trawler *Ulster* sinks.
1927   Loirston House tenanted by William Ellis.
1927   Watch House vacated.
1928   Bus service introduced in the Cove.
1928   Recreation Park (Catto Park) donated to the village by the Aberdeen Fishmeal Company.
1933   Death of William Sinclair.
1936   Wooden shop appears on Loirston Road.
1937   The Aberdeen Fish Meal Company in voluntary liquidation.
1939   Loirston House and bounds purchased by William Ellis.
1939   Catto Crescent constructed.
1940   The steamship *Trebartha* bombed and sunk.
1941   Two converted trawlers sunk off Girdleness.
1941   Cove Schoolhouse constructed.
1947   Prefabricated houses erected by Loirston Road.
1948   Sinclair Crescent constructed.
1948   Initial development of private houses on Loirston Road.
1950   Loirston Stores opened.
1950   Cove Rangers F. C. open Allan Park.
1951   Mowatt's Pioneer Iron Grit Company begins in operation.
1952   Cove Thistle F. C. founded.
1952   6 detached houses on the south side of Loirston Place constructed.
1953   Lady Marjory bell proprietor of the existing housing stock in the old village.
1954   Cove Rangers F. C. defeated in the final of the Scottish Amateur Cup.
1956   Cove Bay Station closed.
1957   Kincardine County Council become the owners of Recreation Park.
1958   Kincardine County Council proprietors of the existing housing stock in the old village.
1959   Sea wall seriously damaged.
1959   Braeheid shop opened.
1962   Running water introduced into the houses in the village.
1963   Stonecraft Fireplaces established.
1963   Fittick Place (first phase) constructed.
1964   Death of Miss Mary Marr.

1964	Manse at St. Fittick's Church demolished.
1966	North Loirston estate purchased by Aberdeen City Council.
1967	Large wooden shop no longer on Loirston Road.
1968	Council houses constructed to the west of the railway, including Sinclair Terrace and Place.
1968	Kincardine County Council construct nine new houses in the village.
1968	Burnbutts Crescent constructed.
1968	Roads in the village given individual addresses.
1969	Braeheid shop demolished.
1969	Cove Primary School win the East Kincardineshire League Trophy.
1969	Facilities for making blinds established on Loirston Road.
1970	Cove Youth Club hold the world record for a marathon dance.
1971	First of the modern houses on Colsea Road constructed.
1971	Removal of the large wooden hut belonging 12th Kincardineshire Boy Scout Group.
1972	Death of John Ellis.
1972	Demolition of Loirston House.
1972	Failure to save the Cove's absorption into Aberdeen.
1973	Cove Bay Station demolished.
1973	Cove Primary School win the East Kincardineshire League Trophy.
1973	Cove Bay Hotel under major renovations.
1973	Joiner's premises established on the Cove Road.
1974	A specimen of Ray's Bream washed up at the Cove harbour.
1975	Balmoral Terrace demolished.
1975	The Small Blue butterfly disappears from its habitat.
1975	Coastal path from Bay of Nigg to Black Cove inlet constructed.
1975	School bell repaired and re-hung.
1975	Scandinavian-type houses constructed to the west of Loirston Road.
1975	Cove now Aberdeen City, Ward 42.
1976	Closure of the signal box.
1976	The Cove designated as a conservation area.
1977	Modern houses on the south of Stoneyhill Terrace constructed.
1977	Altens housing estate constructed.
1979	Joiner's premises on the Cove Road replaced by car repair workshop.
1981	Cove bus service run by Aberdeen Corporation.
1981	Initial private housing development between the Langdykes and the Cove Road.
1981	Loirston Primary School opened.
1981	First amateur sound and vision link between Scotland and Holland, via Cove Bay Television.
1981	Demolition of North East Coast Mission Hall.
1981	Closure of Cove Bay Primary School.
198?	A rotting portion of giant squid washed up at the Crawpeel.
1984	Cove Rangers Social Club opened.
1985	Snooty Fox public house opened.
1985	Death of David Sinclair II.
1986	Cove and Altens Community Council formed.
1988	The Least Sandpiper is recorded at Rigifa.
1989	Salmon bothy and stores demolished.
1990	Skin of concrete applied to the main pier.
1992	Colsea Terrace constructed.
1992	Housing development to the south of the Cove Road.
1992	Braehead Nursery established.
1995	Cove Thistle secure a grant for major refurbishment of the changing facilities.
1996	Catto Park named.
1999	Salmon fishing ceases at the Cove.
1999	Charleston Primary School opened.
1999	Closure of Nigg Parish Church.
2001	Piers and part of the foreshore offered for sale.
2001	Colsea Square constructed.
2002	Cove Rangers F. C. win the Highland League.
2005	Affordable housing constructed by Grampian Housing.
2005	Cove Bay Library opened.
2006	A specimen of Ballan Wrasse caught at the Cove harbour.
2007	Cove Bay Health Centre opened.

Index of Names and Places

de Bernham, David, *1*
Dee, Bridge of, *85, 86, 88, 122*
Dee District Salmon Fishery Board
the, *70*
Dee, River, *1, 7, 8, 9, 63, 86, 90*
Dempster, Bob, *150*
Dempster, Elizabeth, *20*
Den the, *149*
de Nugg, Cormac, *1*
Diamond Street, *19*
Diney, Burn of, *66, 97, 148*
Dog's Hole, *31*
Don, River, *9, 31*
Downies, *23, 47, 80*
Drumforskie, *8, 85, 87, 88*
Drumforskie, Hill of, *85, 114*
Drumforskie Road the, *85, 88*
Drumforskie School, *114*
Drumquhale, *14*
Duncan, Mary Elizabeth, *13*
Duncan, Thomas, *13*
Duncansby Head, *97*
Dunlin (addresses), *165*
Dunnydeer, *16*
Dunstaffnage, *103*
'Dunstaffnage', *103*
Durris, *153*
Duthie, Esq., Alexander, *9, 11, 25, 26, 88, 104, 111, 112, 125, 138*
Duthie, Elizabeth Crombie, *10*
Duthie, Margaret, *10*
Duthie Park, *10*
Duthie, Walter, *10*
Dyce, *95*
Dyce Esq., Alexander, *13*
Dyce, Marjory, *13*

E

Earnsheugh (addresses), *32, 165*
Earnsheugh Bay, *96, 100*
Earnsheugh Circle, *159*
Earnsheugh Road, *173*
East Anglia, *61*
Edinburgh, *8, 9, 11, 14, 86, 92, 104, 125, 138, 152*
Ellis, Dorothy, *20*
Ellis, John, *20, 147*
Ellis, William, *20*
Elmhill House, *19*
Endowed School, *6, 10, 88, 111, 113, 114, 116, 119, 130, 138*

F

Fairweather, Rev. Robert, *19, 104, 116, 117*
Falklands Avenue, *165*
'Family's Trust', *58*
Farquharson, Captain James, *103, 117, 139, 141, 144, 145*

Farquharson, Jane, *144*
Ferguson, Sir Alex, *161*
Ferguson, James, *10, 89, 111, 112, 115*
Ferguson, Jane B., *11*
Ferguson, Dr. John, *13*
Ferguson, Margaret, *112*
Ferguson, Norman, *16, 50*
Ferguson, Peter, *25, 110*
Fernieflat, *9*
Ferryhill, *42, 91*
Fettercairn & Luthermuir (Primary
Schools), *163*
Findon, *8, 11, 44, 45, 47, 66, 80, 96, 128*
Findon Ness, *61, 103*
Findon Point, *37, 79, 101*
Finlayson, Andy, *173*
Firth of Forth, *56, 61, 63*
First Bus, *95*
Fittick Place, *118, 147, 165*
Fittie (Footdee), *23, 29, 34, 38, 56, 80, 170*
Flagstaff the, *31, 126*
Forbes, Alexander Penrose, *106, 107*
Forbes, Andrew, *129*
Forbes, Duncan, *2*
Forbes, John, *112*
Forbes, William, *3, 8*
Forfarshire, *80*
Forties, *60*
Forties, Long the, *60*
'Fort Royal', *154*
Fourdon, *125*
Fowlis Bank, *160*
Fowlsheugh, *96, 128*
France, *103, 133*
Fraser, Walter, *54, 83*
Fraserburgh, *61, 152*
Freeland, John, *53*
Friendly Society the, *24*
Fyfe, John, *27, 50, 51, 66, 106, 123, 124, 125, 149*

G

Galbraith M.P., Sam, *120*
Gallowgate, *12*
Gauldie, Gillespie & Co., *101*
Garibaldi, *63*
Garner, Captain G. (Coastguard), *127*
George Street, *129*
Germany, *133*
Gibb, Alexander, *90*
Gibb, John, *123*
Gibb & Son, *11*
Gin Cave the, *127*
Girdleness, *98, 121, 154*
Girdleness Lighthouse, *96, 128*

'Girl Jean', *83*
Gladstone, Right Honourable,
W.G., *57*
Glasgow, *101, 152*
Glasgow Rangers, 161
'Golden Arrow', *58*
Golspie, *56*
Gordon, Harry, *136, 168*
Gourdon, *33, 41*
Grahame, Alexander, *1*
'Grahmor', *125, 136*
Grampian Housing, *145, 165*
Grampian Land, *165*
Granna Crags the, *79*
Granton, *100*
Graves the, *6*
Gray, Kristofer, *97*
Gray, Rosemary, *154*
Green the, *42, 89, 147, 151*
Greenarbour, *6, 9, 20, 21, 87, 89, 93, 115*
Greenwich Hospital Fund, *53*
Gregness, *47, 93*
Grimsby, *132*
Gritter the, *149*
Groundless Myres, *11*
Guild Street, *91*
'Guthries of Dundee', *24*
Guyan, Alexander, *47*
Guyan, Mabel, *36*
Guyan, Willie, *120, 161*

H

Haig, David, *142*
Hain Steamship Co., *101*
Halyman's Coif, *1*
Halymanis-coif, *2*
Hallglen, Mrs., *18*
Hallglen, Richard, *18, 140, 141*
Halyruidhuis (Holyrood House), *2*
Hardgate, *147*
Hare Ness the, *1, 66, 97, 121, 122, 124, 125*
Harlaw, Battle of, *1*
Harris, G.F., *121*
Hasman Rocks, *24, 27, 61*
Hasman Terrace, *27, 37, 147*
Hay, Will, *93*
Hector, Andrew, *68*
Hector, James, *9*
Hector, John, *53, 68, 69, 70, 104, 110, 136*
Henderson, Cathy, *144*
Henderson, Christian, *144*
Henderson Complex the, *173*
Henderson Jr., David, *106, 120, 144*
Henderson Sr., David, *144*
Henderson, Helen, *142*
Henderson, Mary, *144, 160*

McAdam, John & Sons, *125*
McAdam, John Louden, *85*
McColl, Amanda, *120*
McDonald, Charlie, *149*
McDonald, Fred, *149*
McEwen, Peter, *24*
McHardie's Shop, *154*
McHardy, David & Son, *120*
McKay, Alexander, *145*
McKay, Captain James, *98*
McKenzie, Monica, *118*
McLean Cup, *163*
McLeod, Murdoch, *129, 138, 139, 144*
McPartlin, Michele, *173*
Mearns, *1,*
Meg's Hole, *31*
Mennie, Joe, *128, 129*
Menzies, Alexander, *8*
Menzies, Gilbert, *2, 3, 7, 8*
Menzies Esq., John, *3, 4, 5, 6, 8, 9, 10, 11, 13, 26, 47, 51, 68, 85, 86, 88, 110, 111, 114, 125, 144*
Menzies Road, *9*
Menzies, Thomas, *7*
Menzies, William, *1*
Michie Esq. M.D., William, *19, 38, 39*
Middleton, Colonel, *86*
Middletown, *7*
Midlothian, *145*
Milne, Andrew, *144*
Milne, Agnes, *144*
Milne, Charles, *86, 144*
Milne, David, *116*
Milne, George, *26*
Milne, Hugh, *144*
Milne, Janet, *21*
Mission Hall the, *106, 117, 118, 160, 172*
Mitchell & Muil, *155*
Mitchell, William, *112*
Moir, Colin, *70*
Moir, George, *3*
Moir, Hugh, *54, 70*
Montrose, *41, 90, 98*
Montrose Pits the, *62*
Montrose, William, Earl of, *1*
Monymusk, *3, 8*
Moray, *7*
Moray Firth, *25, 56*
Morrice, Ann, *24*
Morrice, George, *51, 53, 57*
Morrison, Coastguard District Officer, *101*
Morrison, Dr. George, *86*
Morrison, James, *86*
Moscow, *21*
Mountain the, *31*
Mowatt's Pioneer Iron Grit Co., *149*
Muchalls, *47, 75, 80, 141*

Muir, Alexander, 9, *10, 11, 14, 26, 90, 112, 138*
Muir-Arms' Inn, *10, 138*
Muir, George Falconer, *10, 11, 14, 68, 116, 129, 138, 139, 144*
Muir, Patrick Kilgour, *10, 11*
Murdoch's Croft, *39, 167*
Murray, Janet, *22, 106*
'Murraybank', *167*
Murray, John, *110*
Mutton Rock the, *31, 72, 79, 99*
Mythical Wall, *95*

N

National Lottery the, *162*
Nellfield Cemetery, *11*
'Nellie', *58*
Netherkirkgate, *120*
Netherleask, *10*
Neuk the (public house), *75*
Newlands Cottage, *88*
Newlands Croft, *19*
Newlands Farm, *38*
New Park, *11*
Newtonhill, *47, 75, 80, 170*
Nicholas II, Tsar of Russia, *21*
Nigg, *8, 14, 32, 86, 90, 103, 109, 121, 141, 142, 144*
Nigg, Bay of, *46, 47, 70, 88, 89, 99, 103, 121*
Nigg Churchyard, *151*
Nigg Kirk Session Minutes, *109, 138*
Nigg Mutual Improvement Association, *19*
Nigg Parochial Board, *10, 11, 22*
Nigg Parish Church, *45, 88, 89, 104*
Nigg Parish Council, *22, 32*
Nigg, Parish of, *1, 23, 33, 67, 85, 86, 87, 103, 117*
Nigg Parish Parochial School, *115*
Nigg Parochial Schoolmaster, *104*
Nigg Picnic & Games, *19*
Nigg, the Parish of Road Survey, *87*
North Balnagask, *7*
North Blackhill Farm, *97*
North East Coast Mission the, *105*
North Loirston, *7, 19, 21, 22, 31, 51, 70, 88, 89, 111, 114, 115, 165, 168, 171*
North Loirston House, *21, 22, 172*
North Kirkhill, *7*
North of Scotland Amateur Cup, *162*
North Star Steam Fishing Co., *101*
Northern Agricultural Co., *133*
Northfield, *153*
Norway, *60*
Norwood Hall Hotel, *9*

Nunnery Croft, *11*

O

Old Pretender the, *103*
'Ollaberry', *167*
Oranges & Lemons Nursery, *150, 160*
Orkney, *61*
Ottawa, *10*

P

P & O Group, *101*
Paris, *87, 103*
Parker, Leonard, *150*
Parkinson, Renee, *162*
Parochial Side School, *106, 113, 114, 116, 117*
Partan Crags, *66, 101*
Paul, Rev. William, *34*
Penny, David, *147*
Penny, Ian, *147*
Penny, James, *153*
Penny, Jimmy, *147, 154*
Penny, Mary, *147*
Penny, Norman, *150*
Perth, *86*
Peterhead, *61, 152*
Peterseat, *147*
Petrol Jean, *94*
Philadelphia, *101*
Piggery the, *136*
Piper Alpha (tragedy), *107*
Pitfodels, *5, 7, 8, 55, 85, 88, 121*
Point Law, *51*
Pond the, *134*
Poor Man, *31, 170*
Poor Man Rocks, *67, 127*
Portlethen, *8, 17, 23, 40, 47, 75, 79, 80, 170*
Port More, *47, 49*
Portsmouth, *127*
Posties Shop, *37, 85, 87, 145, 146, 155, 168*
Preston, Andrew, *143*
Preston, Helen, *143*
Preston, Raymond, *143, 170*
Preventative Water Guard, *12, 125*

Q

Queen Victoria, *117*

R

Railway, Bridge the, *90, 92, 128, 155*
Railway Cottage, *145*
Ramsgate, *121*
Recreation Park, *152, 160, 161, 162*

Places of Reference

Aberdeen Art Gallery.
Aberdeen Central Library.
Aberdeen City Archives.
Aberdeen Journals Ltd.
Aberdeen Maritime Museum.
Angus Archives, Restenneth House, Forfar.
Forfar Library.
Loirston School, Cove Bay.
Special Libraries and Archives, Aberdeen University.
The George Washington Wilson Database, Aberdeen University.
The Land Registry Office, Erskine House, Edinburgh.
The Leopard Magazine.
The Map Library of Scotland, Edinburgh.
The Mearns Leader.
The National Archives of Scotland, Edinburgh.
The National Library of Scotland, Edinburgh.
The North East Family History Society, Aberdeen.
The Royal Commission on the Ancient and Historical Monument Society, Edinburgh.

Estate Papers and Related Documents:

Kilgour Estate Papers, Special Libraries and Archives, Aberdeen, Ref MS 2769.
Last Will and Testament of Mr. Alexander Muir, NAS, Edinburgh.
Nigg Parish Records, NAS, Edinburgh, Ref CH2/555.
Heritors Records for the parish of Nigg, NAS, Edinburgh, Ref HR/487.
Valuation Rolls, 1862 — 2008, Aberdeen City Archives.
John Menzies Estate Papers, Aberdeen City Archives.
Sasine Registers, NAS, Edinburgh.
The Arbroath Liber, Restenneth House, Forfar.

Bibliography

A General View of the Agriculture of Kincardineshire, or The Mearns, parish of Nigg, Robertson, G., pub. 1808.

A Natural History of Aberdeen, Marren, Peter ISBN 0-907-184-04-9.

A Regional History of the Railways of Great Britain ISBN 0-946537-03-8.

A Thousand Years of Aberdeen, Keith, Alexander ISBN 0-900015-29-2.

A Topographical Dictionary of Scotland (1846), the British Historical Society.

Aberdeen 1800 — 2000 A New History edited by Fraser, Hamish & Lee, Clive H. ISBN 1-86232-175-2.

Aberdeen Before 1800, A New History, Dennison, Patricia E., Ditchburn, D., Lynch, M. ISBN 1-86232-119-1.

Aberdeen and the Fishing Industry in the 1870's, Waterman, J.J.

Aberdeen of Old, Meldrum, Edward.

Aberdeen Street Names, Fraser, G.M., ISBN 0-948246-04-9.

Aberdeen Today, Bon Accord 1886 — 1907, Anderson, Robert Esq.

An Historical Account and Delineation of Aberdeen, Wilson, Robert, published 1822.

Antiquities of Aberdeen and Neighbourhood, published 1913.

Bygone Days in Aberdeenshire, Allardyce, John.

Catch the Bluebird — A Pictorial Transport History, Brown, Stewart J. ISBN 0946265-26-7.

Epitaphs and Inscriptions, Jervise, Andrew.

Farmfolk and Fisherfolk edited by Smith, John S. & Stevenson, David ISBN 0-08-0377335.

Fisherfolk to Torryfolk, Milne, Colin A. ISBN 0-9538921-0-7.

Fishing Boats and Fisher Folk on the East Coast of Scotland, Anson, Peter F. ISBN 0-460-03994-6.

Fisher life and Habits in Relation to Disease… (Thesis) Cook, Robert Haldane, M.D. C.M. published 1895.

Folk-lore of the North-east of Scotland, Gregor, Walter, published 1881.

From Aberdeen to Ottawa in1845, MacKenzie, George A. ISBN 0-08-037983-4.

From Herring to Seine Net Fishing on the East Coast of Scotland, Sutherland, Iain ISBN 0-9508697-2-4.

Granites and Our Granite Industries, Harris, George F.

Harvest of the Sea, Bertram, James, published 1865.

History of the Parish of Banchory Devenick, Henderson, John A.

History of the Valley of the Dee, Macintosh, John, LL.D.

National Association for the Promotion of Social Science, Twenty-first Congress Aberdeen, published 1877.

North-East Lowlands of Scotland, Allan, John R. ISBN 0-7091-3986-1.

Past and Present of Aberdeenshire, Paul, Rev. William.

Primitive Beliefs in North East Scotland, McPherson, J.M. (B.D.).

Recollections of Scottish Episcopalism, Humphrey, Rev. William

Schooling in the Cove, Murray, Janet.

Shipwrecks of the North of Scotland Baird, R. N. ISBN 1-84158-233-6.

Shipwrecks of N.E. Scotland, Ferguson, David M. ISBN 0-08-0412173.

The Aberdeen Granite Industry, Donnelly, Tom ISBN 0-906265-18-5.

The Coming of the Turnpikes to Aberdeenshire, Patrick, John.

The Coming of the Railway to Aberdeen in the 1840's, Waterman, J.J.

The Eastern Counties, Tranter, Nigel ISBN 0-340-16462-X.

The Essence of the Cove, Murray, Janet.

The Fishing Industries of Scotland 1790 — 1914, Gray, Malcolm ISBN 0-197141-05-6

The Kirkyard of St. Fittick's, Nigg, Bain, Gavin ISBN 1-900173-08-5.

The North East of Scotland, The British Association: The Central Press, Aberdeen.

The Scottish Field, March 1944.

The Sea Fisheries of Scotland, Coull, James R. ISBN 0-85976-410-9.

Then and Now 1854 — 1912, The Aberdeen Lime Company Ltd., McRobb, John.